DEMOCRACY AND APARTHEID

Also by Anthony Butler and from the same publishers

TRANSFORMATIVE POLITICS: The Future of Socialism in Western Europe

Democracy and Apartheid

Political Theory, Comparative Politics and the Modern South African State

Anthony Butler
Lecturer in Politics
University of Nottingham

First published in Great Britain 1998 by
MACMILLAN PRESS LTD
Houndmills, Basingstoke, Hampshire RG21 6XS and London
Companies and representatives throughout the world

A catalogue record for this book is available from the British Library.

ISBN 0–333–66593–7

 First published in the United States of America 1998 by
ST. MARTIN'S PRESS, INC.,
Scholarly and Reference Division,
175 Fifth Avenue, New York, N.Y. 10010

ISBN 0–312–21696–3

Library of Congress Cataloging-in-Publication Data
Butler, Anthony, 1964–
Democracy and apartheid : political theory, comparative politics
and the modern South African state / Anthony Butler.
p. cm.
Includes bibliographical references and index.
ISBN 0–312–21696–3 (cloth)
1. Democracy—South Africa. 2. Apartheid—South Africa.
3. Elections—South Africa. 4. South Africa—Politics and
government—20th century. 5. Democracy. 6. Democratization.
I. Title.
JQ1981.B89 1998
320.968'09'049—dc21   98–28376
                          CIP

© Anthony Butler 1998

All rights reserved. No reproduction, copy or transmission of this publication may be made without written permission.

No paragraph of this publication may be reproduced, copied or transmitted save with written permission or in accordance with the provisions of the Copyright, Designs and Patents Act 1988, or under the terms of any licence permitting limited copying issued by the Copyright Licensing Agency, 90 Tottenham Court Road, London W1P 9HE.

Any person who does any unauthorised act in relation to this publication may be liable to criminal prosecution and civil claims for damages.

The author has asserted his right to be identified as the author of this work in accordance with the Copyright, Designs and Patents Act 1988.

This book is printed on paper suitable for recycling and made from fully managed and sustained forest sources.

10　9　8　7　6　5　4　3　2　1
07　06　05　04　03　02　01　00　99　98

Printed and bound in Great Britain by
Antony Rowe Ltd, Chippenham, Wiltshire

Tessa
inja entle kakhulu
something to chew on

Contents

Preface		ix
1	Introduction	1
2	A Periodization of South African History	6
3	Historical Debates and Political Analysis	30
4	Democracy and Apartheid	54
5	Analysing Democratic Transitions	86
6	Political Science and the End of Apartheid	105
7	The Failure of Political Science	127
8	Conclusions	156
Notes		176
Bibliography		197
Index		205

Preface

I have incurred many institutional and personal debts in writing this book. I am grateful to the fellows of Emmanuel College, Cambridge, to the trustees of the Jan Smuts Memorial Fund, and to Nottingham University Research Committee, for invaluable assistance with research expenses. Rhoda Kadalie, Nomusti Ntamo and Zizi Ntamo were immensely kind hosts. South African academics too numerous to mention have been uncommonly generous with their time and professional advice. Julia Jellema-Butler in London offered incisive comments on the final draft, and Cliff Butler was once again an exemplary proof-reader. Anne Jellema has been supportive throughout.

I am grateful to colleagues in the Department of Politics at Nottingham, in particular Paul Heywood and April Pidgeon, for ensuring that a relaxed atmosphere and a lively research culture have remained compatible with the demands of teaching and administration. April Pidgeon also provided invaluable assistance in the preparation of the manuscript.

Apartheid was organized around the classification of a population by race. I use the term 'African' to refer to those officially classified as 'Black'; and I use 'Black' to refer to all those not classified as White under apartheid legislation. I capitalize all such terms throughout in order to emphasize their problematic nature.

Parts of Chapter 7 first appeared in Volume 32 of *Government and Opposition*, Winter, 1997.

1 Introduction

Celebrations of the global triumph of liberal capitalist democracy have been cut short by stark failings in the practice of newly democratic governments. Around half the world's states can now claim to protect basic political rights and to have instituted regular multi-party elections. Yet the new democracies continue to be dominated by clientelism, social division and class conflict. Moreover, they display multifaceted institutional weakness. Political participation remains at a low level, local democracy and civic institutions are fragile, and corruption threatens to negate the gains that democracy might bring.

The established liberal democracies meanwhile are faced with a steady deterioration in their own democratic systems. Popular discontent with political leaders has spread across the whole OECD zone over the past decade. Trust in the institutions of and participants in democratic government has weakened, and faith in the capacity of democratic institutions is failing; anti-party populism has been rising amidst disintegrating party systems; and corruption and extremism have become newly powerful forces in political life. Some analysts even see a longer-term erosion of 'social capital', the quality that supposedly makes democracy possible by supporting cooperation and collective action for mutual benefit.[1]

Western liberal democracy has also become morally exposed in consequence of its very success. The lack of any remaining alternative vision of political order has destroyed the relative attractiveness democracy used to enjoy next to its communist competitor. Moreover, the persistence or deepening of international injustice, the entrenchment of domestic structural inequality and the impotence of democracy in the face of the violence and destructiveness of third world capitalism, have exposed the weaknesses of democratic government to the citizens who live under it.

In the midst of this disheartening tale of growing popular disillusion, the South African election of 1994 had counter-intuitive effects on popular consciousness in the West. In the UK, Scandinavia and North America, publics followed the process of negotiation and election with unusual interest. Democratization elsewhere had been narrated as a morality tale – particularly the transitions from communist rule in Eastern and Central Europe. Other small states' popular struggles against authoritarian rule – such as those in the Philippines – had also attracted widespread attention in the West. But South Africa produced something quite distinct, not just in the degree of international media interest attracted, but also in the significance of the election to outsiders.

In this book, I use the South African experience, and the ways in which it has been viewed within and outside the Republic, to explore the internal strains within political science, and also to reflect more generally on the predicament of liberal democracy. I use the South African case to bring to light failures of understanding that are hard to identify in self-conscious and defensive Western universities. I am also interested in the possible futures of the South African state, and I investigate how changes in the Republic's political institutions are likely to affect the lives of the majority of the population. Democratic transitions generally are explored with a view to explaining how they have come about: I explore the more pertinent issue of the consequences that may follow from the democratization of a polity.

I begin in chapter 2 with an introduction to the political history of South Africa, accomplished by means of a rudimentary periodization. My intention in this chapter is to introduce readers unfamiliar with South Africa to its short history. (Readers familiar with the literature may wish to move directly to chapter 3.) I demonstrate the difficulties that follow attempts to provide South Africans with a common history, while stressing the degree to which the ramifications of the late nineteenth-century mineral revolutions were felt across the many different societies then present in the region. In particular, I emphasize that the existence of the state itself, as a socio-political reality as well as an object of historical analysis, was a direct consequence of the mineral revolutions. For this reason alone, the current reaction against materialist explanations of segregation is likely to prove short-lived.

Chapter 3 explores the development of historical writing on South Africa in more depth, and stresses the richness but also the limitations of historical method in constructing agreed pasts in so fractious a country. I argue that historians have carried the academic burden of critical political analysis in the apartheid state. This has led an extraordinarily rich tradition of historical analysis, constantly energized and energizing, to be shackled to the exigencies of contemporary politics. While in many ways desirable and enlivening of the literature, political debate among Whites, conducted in coded historical language, continues to serve the self-consciousness of only one fragment of South Africa's population. The chapter suggests that there are many reasons why South African historical writing is likely to remain rich, but it argues that rejuvenated political studies can relieve professional historians of their unendurable burden and can achieve much that the historical method cannot.

Chapters 4–7 address the past achievements and future potential of professional political analysis both in and of South Africa. Chapter 4 is the most aggressively counter-suggestive of these chapters, having as its theme the potentially evil consequences of democracy. I take issue with a conventional wisdom that sees democracy as the end-point of apartheid, or as the regime type that replaced it (or even that liberated South Africa from it). I argue, by contrast, that the Union was undoubtedly a democracy from 1910. What is more, I find that no tension existed between the practice of democracy and the large-scale and systematic exploitation of the majority of the population. Moreover, democracy can plausibly be considered to have caused apartheid. This argument takes seriously and elaborates the belief of many White South Africans that they merely reproduced Western European practices. High apartheid, on this reading, assisted the process of decolonization and liberation, so belatedly parallelling experiences elsewhere in Africa. My intention in this chapter is not to celebrate the benign intentions of the creators of apartheid, nor even to investigate the degree to which its apologists were honest in their claims. Rather, I wish to show how limited are the critical resources of liberal democratic ideology in the face of those willing to use it to justify their exploitative practices.

Chapter 5 moves to the glamorous international community of comparative political scholarship. While comparative politics for decades remained a junior branch of North American political science, it has in the 1990s developed its own academic jet-set. Its new expertise, suddenly much in demand, has been in the field of democratization, an evidently important subject upon which deservedly large amounts of time and money have been expended. I explore the (few) high and (many) low points of the literature, and discover that the African continent has not been well represented or respected in mainstream democratization analysis. The literature on democratic transitions is itself a historical product, shaped by the circumstances in which it was formed and by the political imperatives facing its creators. African democratization, belated and largely externally engineered, has not been treated seriously. The experiences of rich or strategically significant states, I argue, are viewed as the raw materials with which a purportedly empirical social science must come to terms. The experiences of African states, by contrast, have been treated as anomalies and have stimulated moralizing, ill-informed criticism and policy prescription.

Chapter 6 turns to the frenzy within political science in the run-up to South Africa's first universal suffrage election in 1994, and examines literature of domestic origin as well as comparative political analysis from Western Europe and North America. The pre-election period was marked by extreme disagreements between analysts. Some saw South Africa as a classic example of controlled negotiation. Others feared that ethnic civil war, explosive mass protest or military coups were dangers soon to be unleashed. I explore the reasoning of the doom-mongers to see whether professional political analysis can provide safeguards against exaggerated hopes and fears, or whether it is likely to fuel them. I find that different schools of academic analysis, tangentially connected yet organizing their thoughts around quite different sets of assumptions and procedures, mutually reinforced one another's least plausible presumptions. Key categories of description, moreover, were drawn from quite inappropriate settings. The relationships between major actors within the alliance between the African National Congress, the Confederation of South African Trade Unions (COSATU) and the Communist Party (SACP), and the role played by youth, civics, religious movements and self-conscious women's organizations were systematically misunderstood by analysts deploying the categories of Western political science.

Chapter 7 looks in greater depth at the immediate concerns of the negotiating parties in the tense period before the election of 1994, and at the efforts of political analysts from South Africa and overseas to facilitate an effective transition to democracy. Political analysts' sophisticated investigations, despite their careful design, often supported entrenched interests and gave voice to the already well represented and powerful. Constitutional designers, in an area of supposedly detached technical expertise, produced a range of feeble analyses which were wholeheartedly supported only by the National Party and Inkatha Freedom Party. The methods of political science seemingly provided no check against the direct reflection of the ideas and interests of the powerful. Domestic political analysts focused on scenarios, which heuristics were supposedly to benefit all groups. Designed and funded predominantly by business, and written by established social scientists, they provided a narrow conception of political possibility, serving to transmit an anti-populist message to African constituencies that did not need it.

My conclusions in chapter 8 are organized into three sections. First, I consider what academic political analyses of contemporary South Africa teach us about the nature of political science as a discipline. Second, I examine what South African experience shows us about the nature of Western liberal democracy, in particular addressing the relations between nation, territory and legitimacy that lie at the heart of Western political theory. The final section uses South Africa in 1994 to help make sense of the modern election. The great festivals of democratic politics, elections, remain poorly understood. The surprising strength of Western popular interest in the election conducted in this medium-sized developing country in 1994 has lessons for the jaded political leaders of the OECD zone.

2 A Periodization of South African History

INTRODUCTION

In this chapter, I provide an introductory periodization of South African history. This will serve three major purposes. First, it will provide the reader with the necessary contextual material to situate arguments of later chapters, and in particular the argument of chapter 3, which addresses conventional academic approaches to South African history and the 'liberal-revisionist' debate within English-language historiography.

Second, this chapter denaturalizes accounts of South African history that have been constructed in support of the historical identity and legitimacy claims of contemporary social groups. Contestation over appropriate periodization of South African history reflects not just antagonisms between the competing intellectual positions of historians and political scientists, but also the diverse attempts to construct coherent narratives of ethnic and nationalist destiny. Many central arguments in South African academic and political debate have turned on the significance of markers of key 'watersheds': 1652, the year of the establishment of the Dutch East India settlement at Cape Town; 1910, the year of formal national unification; 1948, the year the National Party won a general election on a slogan of 'apartheid'; and 1994, the year of the first universal franchise election. Key elements in the historical consciousness of Afrikaner, English and African – the mfecane, the Great Trek, the Zulu and South African Wars, petty apartheid and its legislative Acts, Sharpeville and Soweto – are introduced between and around these central dates in support of often highly moralized narratives which centre on particular population groups.

The third purpose of this chapter's fourfold periodization is to emphasize important but poorly registered aspects of South Africa's history: the dynamism and force of African politics throughout a post-settlement history that has usually been framed in colonial terms; the inescapable causal force of industrialization in the creation of the South African state, and also in the emergence of the distinctive identity-based prisms through which later historians have viewed the past; the logics and essential unity of segregation and early apartheid; and the extraordinary departure, in both comparative and domestic historical terms, represented by the period of 'high apartheid'.

My periodization does not make the (always) unsupportable claim to be definitive, independent of explanatory purpose or of intended audience. It is designed to bolster readers' counter-suggestibility in the face of partial renderings of South African history while steering clear of the identification of identity and historical destiny which have rendered arguments about periodization so intractable in the past. The relevant periods are: South African before minerals (pre-1870); the age of mineral revolutions and unification (1870–1910); the age of established segregation and early apartheid (1910–60); and the age of high apartheid (1960–90).

BEFORE MINERALS: SOUTH AFRICA TO 1870

Modern South African history begins with the discovery and exploitation of minerals in the 1870s, developments which resulted in the creation of the South African state. A great range of issues cannot be understood without reference to the social and political forms present in southern African before 1870: African political systems' ability to adapt and respond to the demands of migrant labour and quasi-proletarianization; Africans' modes of resistance to the apartheid state; Afrikaners' emergent organization around a nationalist political identity and their support for a politics of racial separation; the emergence of English speakers' social and political dominance; and the nature of capitalist development in South Africa. It is not merely that the relationships between different social groups in twentieth-century South Africa were strongly shaped by prior events; rather, it is the creation of those groups themselves and their forms that demand investigation of pre-1870 South Africa.

South Africa before 1870, however, has defied attempts to provide it with a single coherent history. Within the borders of this yet-to-be created state, groups with complex histories and distinct modes of self-understanding were engaged in increasingly harsh competition for resources. The oldest settlers of the area now occupied by South Africa were the hunting and herding societies known today as Khoikhoi, San or collectively Khoisan, who had been present in the west and north-west since around 1000 BC. Hunting and herding societies closest to settlement fared particularly badly during the early period of East

India Company rule: Boer settlers (and the diseases they brought with them) very rapidly subjugated the Khoisan peoples of the Western Cape (written out of contemporary history because of the absence of Khoisan nationalism).

African 'Bantu' political kingdoms had been expanding into what is today South Africa by a process of fracturing and movement, from around the third century AD. Engaged in dynamic processes of political formation and reformation, African polities had spread almost to the west of South Africa by the time of European settlement.[1] This occurred by means of a 'migratory drift' or 'gradual territorial expansion', rather than by means of a wave or waves of migration.[2] Chiefdoms split and new ones arose, inching into new lands, or lands occupied by hunter-gatherers or pastoralists. By the end of the eighteenth century, the population was reaching the limits of the potential of the South African land mass.

The effective political units in mixed Bantu farming societies were hereditary chiefdoms, varying in size from fewer than 1000 members to over 50,000.[3] Chiefdoms were not closed entities, but rather included people of different descent groups, migrants from poor regions and arrivals who had split from other chiefdoms. 'The Western concept of tribalism, which is usually taken to refer to closed populations reproducing fixed cultural characteristics,' as Thompson notes, 'is not applicable to African farmers.' Rather than 'closed reproducing entities, equipped with unique unchanging cultures', such societies were fluid and politically affiliative in composition. 'People interacted, co-operating and copulating as well as competing and combatting, exchanging ideas and practices as well as rejecting them.'[4]

The multiplicity of South Africa's political kingdoms around 1870 demonstrates the viability African polities retained after two centuries of settler expansion. It cannot, however, purport to demonstrate an equality of power, or some openness of historical potential: Afrikaner settlers benefited from technological and military advantages over African states. These latter, moreover, had undergone traumatic dislocations in the 1820s and 1830s, during the period known as mfecane or difaqane: and the admittedly far less numerous British settlers were backed by a great imperial power with the potential (albeit one it was very unwilling to exercise) to dominate the region militarily. Nevertheless, the map indicates the presence of powerful political structures, none of which achieved dominance over the others. Each contained its own histories which would come to influence later responses to political opportunity and historical crisis.

Both Africans' and Afrikaners' pre-1870s histories were open to romantic and teleological rendition, and this came to pass in the twentieth century, especially in the case of the Afrikaners. Boer nineteenth-century experience is marked more by its similarity to than its difference from African experience. The expansion of the Boer population north and east into the areas occupied by Bantu polities began in the late eighteenth century. White settlers achieved advances through a combination of factors: exploitation of divisions in African society, (uneven) cooperation between Whites, the technological superiority of firearms and the ability to store wealth in a more sophisticated economic system.

A major transformation occurred with a series of devastating conflicts centring on the region between the mountain escarpment and the Indian ocean. This process was driven by a centralization of the Zulu kingdom. The causes of the series of displacements called the mfecane (Zulu) or difaqane (Sesotho) are controversial: most analysts see the process as internal to mixed farming society – a collapse of the existing system of accumulation as the relationship between population level and environment changed. Fresh territory for exploitation became exhausted, and competition for land and water supplies grew. Severe droughts in the early nineteenth century triggered a process of concentration of power, and led to the emergence of a new scale of standing armies. A series of major conflicts led to the dislocation of the region's economies and the displacement of great bodies of refugees.[5] Other historians argue, by contrast, that it was foreign trade that lay behind the process of Zulu state centralization.[6] On this reading it was competition to control trade routes to Portuguese settlers on Delagoa Bay that spurred militarization.

Whatever the dynamics of dislocation, the resulting turmoil presented White settlers with an unprecedented opportunity. The sparsely populated central highveld in the aftermath of these massive conflicts gave Afrikaner travellers the impression of an empty land – uninhabited and unclaimed. Simultaneously, the Cape colony became increasingly inhospitable to Afrikaner settlers. Britain had taken direct control over the Cape in 1795 and permanently controlled it from 1805. It was introducing cultural and legal changes which damaged Afrikaner interests and weakened their power over their labourers from 1833. The growing influence of the ideals of the French Revolution and the growing influence of evangelical opponents of exploitation threatened further damage to Afrikaners' customary practices of dominance. The option of migration to the immediate east, moreover, was blocked: the frontier wars with Xhosa speakers had shown them to be politically and militarily highly resilient.

The 'Great Trek' – in reality a series of episodic migrations totalling about 12,000 persons (half of whom were Khoi servants and former slaves) – left the Cape between 1836 and 1840. Conflicts with African polities ensued, followed by settlements, first in Natal and then (after British annexation) in the highveld. While they secured effective independence from the British, as London no longer viewed protection of African against Afrikaner as worthy of expense, they remained poor and vulnerable, and in incomplete control over the territory which they had claimed the right to rule.

British behaviour was driven by an unwillingness to expend resources on this unimportant region. The Cape Colony had been occupied in 1795 to prevent it falling to the French; its consolidation as a British possession from 1806 to 1814 followed the Cape's strategic location on the trading routes of the English East India Company, notably to India. 'Like the Dutch before them,' Thompson remarks, 'the British had no vital material interest in South Africa beyond the peninsula. But appended to that strategic prize was a complex, violent, and largely anarchic society, scattered over a vast hinterland.'[7]

The profound unimportance of South Africa, beyond its immediate role as a staging post, was reflected in the small proportion of British overseas capital attracted to it, the very small number of British emigrants in comparison to other colonies, and the paucity of British commitment of manpower and resources. By 1870, the United States had 32 million inhabitants of European origin or descent and 53,000 miles of railways; southern Africa as a whole was occupied by 250,000 White people and possessed around 70 miles of railways.[8] The total value of imports was only £3 million per annum; exports were even less.[9] The biggest town housed just 50,000 inhabitants.

The marginal status of the turbulent hinterland persisted through the early and mid-nineteenth century. In the face of potential alliances between Sotho and Trekker, indeed, the British were willing to concede Boer independence in the South African Republic (later Transvaal) in 1852. Further Sotho resistance led to a truce and colonial withdrawal.[10] Indeed, the mid-nineteenth century is often viewed as a time of general withdrawal from commitments by the colonial power. British migration, moreover, remained at a low level. In 1820, a Conservative government eager to placate domestic critics, funded the migration of 4000 settlers from the British Isles. These were settled in the Eastern Cape agricultural belt, but rapidly adopted trading and commercial occupations.[11] They added new complexity to southern African society, and remained culturally distinct from Afrikaner settlers, so creating a nascent ethnic division and antagonism within the White population.

While reform influences in Britain had repercussions in South Africa as in other British colonies, these were not decisive in dividing Whites. Participation in the slave trade was outlawed in 1807 (depriving Cape farmers of easy labour access), and in 1823 minimum standards of food, clothing and maximum working hours and punishments were imposed (albeit grudgingly and patchily enforced) as a spillover from a tax on slavery in the Caribbean. Further legislation secured the legal position of the Khoi-Khoi and former slaves, although it could not remove their poverty and economic dependence. As Thompson put it, 'the reforms were the reforms of freedom, but the facts were still the facts of exploitation'.[12]

The tide of philanthropy, in any event, had ebbed in Britain by the mid-nineteenth century. The British settlers were themselves faced with the same conditions as Afrikaners: insecure frontiersmen fighting against Africans for land legally granted to them without the consent of its customary inhabitants. They brought with them the distinctive racism of mid-Victorian Britain and adapted it to these new circumstances.

The seeming withdrawal of British colonial power in the mid-nineteenth century, as Worden explains, was belied by the establishment of considerable colonial economic influence by the 1850s.[13] While Afrikaners lay beyond the reach of systematic imperial interference, the colonial heartland was increasingly incorporated into the Empire. Trade was centred on the Cape, and migrant labour had been drawn to the colony from the 1840s. Where Cape interests were threatened, intervention was rapid and effective. Moreover, the very fact of possession brought with it inescapable responsibilities: notably to provide a modicum of law and order in the frontier zone. These pressures, mediated through military, evangelical and commercial interests, resulted in a continuous stream of (to Boers) unwanted interventions by the British authorities.

Up to 1870, it is extraordinarily difficult to identify the elements of a common history of the African peoples of South Africa. Many African polities remained little affected by settler penetration, and there was little sign of disintegration or of the collapse that had affected the indigenous peoples of other colonies. Like Boer republics and colonies, they faced an inhospitable physical environment and endured the unwanted attentions of settlers increasingly frequently and disruptively across the decades. African societies, furthermore, were constantly changing, and the rate of change accelerated in the early nineteenth century with the rise of the Zulu kingdom.[14] In such circumstances, the part-mythical histories, by means of which rulers justified their claims to obedience, were themselves ever changing. African polities, however, were usually robust, and existed alongside republican states that were fragile and vulnerable, and colonial states with few resources of the imperial power at their command. Many Africans, furthermore, were using the opportunities presented by settlement to their advantage.[15]

Southern Africa's relatively small quasi-states were influenced in diverse ways by their relations to each other and to the forces of settler expansion and trade. All of these republics, colonies or polities were multi-ethnic and multi-lingual.[16] Experiences had been diverse and incorporated into political behaviour and institutions in different ways. Most polities lacked the bases of political and cultural unity and limited political self-consciousness was the rule. The history of the polities in the 1870s could never be told as an attempt to master collective destiny since political leaders were attempting to survive in unforgiving circumstances: there was no South African history to tell.

THE MINERAL REVOLUTIONS AND THE CREATION OF THE SOUTH AFRICAN STATE: 1870–1910

If southern Africa before 1870 contained myriad interrelations between changing political communities, then post-1870 South Africa was marked by a quite different relation between collective self-understanding and social change. From 1870 the populations of the area covered by presentday South Africa were driven by a common series of impersonal forces. South Africans faced novel social experiences and a realm of malevolent economic causality which imposed social transformation. The roots of this upheaval lay in the finds of diamonds and gold, and the responses of the British colonial power to these discoveries. Four massive processes marked the transformation of South Africa over this period: war, unification, economic development and quasi-proletarianization. Each can be traced directly to the discovery of diamonds and then gold; and each can be seen to have unleashed processes beyond the control and imagination of political actors.

Diamonds were discovered in 1867. By 1871, 75,000 people had flocked to the diamond fields. These discoveries, by attracting investment from overseas and spurring industrialization, can be said to have initiated modern capitalism in South Africa. With the development they brought came greater labour demands – not only directly in the mines, but also on the farms, on the railways and in public works. These demands for labour, and the greater economic significance to outsiders that diamonds gave to South Africa, led to British attempts to break the Zulu, Sotho and Afrikaner polities' resistance.

Diamonds, however, were small beer compared to gold. Discovered in 1886 on the Witwatersrand, gold mining proved to be the principal spur for the transformation of the region as a whole. The gold was of low quality, difficult to extract, but immensely plentiful. Potential gold wealth was vast. The metal, moreover, played an important role in the international economy and its effective exploitation was a British imperative. Mining and associated industrialization demanded vast domestic as well as skilled foreign labour together with an integrated state infrastructure.

The demand for labour was justification enough for breaking the resistance of African polities. The defeat of the Boers, by contrast, was arguably unnecessary. While not ideal midwives of industrialization, and still attuned to the voices and interests of dispersed settlers, the Afrikaner republics might have come to a negotiated settlement. The defeat of Boer forces in the South African war cemented ethnic antagonism between Britain and Afrikaner, at the same time as it created the single South African state within which both would coexist.

Unification was the ultimate goal of war. Far from merely representing a legalistic or constitutional device, unification was a comprehensive process of state creation. The British developed the logistical power of the state to control, tax, enforce contracts, secure transport links, control and regulate labour and business, and ensure strategic security across the state as a whole. By so doing it ensured that the mineral inheritance of South Africa could be exploited safely by British-based conglomerates.

Economic development in the new urban areas, the third key process of change, was signalled by the extraordinary growth of the Johannesburg and the Witwatersrand region, and by the wholesale transformation of the economic geography of South Africa. Johannesburg did not exist in 1880. By 1911 it contained 240,000 inhabitants, and the Witwatersrand as a whole twice that number. By contrast Cape Town contained fewer than 200,000 people. The creation of urban areas from scratch in very short order accompanied the incorporation within them of a vast and diverse range of labour: low-skill and low-wage mine labour from across the region, service workers and new migrants.

These events were new in scale and reach, but drew on earlier practices and ideologies. Reserves, urban influx control and the manipulation of chiefs had all been recognized by Britain's unification High Commissioner Milner as vital for an industrializing state. Social Darwinism helped justify the policies of the colonial state, and further ideological support was provided by new segregationalist terminology from the United States. What made South Africa's segregationist policy unique, however, was how closely it followed the needs of the mining industry and how adaptable it had to be made to the demands of agricultural capital.

The fourth major process of change in South Africa lay beyond the town. South Africa developed a system of migrant labour that was to mark its later twentieth-century history. Migrancy began in the sugarfields of Natal to which migrant workers from Mozambique had been drawn. It was to become a system of cheap labour feeding the Witwatersrand mining, commercial and agricultural sectors – by 1910 90 per cent of the Black population of Johannesburg was male – and later the backbone the industrial and commercial systems of apartheid as a whole. The mine owners' initial preference for such migrant labour, primarily because it was cheap, meshed with African interests since labour by young men provided money for chiefs and fathers. Only gradually did money become necessary for survival. By the 1920s, 30–40 per cent of all active men in rural areas were away working at any given time.

These massive changes – warfare on a grand scale, the creation of a modern state, the new economy and the transformation of rural areas by migrancy – were wrought over a short period and by forces that can only be conceived as abstract: markets, imperial power, capital. Without these changes there would be no South Africa; no need for the investment of resources and the expenditure of violence that created the modern South African state.[17]

The Act of Union of 1910 cemented a political arrangement compatible with these vast changes. It served, moreover, to entrench the privileged interests of Whites by means of the electoral machinery of democracy. Whites secured a virtual monopoly of electoral power, with a property franchise retained in the Cape Colony alone. This period of South African history, therefore, saw not merely the institutional foundations of segregation laid, but also the political institutions by means of which competition for power could be accommodated – without permitting any legitimate contribution from non-Whites.

SEGREGATION AND EARLY APARTHEID: 1910–1960

The modern South African state developed from unification in largely unsurprising ways until the 1960s. Only in retrospect have segregation and early apartheid come to seem somehow natural precursors to the extraordinary perversity of high apartheid which followed them. Postwar reconstruction was shaped by powerful links between the new state and the mines, in tandem with the entrenched role of farmers in the new political dispensation through the electoral system. The state–mine relation kept the question of labour supply at the heart of government policy. Reserves, influx control and the manipulation of traditional authority were re-attuned to the needs of state-sponsored industrialization. Social Darwinism and liberal-democratic ideology turned the new segregationist policy into a reliable servant of mining and agricultural capital. The decade after 1910 saw continued English dominance and deepening racial segregation under the auspices of a political alliance between Afrikaner agriculture (with its disproportionate electoral power), White mine owners and those dependent on them.[18]

The African population was further regulated where it remained on the land, and further proletarianized through the migrant labour system. The Natives Land Act of 1913 allocated 87 per cent of land to Whites – albeit including much of the most fertile land and leaving many Africans on speculatively held land on White farms – and moved to prohibit native land purchase and non-labour based tenancies. The Urban Areas Act, enacted in 1923, laid down the legal tools to entrench further the practices of segregation and influx control. The formative phase of influx control had been the 30 years following 1890. Initially a discretionary process, by means of which cash income was chosen as a supplement to rural economic activity, it eventually became unavoidable as taxes, dispossession and population growth squeezed rural populations. The Chamber of Mines used chiefs, traders and criminals to recruit young, male workers, and from 1910 became increasingly cost-focused and geographically ambitious in recruitment. A centralized and effective system was in place by 1920 – by which time 200,000 workers were involved in migrancy in any year – and this eventually grew to some 430,000 workers in 1961.

1922–33 was a period of economic nationalism and class conflict between mining capital and White workers. The 1922 Rand revolt, in which Afrikaans- and English-speaking Whites fought against capitalism but also against Blacks, was crushed only by considerable military firepower and at the cost of more than 200 lives. The government of 1924, which combined Hertzog's National Party with the Labour Party, pursued an import-substitution strategy and oversaw the foundations of an Afrikaner welfare state. The emergence of Afrikaner nationalism, itself a creature of social dislocation, served as a bridge across regional and class divides.

Between 1933 and 1948, South Africa emerged from the depression into a second industrial revolution. On the back of the rise in the gold price which followed the collapse of the Gold Standard, and further bolstered by increased demand for manufactured exports as the North prepared for global war, the economy grew rapidly, with English interests spreading out from their heartland in the gold mining economy. General economic affluence, fuelled by gold and the export boom, helped to fund government welfare and agricultural support programmes, but did not prevent the growth of Malan's 'purified' National Party and the shattering of White unity over the course (and the issue) of the war. After the 'fusion government' was formed in 1934, this breakaway National Party managed, with increasing success, to deploy cultural and educational organizations, Afrikaner unions and business groups (with representatives from both Cape and Transvaal Afrikaner elites) in national Afrikaner mobilization. Despite the benefits that the fusion government sought to bring to these groups, farmers, civil servants, teachers and poor Whites turned increasingly towards the Nationalists.

The mid- to late 1930s marked a first high-point of segregation. The Economic Commission of 1930–2 had resurrected the notion of African tribe and bolstered it with theories of native mentality, rural dependency, propensity to violence and 'cattle complex', which had been defined and explored by anthropologists.[19] Acts passed in 1936 consolidated the reserves and removed Africans from the Cape franchise.

This high point of segregation was also a low point of Black resistance. The ANC had remained elitist, isolated from labour and radical protest throughout its existence; and Indian and Coloured political movements organized around particularist concerns. Political organization in the remarkable Industrial and Commercial Union (ICU) in the 1920s never threatened the South African state;[20] and political resistance was largely expressed within churches and by means of widespread non-compliance and resistance of individuals. Politics for Africans was a defensive process: the use of forms of traditional authority and religious belief to defend land rights and grazing, and to advance localized interests in urban situations.

1939–48 saw a relaxation of segregation and an inexorable urbanization. White and Black were drawn to the towns, but the change in Africans' situation was striking. Between 1936 and 1946, the number of Africans in urban areas grew from 139,000 to 390,000, many of whom were women. The presence of Africans in the urban economy was expressed politically in a number of ways: Black trade unions blossomed; higher-skilled jobs were opened to Africans and colour bars in many sectors floated upwards; and the formal organizations of African politics – notably the ANC Youth League from 1942 – began to organize deliberately integrative protests to draw together the opponents of segregation. The South African Communist Party arranged anti-pass protests in 1943–4; bus boycotts became a major instrument of protest; strikes escalated across the war years; and thereafter the turmoil continued into the peace as the younger generation of Nelson Mandela and Oliver Tambo galvanized the ANC into action with the use of strike and squatter methods on the Rand.

1948 is signalled by many analysts as a turning point or a pivotal date in South African history. It is, however, misleadingly ascribed this status, and the continuities across the period to 1960 were more striking than the discontinuities. Only in the 1960s, with the second phase of apartheid, did Afrikaner power exert itself to produce the unprecedented social deformation of high apartheid. Why, then, has 1948 been taken to be the key date in South African twentieth-century political history?

There are three reasons: an election, a slogan and a moral repugnancy. The election of 1948 represented the first major triumph for a new and non-conciliatory generation of Afrikaner politicians. This victory was a slender one and represented no massive swing in White (or even Afrikaner) sentiment. Smuts lost many Afrikaners' support because of 'swamping' fears associated with Black urbanization, economic austerity and the presence of Africans in jobs formerly reserved for (war-mobilized) Whites. Local issues made a major impact in Natal where anti-Indian land restrictions played a central role; in the Transvaal and Orange Free State, doubts among farmers about labour supply and the intentions of the United Party led to a swing to Malan's NP, despite the latter's Cape origins and core support. Nevertheless,

40 per cent of Afrikaners voted for the UP, and the NP relied on the votes of 20 per cent of English speakers to achieve their overall 39 per cent.[21] Here again, good fortune played a role. While the UP and Labour won 53 per cent between them, the NP secured narrow victories in weighted rural and peri-urban constituencies.

Thus, while 1948 is seen as important in part because it was a pivotal election, this election secured a tenuous and fortuitous victory on a minority and protest vote. The changed electoral coalitions that secured long-term NP power came earlier and later: earlier in the creation of Afrikaner nationalism as a cross-class and inter-regional force that could potentially unify labour and agriculture around the policy of segregation, and later in the establishment of core Afrikaner control over the White electorate as a whole.

The second reason for the predominance of 1948 as the key date in twentieth-century South African historical writing was a slogan: 'Apartheid'. Apartheid as an all-encompassing system of institutionalized racial segregation is undoubtedly the phenomenon that must above all others be explained in South African history: it is the unavoidable problem around which a coherent history of South Africa must be organized. The term first rose to prominence in the National Party's electoral campaign of 1948 and became a common figure of speech across White South Africa in that year. Therefore, many analysts have supposed that this campaign in this year must be pivotal.

This is to read history backwards. The slogan 'apartheid', along with the fears of Black urbanization and job competition to which it drew attention, was an important asset of the National Party in its marginal minority win in 1948. While the word was widely used a decade before the system of high apartheid was put in place, its importance lay in its very ambiguity. NP supporters agreed that Africans should continue to be excluded from political power and that White supremacy should be maintained. Beyond this, however, apartheid provided a means of papering over great differences. Should Afrikaners strive for total segregation, with the replacement of African labour by White labour (by birth or migration), as many intellectuals, clerics and teachers argued? Or should businessmen and agriculturalists continue to have access to Black labour in a pragmatic and moderated form of segregation?[22] Alternatively, should apartheid consist in the rebuttal of African advances in the labour market? Appealing to new voters and war returnees, enabling cross-class and cross-regional support from electors who might otherwise split along class and regional lines, the slogan 'apartheid' was an accident of political rhetoric.

A third reason for the significance attached to 1948 is a sentimental one: the National Party enacted a vast body of repugnant legislation in the period immediately after its first electoral success.[23] In this mass of legislation, the Population Registration Act enforced the classification of people into four strict racial categories: they were to be white, Coloured, Asiatic or native (later Bantu or African). In the first period of NP rule, however, the focus was on symbolically important aspects of life as much as upon the economics of the labour market. 'Mixed marriages' were prohibited in 1949, and in 1950 all sexual contact between Whites and other South Africans was prohibited by the Immorality Act. Likewise, residential segregation became a key target of legislative activity. The Group Areas Act of 1950 enforced separate residential areas by race comprehensively across the country.[24] The Reservation of Separate Amenities Act of 1953 segregated transport, cinemas, restaurants, sporting facilities, and so on. A series of Acts enforcing segregation in schools, colleges and universities were passed through the 1950s.

Those who gained most from substantive apartheid legislation achieved major gains at the cost of a massive loss to the victims of the legislation. Much segregationist legislation was designed to reshape South Africa's structures of economic opportunity. Petty apartheid legislation after 1948, by contrast, lacked this hallmark of systematic exploitation. Legislation was distinguished by blatant racism and by the transparency of connection between legislation and human suffering. Translated into human misery and apportioning this misery strictly according to 'race', this programme lacked a cushion of instrumental rationality to soften its evil.

Three factors in combination – the electoral win of the National Party, the later importance that the term apartheid adopted and the moral repugnancy and seeming triviality of early NP legislation – made 1948 a year of seemingly unprecedented importance. The myth of 1948 as the great break in South African history has been manifest in the notion that apartheid was a 'grand plan', unfolded by NP leaders in the 30 years following 1948. Recent scholarship, however, has shown that NP policy represented a pragmatic continuation of pre-1948 government strategy – albeit an intensification of it – and a reactive series of responses by the party. The notion that 1948 saw an intensification rather than a turning point was pushed forcefully by Wilson in his analysis of the extension of mining labour practices across the South African industry as a whole. Wilson identified the entrenchment of the colour bar by 1926, the strength of the 'civilized labour policy' of

1924–36, the Wage Act of 1925 and the role of education as a barrier to apprenticeship as precursors to early apartheid. Retaining the notion of design, Wilson argued that the architects of apartheid took the gold mining industry as their model.[25]

Not merely in the economic sphere, but more generally across the fields of social policy, apartheid in the 1950s represented rather a series of *ad hoc* attempts to resolve embedded problems. In urban areas, Nationalists wanted to restore control over population growth and Black politics, and embarked on a 'stabilization' strategy of squatter camp destruction, the purification of White areas and township construction. In rural areas, the messy compromises of retribalization were formalized through the Bantu Authorities Act of 1951 into a distinct realm of African politics with an associated 'traditional' system of administration and authority.[26]

The idea of a grand plan became established because of its attractiveness to both liberals and Afrikaners. The former used the notion to condemn Afrikaners as fanatical imposers of a systematic oppression; the latter liked to believe in their own foresight and in the destiny they saw as embedded in this process of social engineering. Moreover, they could endow the messy reality of oppression with the moral perfectionism that could accompany complete separation and independence.

As Posel has shown, however, the steady consolidation represented by the policies of the 1948 government's legislation does not imply a great degree of planning or control. Proponents of the NP's ability to plan systematically have always advanced as evidence the Sauer Report of 1947 – a document that attempted to give substance to the slogan of apartheid while uniting the farmers of the Transvaal, Orange Free State and the Cape, with White labour and the Afrikaner petty bourgeoisie. Posel demonstrates that this report reproduced divergencies within Afrikanerdom rather than settling them. The total segregationalist aspirations of intellectuals and petty bourgeois Afrikaners were irreconcilable with the practical designs of prosperous Afrikaner industrialists and financiers; their combination created an 'ambiguous combination of purist and "practical" recommendations', leaving the 1948 government lacking any 'compelling, unambiguous, and uncontested blueprint from which state policies could simply be read off.'[27]

Not only was there no consistent plan, there were immediate and inescapable pressures on NP leaders. Policy had to satisfy not merely Afrikaner interests but also English capital and the largest local authorities (which remained UP-dominated). They also faced the threat of

African resistance and the nagging danger of electoral desertion: 'Uncertain of its reelection in 1953,' as Posel reminds us, 'the newly elected Nationalist government was anxious to consolidate its power base within the state and the electorate at large.'[28] In chapter 4 I shall argue that neither this strong continuity between the 1940s and 1950s, nor the impact of competitive liberal democratic policies, has yet been reflected fully in the literature. However, the 1960s represented a genuine departure, and one for which three preconditions were in part laid by the policies and practices of the 1950s.

The first precondition for high apartheid was the consolidation of the electoral constituency of the National Party. This was accomplished with speed and skill: the abolition of the Cape franchise and the rigging of the Namibian constituency contribution quickly enhanced the party's uncertain electoral potential. A second precondition was the creation of a new moral climate among White electors as a whole. The blatant and systematic racism of the legislation of the 1950s, combined with the potential created by effective population classification, made possible the conception of quite distinct social lives being created for distinct racial and ethnic groups.

A third prerequisite for the creation of high apartheid was the sidelining of English-speaking bureaucrats and their replacement by Afrikaners – and, in particular, by the members of the Broederbond – as the instruments of Afrikaner political will. By the 1950s, the Bond was in control of the heartlands of executive power in the South African state, and the Native Affairs Department (NAD) had grown to be a state within a state. It was within NAD that the policies of the 1960s fomented.

Statism was a defining theme of 1950s politics. Bonner et al. comment that the Nationalists were convinced that 'most of the problems [the state] confronted in 1948 could be solved effectively by simply expanding the scope and intensity of state intervention on the social, political, and economic fronts'.[29] However, even where the NP appeared to be following a new and distinctively statist route, it seems very likely that a United Party government would have followed very much the same one. Nattrass argues of the 1948 government that 'the structural problems facing the economy...were those which would have faced any government and would probably have been dealt with in much the same way.'[30] The Fagan Commission of 1946 had recommended 'ideally voluntary' labour bureaux and identity documents in its prescriptions for the control of African urbanization (even while admitting that such population movements had to be tolerated). The UP put its name to Fagan's recommendations. 'Had the UP won that election,' as Bonner et al. point out, 'there is good reason to suppose that the shift into a more statist era would have happened anyway.'[31]

SOUTH AFRICA FROM 1960: THE RISE AND COLLAPSE OF HIGH APARTHEID

The retrospective reading of 1948–60 as a period of grand plan and strategic statism is thus a misconception, supported by a misplaced emphasis on 1948. The 1950s in reality saw a government addressing serious difficulties with a series of *ad hoc* responses, in a context of intense electoral and administrative pressure, and with Afrikaner economic interests ultimately protected by pragmatism. The legislative programme was never able to do more than scratch the surface of South Africa's structural economic and social problems. The governments of the 1950s, moreover, do not appear bizarre in comparative terms. White supremacy and the exclusion of minorities from participation in formal political activity remained commonplace, and were not absent from even the advanced liberal democracies.

The 1960s, by contrast, were a qualitatively distinct period in South African history, and indeed a unique episode in world political history. They are the years of most significance for those trying to understand the moral and political significance of apartheid. The emerging academic consensus that the policies of the 1960s were a change of direction rather than a cumulative process of deepening segregation is well founded. Fresh and distinct elements emerged: the abandonment of White supremacy for the pervasive and far more dangerous notion of self-government; the creation of a doctrine of 'separate development', with its corollary of industrial decentralization; the introduction of mass forced removals and the changed class structure and re-tribalization that the homelands brought with them. In apartheid's second phase, the reach of the state increased, the policing system intensified and distinct security and military apparatuses competed increasingly to dominate the South African's state executive core; and influx controls were re-entrenched and strengthened.

Separate development was the key concept in this phase of apartheid. Africans' political rights were transferred to a series of quasi-states under the Promotion of Bantu Self-Government Act of 1959. These homelands were to serve political rather than merely economic functions, and African political rights were to be confined to them. Ten were eventually established, and in 1970 homeland citizenship was imposed on all Africans. In the following decade, four of the homelands were nominally, and without international recognition, declared independent.

The idea that Africans and others should live and enjoy political rights in distinct ethnic homelands was a change of great significance. Whereas White supremacy and segregation had involved an explicit racial hierarchy in legislative and political practice, the NP from 1961 was committed to formal equality between groups understood in ethnic terms. The inspiration for these moves was in part the decolonization movements elsewhere in Africa. If African nationalists could press for the independence of artificial and arbitrarily defined states, then why could not equally artificial states be granted independence within South Africa itself. Such 'internal decolonization' was inspired particularly by the experiences of the former British protectorates of Botswana, Lesotho and Swaziland, which many Afrikaner political leaders had hoped to incorporate into South Africa (in recognition that they were economically dependent on it). The abandonment of White supremacy in favour of self-determination drew on an extended intellectual history, however. Cape liberals had advanced a very similar understanding of a relationship between a collectivity and the process of self-determination.

As I shall argue later, moreover, the idea that distinctive political rights should be allocated in accordance with pre-existing territorial affiliation is a mainstay of European liberal democratic thought. The champions of democracy, and notably its idealist proponents, have always advanced democracy as the ideal political form *for* a political community; its properties as the creator or destroyer of political communities have been less carefully explored, in part because it has grown and spread from areas of the globe in which nation-states (or state nations) have been the characteristic political form of the state.

SEPARATE DEVELOPMENT AND 'TRIBALISM'

The doctrine of separate development provided the economic and territorial rationale for these homelands and itself rested on the bizarre notion that ethnicity (or tribe) might be ascribed to all African South Africans. Ethnic categories were to be enforced by means of comprehensive social engineering. Communities, and even families, were divided as the intellectual servants of apartheid categorized everyone in accordance with rules of descent. Population removals, simplified now by a simple classification by race and ethnic group, could adopt a stark brutality. Between 1960 and 1989, 3.5 million people were forcibly removed, having been found to be of inappropriate ethnicity for their location.

The homelands were never in danger of acquiring economic self-sufficiency. As a contribution to their viability, the South African government introduced location incentives to business on the borders of each homeland. This 'industrial decentralization' and investment in the institutions of homelands self-government did not make the homelands self-sustaining, but it was substantial enough to create perverse incentives which remain in place today.

Another necessary and related policy was the systematic 're-tribalization'. Ethnicity was established as the principal foundation of homeland self-government, with ethnic affiliation designed to displace South African nationality as the proper political identification of Africans. A successful reorientation of Africanist and African nationalist political activity, to accommodate it to the historical peculiarities of the Bantustans, evidently require systematic propagation; re-tribalization was the state's response.

'Tribalism' has caused political analysts great difficulty in sub-southern Africa, with South Africa as no exception. On the one hand, politics based on ethnic affiliation and traditional systems of authority seems an obstacle to any benevolent political settlement; ethnic attachments have been viewed as a hangover from the past, and 'tribal' divisions have been viewed as a continuing bar to the development of liberal democratic politics. The official ethnic divisions of 1960s South Africa had plainly been defined, and to a great extent shaped, by European academics and missionaries who in earlier decades codified, recorded and disseminated tribal languages, cultures and national histories. Yet, at the same time, academic analysts were aware that ethnic self-understandings could not be imposed on an unwilling population and must therefore gain some purchase in existing affiliation or interest.

In consequence, there have been broadly three ways of understanding tribalism and its importance: an essentialist view, an instrumentalist view and a historical-constructivist position. Essentialism, expunged from international scholarship, remains the 'common-sense' view of ethnicity in White South Africa (including its universities).[32] On an essentialist view, tribes are timeless, ahistorical collectivities: social groupings with common languages, cultural practices and physical features. With their exclusion of outside cultural, political or linguistic influences, such 'tribes' were inherently antagonistic and prone to engage in bouts of warfare. Such a view of ethnicity can be labelled 'essentialist' because it supposes that there lies within a community some common core or essence, made up of language and social practices, that is passed on from generation to generation across an unchanging cultural terrain.

The second, 'instrumentalist view' considers human identity to be plastic. Drawing on the history of colonialism, instrumentalists argue that the modern tribe is a creation of colonial rule. The interrelated languages and cultural practices of southern Africa, on this view, were the creations of the great social fluidity that accompanied migration, conflict and political disintegration and reintegration. African societies were the creations of affiliation to political structures, rather than linguistic, cultural or historical unities. Academics, missionaries and colonial administrators were the creators of tribalism. Academics examined and codified the practices of African peoples. Drawing upon a model of societies as self-sustaining and timeless, they conjured up pseudo-languages out of dialects; they invented their histories; and they created a new class of African leaders, drawn from those in power when their colonists arrived, and turned them into timeless ruling clans. Missionaries likewise recorded languages and practices. They also ran the major institutions of socialization of later generations of African political leaders. Most importantly, however, for instrumentalists, tribalism's role lay in assisting colonial strategies of rule and exploitation. The overstretched and under-resourced administrative structures of British rule could not cope with the maintenance of law and order, the collection of taxes, the extraction of labour and the whole host of other state functions. Rather, like other colonial powers, they had to rely upon local systems of authority; if these 'traditional' institutions were absent, they were created.[33]

The third, 'constructivist', view of tribalism recognizes the unsustainability of the naive essentialist thesis, but nonetheless rejects the instrumentalist account as crude, ahistorical and silent on the motivations of Africans.[34] Ethnic identification could never simply be imposed, but had to be consciously and deliberately created out of patterns of experience and affiliation. In South Africa, the industrialization and quasi-proletarianization of the late nineteenth and twentieth centuries dislocated pre-colonial polities and destroyed the conditions of viability of local political affiliations. Constructivists agree that outsiders created the formal linguistic and cultural materials around which modern tribalism could be organized. Formalization in teaching of written African languages secured the preconditions for ethnic divisions along linguistic divides. Native administrators, concerned to bolster traditional culture and overcome class divisions,[35] found these ideas useful.

Constructivists agree with instrumentalists that divide-and-rule strategies, and the need to secure labour supplies and tax revenues, drove much of the historical process of created tribalism. Nonetheless, the perceptions and interests of three African groups – local chiefs, middle-class Africans and migrant workers – were at the heart of the emergence of tribalism. Local chiefs, leaders of the clans or alliances on top in power struggles during the formalization of ethnicity, used creative histories and the idea of timeless ahistorical systems of African power to entrench their own positions, and to turn a temporary hegemony into a permanent rule. The new African middle classes – notably the teachers and intellectuals who were most exposed to the colonizers' interpretations of African history and social structure – could benefit from these processes by acting as both the interpreters of tradition for the colonizers and as interpreters of colonial practice for 'traditional leaders'.

A third key group for constructivists were migrant labourers. The experience of competition for resources in the cities and in their workplaces, and the importance for survival of networks of support in the cities, hostels and squatter settlements, gave place of origin and nuance of language new salience. The reserves, as the only feasible sites of economic accumulation, retained economic and hence social significance. Some reserves, moreover, perhaps particularly those that were to comprise Transkei and KwaZulu, retained mechanisms of self-government and narratives of collective self-description and understanding from the nineteenth century.[36]

The development of the homelands also created another group to complicate class structure and further spur tribalization: the political and bureaucratic elites of these quasi-states. Each Bantustan, destined for political independence, required separate political, judicial and executive institutions, together with a political elite (often drawn from existing 'traditional leaders') to exercise government. In addition, a new homeland-based African business class emerged, advantaged by the withdrawal of White traders and businessmen, and supported by investment subsidy.

'Constructivist' analysts of ethnicity plainly occupy a wide range of intellectual positions, united, if at all, by their rejection of the crass simplifications of essentialist and instrumentalist commentary, and by a commitment to the historical investigation of the self-understandings of particular human collectivities. The dismayingly open-ended nature of constructivist analysis has proved too much for the vast majority of professional political analysts, for whose analytic methods, as we shall see in chapters 6 and 7, a simplistic and static essentialism has proved amenable.

High apartheid thus entailed the abandonment of racial hierarchy for the setting of Africans free; the economic and political development of the homelands; industrial decentralization; forced removals; stricter labour movement controls; and a growth in state coercive capacity. These attempts to externalize the problems of the 1950s – to allocate the pains of industrialization both racially and spatially – were unprecedented. Whereas the NAD had accepted the inevitability of economic integration, its successor, the Bantu Affairs Department (BAD), reversed this decision even though the circumstances were now less favourable to a successful outcome. There was now a greater urbanization of Africans, and the dependence of White society on Africans was far greater. How, then, could such a departure have occurred?

The answer must lie in a combination of felt necessity, inspiration, and a newly perceived possibility. Necessity lay in failure: the programmes of the 1950s, the first phase of apartheid, could never solve the problems of segregation. It was plain that new methods were required to address them. Inspiration came from decolonization, and the notion of self-government. Independent sovereign states in an interdependent economy were not abhorrent creations of Afrikaner ideologues: this was, then and now, the prevailing liberal conception of the democratic political community. White supremacy was attacked as a gross evil, even in United States where its practice continued virtually unabated. Self-government in accordance with *unchosen* but pre-ethnic or linguistic affiliations, historically justified, was common practice. 'Internal decolonization' was a logical extension of decolonization itself, in circumstances in which decolonized states were destined to be dependent on an economic world they could not control or even much affect.

The possibility lay in South African politics. Democratic elections had furnished the NP with the power to entrench its rule. The Broederbond, and the ideologues of the South African Bureau of Racial Affairs (SABRA), had by 1960 established themselves in the heartland of the South African executive; the NP was fortified against electoral opposition; the South African Agricultural Union (SAAU) was newly amenable to the extension of state control, and to the project of separate development.

Added to this was an ambitious centralization of state powers. The local authorities obstructed influx control in the 1950s, but by 1960 the central state had acquired the machinery to run influx control virtually independently of them. African resistance played twin roles in this process and in its collapse. Overt political resistance strengthened the hand of those arguing for new measures, and for the far-reaching revolution that was separate development. It was individual acts of defiance of influx control, however, repeated by millions of workers, that made the system ultimately unsustainable.[37] Between 1960 and 1970, while the African population in White urban areas fell by over 200,000, the population of the Bantustans grew by almost 1 million. The extreme overcrowding and impoverishment that resulted in the reserves, and the artificial reduction in available labour in the White urban areas, created a strong incentive for millions of workers to defy the system of influx control.

The final stage in this periodization of South Africa has been left open-ended for now. The energy channelled into separate development could never resolve South Africa's social and economic problems. As elsewhere, however, it was the end of the postwar economic boom that brought underlying structural problems into clear focus for South Africa's ruling elite. Rapidly decelerating economic growth, and the increasing irrationality and economic unsustainability of the high apartheid state, led first to further centralization and militarization, but eventually to crisis and near collapse. I discuss the dynamics of this process, and the ways in which it has been analysed by political science, in chapters 6 and 7. However, apartheid did not cause a mere *deferral* of democratization and liberalization. It shaped South African institutions in such a way that it permanently changed the potential historical paths open to the country, closing off all the more attractive of them. South Africa remains in a historical era that is the creation of high apartheid.

CONCLUSION

In this chapter, I have advanced a fourfold periodization of South African history in order to establish both negative and positive theses about historical writing on South Africa. Negatively, I have argued that pivotal dates and conventional narratives in English and Afrikaans historical writing are elements in collective national self-understanding for select groups only. Events are organized in support of assertions about ethnic or nationalist destiny, rather than according to any compelling South African nationalist framework. Positively, I have organized South Africa's past into four phases in order to stress insufficiently registered truths about its history. First, the dynamism of African polities prior to and after the mineral revolutions, and the openness of historical possibilities by 1870. Second, the inescapable import of the economic causality unleashed by the mineral revolutions themselves, both through the dynamics of rapid industrialization and labour shortage and through the changed structure of incentives facing the imperial power. The mineral revolutions both drove the creation of the South African state itself, and also moulded the central identities in terms of which that history itself came to be interpreted. Third, the development, persistence and essential unity of a segregationist system across the decades between 1910 ands 1960; and finally the historical and comparative uniqueness of the unprecedented social experiment that was high apartheid.

3 Historical Debates and Political Analyses

In this chapter, I build on the periodization of chapter 2 to assess the weaknesses and strengths, from the perspective of political analysis, of the existing academic literature on South Africa and its history. South Africa possesses one of the world's richest traditions of English language historical analysis. I begin by exploring the roots of this strength and then go on to contrast it with the weakness of political science.

In the first section, I investigate the development of Afrikaner nationalist history, and the contrasting weakness of self-consciously African, Coloured and Indian historical writings on the South African past. The second section examines the English language literature in greater detail, investigating the evolution of the liberal/revisionist debate and its analytical and political core. Section three discusses the advances within the English language historiography of South Africa which have resulted from this debate, and explores key ways in which the argument has moved beyond its initially limited terms. The fourth section examines broader advances in the study of South African history since 1970, and shows how these have challenged liberal traditionalism but without adopting a crude historical materialism. Section five investigates key lacunae in this literature, understood on its own terms: a failure to locate South African history within a wider international context; limited attention to the relations between state and industry; submerged or moralized questioning of sites of moral culpability; and the absence of adequate historical institutionalist analysis.

The final section argues that investigation of political behaviour remains profoundly underdeveloped in South Africa. Once one moves outside academic history, the debate usually develops within a crude functionalist framework and covers extended historical periods retrospectively and without consideration of counterfactuals. Political conflict, and the contingency it brings with it, together with the vagaries of electoral politics and wider democratic struggles, have not received adequate recognition. Chapters 4–6 seek to show the potential heuristic benefits of closer attention to conflict, institutional innovation and liberal democratic practices.

NON-ENGLISH LANGUAGE HISTORIES OF SOUTH AFRICA

Modern South African history is often viewed as a struggle for mastery between distinct social groups: between Afrikaner, Briton, Zulu, Xhosa, Tswana, Indian, and so on; and at national level, between coalitions of such groupings, developed into an opposition between White and Black. Where political struggle can be conceived as conflict between groups defined in linguistic or cultural terms, it is common for a wealth of historical writing to be produced. It is in great measure through a consciously disseminated history that self-conscious social formations are able to make sense of their attempts to act together in pursuit of collective goals, and to understand the significance of their collective resistance to some external threat. Histories serve distinct audiences and are concerned with diverse purposes; and they are created in part to make natural the idea of a collectivity, rather than simply to record the activities of a prior social and historical entity. They cannot, therefore, be treated as the means by which given peoples give voice to their collective understandings. Nor can they be viewed as 'perspectives' on a single historical reality.

In South Africa, however, historians and myth-makers of whatever background and audience have inevitably shared a common preoccupation with the creation of apartheid, culpability for the human suffering this system produced and the nature of political activity appropriate to its overthrow (or defence). The South African case, moreover, provides particularly fertile ground for materialist analyses of systems of collective beliefs.[1] Black and White nationalisms, and the histories associated with them, are closely related to changes in the social and economic structure of South Africa as the state was created in the first decade of the twentieth century.

Afrikaners have been the primary generators of self-conscious justificatory tracts. A body of Afrikaner historical writing developed from the late nineteenth century, and Afrikaner perspectives on history were formalized in academic departments, schools and publishing houses. The most significant Afrikaner history was concerned with identity. Worden summarizes Afrikaners' self-understandings of the unified experienced of the Volk thus:

> Born on the old Cape frontier, trekking away from the British in 1836, surviving attacks by hostile Africans in the interior, defending themselves against the British in the 1870s and again in the South African war, suffering maltreatment in British concentration camps,

rebelling against South African support for the British cause in the First World War, partially triumphing in the 1920s under the Hertzog government which made Afrikaans an official language, reacting against the English-dominated Fusion government of Hertzog and Smuts in the 1930s and early 1940s, finally winning the election of 1948 and – the ultimate achievement – breaking from the Commonwealth and establishing a Republic in 1961.[2]

Powerful mythologizing Afrikaner histories can now be written with only very limited reference to non-Afrikaner sources.[3]

Most contemporary analysis views Afrikaner nationalism, like its African counterparts and emerging nationalisms elsewhere, as a response to the social dislocation that came with industrialization and the modernization of the state. The processes inaugurated by the mineral revolutions ran beyond the control and understanding of South African actors. The construction of nationalism can in such circumstances help to recreate social cohesion out of an incomprehensible social turmoil.[4] Such nationalism emerges first in the intelligentsia, in the Afrikaner case in the experiences of middle-class teachers and clerics in late nineteenth century western Cape. One figure, S.J. du Toit, stands out retrospectively for his creation of a distinctive, 'idealistic paradigm'[5] within Afrikaner nationalism. In his *Die geskiendenis van ons land in die taal van ons volk* (The History of Our Country in the Language of Our People) he traces Afrikaner history as the expression of God's will. Predestined to rule and to civilize the African, according to du Toit, these chosen people were to unite around the Afrikaans (rather than Dutch) language and through the religious observances of the Dutch Reformed Church. This work set a pattern for later Afrikaner histories: parochial, idealist and blinkered to the world outside Afrikanerdom.[6] This idealism had few immediate political ramifications, with Afrikaner leaders continuing to operate pragmatically in alliance with English language interests to secure their common goals of White supremacy, access to labour and resistance to British interference in domestic affairs (while maintaining trade and defence links).

The creation of a cross-class Afrikaner identity proved increasingly problematic with the growing urbanization of Afrikaners and the Anglicization of state-funded schools during the period of reconstruction. Transvaal Afrikaner nationalism advanced by means of popular magazines which spread the notion that Afrikaners shared a common history; meanwhile, the Afrikaner nationalist bourgeoisie in the Cape was developing the media and academic infrastructure, along with nationalist financial institutions, to embed further Afrikaner identity.[7] Nonetheless, socio-economic (and notably class) developments militated against success.

It was only in the 1930s that the conscious effort by the National Party to mobilize Afrikaner ethnicity began to make headway. Afrikaner cultural and religious institutions pressed harder the need for unity of the Volk in the face of party division.[8] In particular, the celebration of the centenary of the 'Great Trek' in 1938 was used to catalyse wider ethnic mobilization. The Afrikaner working class, moreover, was courted by new Afrikaner trade unions, in an increasingly successful attempt to break the class unity of the White working class (and in consequence electoral support for the Labour Party). Furthermore, Afrikaner capital was increasingly effectively portrayed as the supporter of Afrikaners as a whole, and not merely of the Afrikaner bourgeoisie. *Volkskapitalisme* had supplanted the idealized pre-capitalist visions of *Volkskultuur* at the centre of Afrikaner nationalist strategy.[9] These efforts, although built on and developing a conception of the history of the Afrikaner peoples, were compatible with many different interpretations of that history; but it was a single recognizable story.

'Coloured' South Africans, by contrast, have never come close to developing a single account of their (purported) identity and their (arguably) unique experiences. Here, neither the historical myths needed to support the notion of a common identity, nor the political unity required to respond collectively to political challenge, have ever been present. 'Coloured' is a term of self-description, but not a reliable marker of political behaviour or of self-understanding. It is a lived category and not merely an imposed one, but nevertheless a contested and often rejected one. Coloured came to be one of South Africa's apartheid racial categories.

'Coloured' South Africans had complex descent, including Khoisan, slaves of the Dutch East India Company, Indonesian Muslims, Whites and an extraordinary variety of other migrants. Those labelled and self-consciously Coloured need share nothing in culture and descent. While mid-century Coloureds in Cape Town had long experience of urban life, shared the cosmopolitanism of the dock city and possessed a range of artisan crafts and skills, those in the distant northern Cape were the products of extended and unalloyed subjugation. It was difficult to believe that any history could be written that might claim, let alone succeed, in uniting so diverse a range of human experiences.

Coloured political ambitions, moreover, had led them in many directions and at different times: towards Afrikaner, British and African allies, but most especially towards obtuse leftist ideologies. While Afrikaans is derived from a Coloured patois, those classified as Coloured have continued to speak in diverse ways, with both Afrikaans and English as substantial first languages. Christian and Muslim religious affiliations both remain significant. Political attitudes and behaviour today are hard to predict on the basis of religion, language or even class. Coloured South Africans divide, moreover, between support for the ANC and the NP.[10]

Before Union, there was no discrimination formally against Coloured people in the Cape. As Thompson notes, '[u]nder favourable [sic] circumstances, the people who became known as Coloured People might have been expected to merge socially and biologically with the Afrikaners.'[11] By the mid-nineteenth century, however, Afrikaner race consciousness and social pressures led to the separation of church congregations and then to the banning of Coloureds from state-run schools. These changes prefigured wholesale discrimination and the marginalization of Coloured influence within Afrikaner political circles. The only effective Coloured political organization of the early twentieth century, the African People's Organization, placed its faith, by contrast, in the force of British liberal principle. The British, however, paid little heed to Coloured interests despite the APO's support for Britain in the First World War; just as, a decade previously, pledges to treat Coloureds well after the end of the South African War carried equally little weight.[12] Coloureds in the Western Cape, indeed, even adopted some of the 'Social Darwinist' ideas that had been used against them, and by the 1920s, many were advancing these ideas to differentiate themselves from Africans.

Coloured people later played a very significant role in the anti-apartheid movement, and, in particular, in the United Democratic Front of the 1980s. The UDF, as we shall see in later chapters, was uniquely active in the Western Cape, and here four ideological strands were especially important among politicized Coloured activists: Trotskyist socialism, Charterism, Africanism and Black Consciousness.[13] Even in active resistance, the ambivalent position of Coloureds shaped their politics. Trotskyists, associated with the unity movement, which had its origins in the Non-European Unity Movement and which flourished between 1943 and the early 1960s when it was suppressed, were predominantly middle-class intellectuals (and especially teachers) who espoused the unity of the oppressed. The Charterist tradition, despite limited ANC effort prior to 1980, nevertheless attracted many Coloured youth to the ANC banner in the following decade, perhaps, in part, as a result of its ambiguity and vagueness. Black Consciousness, with its unambiguous embrace of Coloured and Indian South Africans, treated 'Blackness' as political rather than biological, racial or cultural.[14] Coloured South Africans could be Black too – as could Indians – and this usage became a marker of political affiliation rather than one of cultural identity.[15] Africanism, with its more ambivalent attitudes towards Coloureds, also attracted some strong Coloured support. Whatever their political affiliations, Coloured South Africans have always returned to the question of identity.

Coloured South Africans therefore often share a common language and many have shared the same experiences of segregation and oppression. They may share some common aspects of self-description. But, for the foreseeable future, nobody is remotely likely to attempt a history of Coloured peoples that defines their unity through some common historical experience. Slavery, East Asian Islam, Khoisan heritage, Afrikaner culture, Western values and Black resistance, have each influenced those labelled Coloured South Africans. Coloured political activists have returned repeatedly to the validity of notions of racial and ethnic difference, the coherence of the idea of multiracialism and the ambivalent embrace (or threat) of Dutch Reformism, Africanism and Black Consciousness. Just as Coloured youth culture turned to the symbols of a distant American Black culture, its political resistance gravitated towards the detached analyses of Trotskyism or the rarefied analysis of the meaning and significance of racial difference.

The diverse experiences of Indian South Africans led to equally complex collective orientations towards history. Lacking religious, cultural and political unity (despite the presence of many commonalities) and composed of descendants of quite different groups of indentured labourers and descendants of low Hindu, high-caste Hindu, Muslim and Christian from the Indian subcontinent, South Africa's Indians have no unifying narrative by means of which to comprehend a collective past. Like Coloured South Africans, Indians were turned in two directions by segregationist ideology: by the need to secure equality of opportunity and legal standing with Whites; and by the (corresponding) need for distance from, and privilege over, Africans.

Written African histories of South Africa have been equally absent. At the beginnings of the mineral revolutions in the 1870s, certain preconditions for the construction of self-conscious histories of particular 'African peoples' seem to be fulfilled, or about to be fulfilled, in the Eastern Cape and Natal. In the late nineteenth century Eastern Cape, the franchise allowed propertied Africans to vote. The Cape Town municipality franchise of 1839 and the Cape government franchise of 1853 were not racially defined; rather they were based on moderate levels of £50 per annum earnings or £25 holdings of property. As such, they admitted a substantial proportion of Afrikaners, and a fair number of African and Coloured voters. A mission-educated elite of Africans engaged actively in the pursuit of middle-class interests, forming the South African Native Congress to seek an extension of British protection and a widening of the property franchise. The residual coherence of the Xhosa polity and extended memories of self-government made possible self-consciousness about political history. Likewise, in Natal clumsy attempts to destroy the Zulu monarchy, and a firm continuity in institutional forms of Zulu authority, permitted self-consciousness even in the absence of the possibility for formal and constitutional political activity. In both cases, and elsewhere in African South Africa, the emergence of a literate, educated, African middle class provided potential interpreters of African history to modernity.

The intellectual self-consciousness of the African elite, however, reflected its position within colonial society. Isolated from rural protest and emergent quasi-proletarian politics alike, and distinctive in mission education and 'respectability', this elite was unable to conceive a challenge to White paternalism. Reassuring the British Colonial Secretary that independent African churches were no threat to White ecclesiastical authority, the executive of the South African Native Congress in 1903 wrote: 'The Black races are too conscious of their dependence upon the White missionaries and of their obligations towards the British race and the benefits to be derived from their presence in the general control and guidance of civil and religious affairs of the country to harbour foolish notions of political ascendancy.'[16]

The first and second decades of the twentieth century brought accumulated rebuffs: the failure of the British to extend the Cape franchise, rather settling upon a constitutional framework amenable to the Afrikaner republics; the formalization of a patently inequitable apportionment of reserved land; and the Mines and Works Act. Nevertheless, the African intellectual elite remained largely isolated from wider political protest. It continued to represent the forces of conservatism and middle-class interest, and was concerned to avoid regression into an African society (and re-tribalization) that was anathema to them.

The ability of Afrikaners to construct an extensive written history of their own past, and the failure of others in South Africa to sustain such a project, reflect three factors: the success of Afrikaner political strategy, techniques of cultural dissemination and imbalances of power. Afrikaner political achievements were doubtless based in some measure on luck. But the National Party's building, from the 1930s, of a cross-class alliance around Afrikaner identity was decisive. As this came to full fruition in the 1950s, it retrospectively validated the Afrikaner notion of collective destiny. (Nothing confirms that God is on your side as effectively as the confirmation of history.) But Afrikaner history was also a mass history. Quite deliberately constructed by intellectuals, clerics and party figures, and based around a championing of Afrikaans as the language, Afrikaner history differed from its counterparts in its dissemination through schools, cultural organizations, magazines, newspapers and churches to the mass of Afrikaners.

Afrikaners, however, secured access to power in a way that reinforced their sense of collective identity and rendered meaningful the historical stories that had traced their rise. Afrikaners could understand themselves to be acting as a collectivity. By contrast, even where other groups developed emerging senses of commonality of experience, culture and interests, they were always politically vulnerable and unable to apply what might seem to them a collective will to shape events. Buffeted by change, and engaged predominantly in defensive political strategies, Indian, Coloured and African histories could not be written as the tales of advances secured.

The rudimentary identities around which a history might have been written, moreover, were always in themselves problematic in ways Afrikaners did not have to face. Any identity is to some degree subject to arbitrariness of boundary and of content. But ethnic categories – Indian, Coloured, African, Zulu, Xhosa, Tswana – were to varying degrees inevitably contested by those to whom they were applied. They were also, moreover, in terms of the language and cultural practices that such identities implied, coercively enforced and externally legislated.

Afrikaners' categories of self-understanding entered a perpetual virtuous cycle. A propagated idea of community, with an increasingly tightly institutionalized linguistic, religious and cultural unity, conceived itself to be acting concertedly in politics. It was achieving its collective aims. Such perceived collective achievements validated and strengthened Afrikaners' sense of themselves as a unity. For others, ethnicity and nationality could be experienced as burdens, or even as impositions; and never could they be embraced as unproblematic expressions of a natural unity.[17]

ENGLISH LANGUAGE HISTORIES OF SOUTH AFRICA

The 'Liberal/Revisionist' Debate

For the first half of the twentieth century, English language histories of South Africa followed a conventional academic pattern. Political events and 'turning points' were studied in detail, as were the (purported) actions of the powerful. The 'making of the nation-state' – a theme somewhat inappropriate to South Africa's single state but multiplicity of nations – was an organizing principle as elsewhere in the Empire. Afrikaner historians traced the internal history of Dutch Afrikaans-speakers virtually alone; and English speakers, while less parochial, likewise focused much energy on the British government and settlers.[18] This focus, however, was analytically propitious: the pivotal relationship between the imperial power, the international economy, domestic mineral revolutions and state formation was inescapably at the heart of this analysis.

From the mid-point of the twentieth century, however, it became increasingly evident that South Africa was set upon a different path from other colonies and former colonies. White supremacy had turned to segregation; and segregation was deepening rather than breaking down in the first decade of decolonization. Racism and systematic segregation became the historians' key explanandum. English-speaking historians followed what can be described as a 'liberal' paradigm: an explicit understanding of European civilization was counterposed to the stagnation and pre-capitalist superstition of the African; the dynamism of the capitalist economy was contrasted to the inertia of the traditional reserve. Segregation and apartheid were viewed as irrational impediments to human progress and to the civilizing of the African inhabitants of South Africa. Culpability for these impediments was ascribed to Afrikaners. Vehicles for the pre-Enlightenment values of racism, intolerance and bigotry, they were purportedly shaped by the conflict and isolation of their frontier existence.[19] The religious and social principles of Calvinism reinforced these regressive systems of belief, and the whole was hardened by the stubborn and counter-suggestible temperament of the Boer. Often ascribing contingency a major role, liberal historians saw this archaic value system transplanted by electoral good fortune, fear of the 'black hordes' and a myth of the Volk, into control of the levers of power in a British-engineered state machine – one that they were to turn to their own retrogressive ends.

To operate as indictments of the Afrikaner, of course, these accounts required a counter-factual. Here it was the wasted promise of 'Cape liberalism', with its benign recognition of the dignity of every culture, and its franchise operating according to property rather than race. The liberal account reinforced, and was reinforced by, its overlap with central themes in Afrikaner history. Afrikaners, too, saw a special set of beliefs and an ethnic destiny translated into a political project; and this project as responsible for the nature of the South African state under early apartheid. Continuity in the peoples and the beliefs of the Volk, and the joint struggle against Black backwardness and British imperialism, animated their narratives too.

From the early 1970s, these accounts were subjected to both internal and external questioning. The most fundamental challenge came from a quasi-Marxist 'revisionist' or 'radical' school of scholars. Demonstrating the potential long-term intellectual rewards that can accrue to a tactical strategy of dogmatic and crude structuralism, a relatively small number of academics transformed the explanation of segregation and apartheid by placing cheap labour and labour migracy at its heart. Analysts argued that the key to increasing returns on capital in the late nineteenth and early twentieth centuries in South Africa was cheap labour. Without low-wage, unskilled, disenfranchised labour, the gold finds could not have been exploited. At the same time, agrarian capital relied on cheap unskilled labour. The migrant labour system, which externalized the costs of the social reproduction of the labour force to the reserves and to neighbouring countries, permitted the payment of meagre, 'bachelor wages' to mine and agricultural labourers. This made possible the particular path of industrialization in South Africa.[20] Early revisionist arguments were both necessitarian and crudely instrumentalist: African labour migrancy was determined by the demands of the mine-dominated capitalist economy; and the South African state was the instrument of fractions of capital.[21]

Beyond the Liberal/Revisionist Debate

The dogmatism that marked early publications in the revisionist tradition dissipated, and materialist authors, like their counterparts elsewhere, developed more nuanced accounts of the relationship between economy, class structure and social life. The liberal/Marxist debate eventually produced something close to a new scholarly consensus. Materialist accounts directed scholarly attention towards the (inescapably materialist) economic revolutions of the late nineteenth and early twentieth centuries, and rendered impossible traditional liberal historiography. Even Lipton's impressive attempt to return liberal themes – the importance of politics, progress and the irrationality of apartheid – to centre stage, relies on detailed analysis of material conditions and of how apartheid policy affected industry by sector.[22] Nevertheless, materialist analysis rather than historical determinism became established: few authors would claim that South Africa was impelled along a single, predestined historical trajectory. The persuasiveness of materialist analysis, moreover, is greatest for the period of mineral revolutions and state formation. From 1920, the factors indicating the disutility of segregation to capitalist interests are always as plentiful as those suggesting its benevolence.

A second field of consensus concerned the nature of the South African state. The early radical school saw the central dynamic of apartheid as conflict over the control of labour and the distribution of labour power, with segregation and apartheid as (temporary) resolutions to this conflict.[23] This account, as Bonner et al. insist, is essentially functionalist, treating state policies as responses to the demands of capital accumulation. As such, it is in danger of merely substituting for the liberal picture of the state as instrument of Afrikaner nationalism an equally crude vision of the state as the tool of the capitalist class (or, hardly more subtle, of 'fragments' thereof). Revisionist-inspired historical analysts now characteristically view the South African state as internally 'differentiated' and as a site of conflict. On this view, moreover, the state is treated as a locus of power, with early clumsy attributions of 'relative autonomy' replaced by a more confident treatment of the infrastructural capacity of the state. Analysts have shown that the South African state has contained distinct centres of influence with conflicting strategies.[24]

Perhaps still more importantly, recent analysis has separated the conscious construction of state purposes from '[t]he unintended ways in which the influx control policy of the 1950s functioned in practice'.[25] Allowing for the chasm between design and practice in any modern state – and perhaps most strikingly in utopian and authoritarian social engineering states like apartheid South Africa – analysts have been freed from dogmatic functionalism. As Greenberg insisted in 1987, 'the South African state is no unity or simple instrument. It is a complex terrain shaped by the interplay of political leaders, officials, class and allied actors, and social division.'[26]

Parallel Advances

If the liberal-revisionist debate has been the central intellectual battleground for scholars fighting over the origins and causes of segregation and apartheid, it has been far from the sole field of conflict. A whole range of parallel debates – some influenced by changes in historiographical fashion elsewhere, but others specific to South Africa – have driven professional research agendas. These investigations have often been independent of, or have run counter to, conflicts across the central liberal/revisionist axis.[27] In this section, I outline four of the most important debates.

A first set of arguments have turned on the purported historical responsibility of the Afrikaner people for the creation of apartheid – an indictment that underlies much liberal writing. One challenge to this indictment has been to reassess the impact of British rule. While continuing to view empire, markets and British administration as agents of change, many accounts from the 1970s and 1980s saw them as ultimately malign rather than as the vehicles of progress. In one theme that has reverberated to the present day, Welsh focused attention on the mechanics of British colonial administration and argued that segregation had its roots in the system of reserves and rule through traditional leaders by the colonial power.[28] Marks's analysis of the relative weakness of the colonial state in Natal, and the dependence of the authorities on forms of rule that were economical of resources while deriving maximum taxation revenue and labour access, reiterated and developed this analysis of the role of the British colonial power and its ramifications.[29]

Further studies traced the role of particular British appointees and officials in elaborating both the institutional foundations and the ideology of segregation. In particular, the period of reconstruction provided British officials with the opportunity to redefine the nature of 'native policy', a chance they seized and which resulted directly in the precepts of territorial separation between races, cheap labour and the exclusion of Blacks from political participation.[30] The most important legacy of British conquest and reconstruction, however, is perhaps one of those least observed. As Beinart notes, 'the economic muscle and bureaucratic sophistication of an advanced capitalist country was transferred to the region and helped to bequeath a powerful state structure ... the very solidity of the state provided the stepping stones for Whites, both English and especially Afrikaans speaking, to take power and entrench a system of racially based dominance that was unique in its rigidity.'[31]

In support of this shift of emphasis towards the colonial power during the reconstruction period, historians reassessed the received wisdom about racial conflict on the frontier. Afrikaner and African had a complex and fluid set of relationships that varied from place to place and involved interdependence, trade and mutual cooperation. According to Legassick's decisive contribution, the relationship between Afrikaner and African was one of dependency and not one of servitude. The origins of White supremacy could not reliably be traced to the history of the Boer republics.[32]

Other scholars explored the derivation and history of the systems of ideas upon which segregationist and apartheid thinkers drew, many of which turned out to have roots in mid- or late Victorian Britain. In particular, scholars have shown how Social Darwinist thought was used by Cape Colony authorities to justify residential racial segregation.[33] Forms of non-oppositional liberalism and self-consciously liberal paternalism among English South Africans also may have played a role in the construction of segregationist ideology.[34]

The second set of debates developed in the 1960s in the new subdiscipline of African history, with its insistence that colonial countries' history could not be understood as the actions of settlers upon a passive native population and environment. Developed in part in response to decolonization further north in the continent, and initially forcing a rethinking of the historical dynamics of African societies before colonialism, this sub-discipline brought fresh attention to the origins of the migrant labour system. In the early years of labour migrancy, in some cases preceding colonial control, chiefs exchanged male labour for money and hence firearms and traded goods. Subsequent pressures on rural men to earn wages made the exchange compulsory. As Beinart and Dubow note, migrancy could be seen as 'having arisen as much out of the dynamics of African societies as the demands of the mines'.[35] If the dynamics of African society shaped the initial stages of the migrant labour system, then resistance to incorporation into colonial society continued to shape it in later decades. 'Hidden struggles' in rural South Africa, in particular, while in some ways compatible with segregation, represented efforts by Africans to retain some control over their own destinies.[36]

This emphasis on Blacks as agents rather than as the vectors of social forces profoundly influenced historical writing. Students of postwar internal protest and the mass opposition of the 1980s, however, often merely pay lip service to the new orthodoxy that Black political action 'made a difference'. Black political agency is still often derived from structural change in the South African socio-economic system, rather than being viewed as a set of causes in its own right.[37] Where political science has sustained a focus on the internal politics of resistance, analysts have misleadingly emphasized Black Consciousness and the strategic skills of the organizers of mass action.[38]

Nevertheless, this focus on the politics of resistance has been bolstered by two further developments in the fashionable styles of historiography. While these have swept across the Anglophone historical academy, they are of particular importance to South African history: the move towards 'social history', and the introduction of gender as an analytic category. Social historians everywhere have sought to give voice to the oppressed, and to uncover the texture of everyday life, rather than merely to relay the activities of the powerful. In South Africa, however, efforts to relate the experiences of Black South Africans to a predominantly White audience have themselves represented problematic exercises in communication across considerable social divides.[39] Such social history, moreover, draws attention to the purposes of historical analysis. Earlier historical analysis was exposed as either a self-indulgent wallow in the liberal guilt of Whiteness, in a world whose suffering had been predominantly allocated to the poor and the Black, or as a naive attempt to deliver objective analysis to guide political strategy. Social history and the new focus on African political traditions were, in any event, mutually reinforcing developments in understanding social change in twentieth-century South Africa.

The advance of gender as an analytic category has been episodic and contested in South Africa, just as elsewhere. The analysis of African societies, however, is impossible without approaching at least their patriarchal inheritance; and the role of gender as a category of political organization is pivotal to understanding both the history of resistance to apartheid and the dynamics of oppositional politics up to the present day.[40]

TOWARDS A HISTORY OF SOUTH AFRICA?

As I have organized these debates within South African historiography, it may appear that a convergence between viewpoints is underway, and that a single coherent history of the peoples of South Africa is just over the horizon. Certainly, South African histories of whatever kind cannot easily evade one set of central experiences that have profoundly affected all members of the population: the mineral revolutions and their socio-economic consequences in the emergence of race as the central principle of social organization; and the development of segregation and apartheid as systematic expressions of racial division and then of social engineering. Moreover, no historian can avoid the question of responsibility, causal and then moral, for South Africa's unique system of apartheid. Inevitably, furthermore, the desirability of a politics of reform or of revolution was an implicit theme in historical work – whatever its political stripe. Nevertheless, there are three broad categories of reasons to expect the historians of South Africa to remain more sharply at odds with each other than one would expect in a unitary state with an extended political history. These include difficulties of a technical and intellectual nature; the ever-changing but ineliminable relations between the politics of the present and contemporary understandings of the past; and the immense social, cultural and cognitive divides which remain and are likely to persist in the 'new' South Africa.

The technical and intellectual difficulties are profound despite the remarkable richness of intellectual production over the past 30 years. Three weaknesses in particular are striking: the location of South Africa's history within a changing global environment; the relations between the South African state and its corporate sector; and the wider relationships between the products of different schools of historical analysis.

South Africa's international context has predominantly been understood from the perspective of the imperial power. In particular, the ways in which British colonial rulers viewed South Africa as a strategic asset have been a focus of much work in both liberal and 'radical' traditions.[41] However, revisionist authors' need to establish a materialist historiography, and later their attempt to develop Althusserian variants of Marxist analysis led them to put aside investigation of the inherently opaque realm of geo-economic causality for the more reliable tracing of causes and correspondences within the domestic socio-economic sphere. Likewise, themes in global underdevelopment and later globalization which have provoked intense debate elsewhere in the South have only belatedly made an impact on an intellectual community which conceives South Africa as an extension of the developed world.[42] At a most basic level, the role of changes in international commodity prices, and trade and capital flows in the mid-1970s, and again in the early 1980s, were misread by historical analysts whose focus was domestic. Among the consequences of this involution of perspective was a failure to recognize that the patterns of boom and recession experienced by South Africa between 1950 and 1985 were typical and therefore not readily understood as the products of a distinctive apartheid economy.[43]

A second intellectual weakness in the historical literature lies at the domestic heart of materialist analysis and relates to the nature of the relationship between South Africa's major corporations and its state. This weakness is two-sided, affecting analysis of the state as well as of the corporations. The South African state throughout its existence has been associated with the needs of a racial minority; state and nation have been identified openly with a racial minority since the Act of Union in 1910, and this identification has pervaded the symbolism and ideology of the state as much as its practical activity. The enforcement of labour control and repression, in particular, have signalled clearly and continuously the interpenetration of economics and politics in South Africa. As has been noted by Greenberg, the most impressive student of this interpenetration, the legitimacy of the modern state rests on its seeming to belong equally to all its citizens and not merely to its powerful. South Africa has never achieved any moment of seeming separation in which state and market could be seen as distinct, and so have conferred upon themselves legitimacy.[44]

If the state has been caught in a web of labour market intervention, influx control and authoritarian policing, then South Africa's commercial activities have likewise been entangled with the state to an unrecognized extent. The literature still counterposes 'state' to 'market', and ascribes distinct rules of behaviour and modes of proper analysis to each. The distinctiveness of South African capital lies not just in its remarkable concentration and the degree of cross ownership and control that emerged in the postwar economy; it also lies in the distinctive nature of mining, the key South African economic sector, as an activity. Mining corporations are special economic animals in any context: they rely upon immense investments of capital and have extraordinarily extended time horizons; they depend more than any other industry upon favourable infrastructural provision; they are tied to the most international of markets. Exceptionally, as is often noted of the South African case, they can also have very particular labour demands – for international skilled labour or for cheap domestic labour. All these factors have made South African mining corporations, and Anglo American and its affiliates in particular, entities as much political as economic. Such corporations have been competitors as long-range planning agencies and social engineers to the core executives of substantial modern states.

The role of mining corporations in the evolution of the South African state is very poorly understood. While there is much interesting analysis of the evolution of labour control mechanisms on the minefields, little is known about the high level relationships between political and industrial elites over the twentieth century as a whole.[45] The continuous and powerful influence of business is often treated, misleadingly, as a series of discreet interventions.[46]

Here the academic literature reflects a more widespread oddity in South African political debate. While indictments of the 'capitalist' system or the 'apartheid' system have been commonplace, the concrete manifestation of capital on earth in South Africa – Anglo American Corporation – has been spared vehement attack. Attempts to apportion blame for the evils of apartheid have likewise largely left business corporations untouched.[47] Historians have special difficulty addressing the role of corporations, since these maintain a close and professional control over their archives and disseminate calculated myths about their own histories. For social scientists, the problem has perhaps been still greater: a network of conservative sociologists has cornered the major funding sources within South Africa, and these sources have been the major corporations themselves, together with the quasi-state apartheid legitimating body, the Human Sciences Research Council of Pretoria.[48]

Posel rightly suggests that analysts of the South African state have failed adequately to distinguish between the state's institutional self-interest in accumulation and its responsiveness to particular capitalist interests.[49] It may also be true that the power of the mining corporations has been such that their interests have been almost universally perceived to be at one with the national interest. Echoing public debate, and mirroring the evasions of government policy makers, academic analysts have failed to keep business activity and culpability on the intellectual agenda.[50]

The third major area of intellectual difficulty is perhaps the most intractable. While there have been impressive general surveys of South African history covering the entire modern period, these have not been able to advance a consistent theoretical position.[51] The multiple riches of liberal historiography, revisionist quasi-Marxism, social history and politico-economic analysis – inevitably given their contradictory theoretical foundations – have not produced anywhere a fluent synthesis.

Two historical conjunctures, as I indicated in my analytical periodization in chapter 2, are especially problematic. The first is the period of social change around the mineral revolutions. The distinct trajectories of the political entities existent in the 1870s – African, British and Boer – are viewed through a series of prisms: these highlight now the dynamism of African politics, then imperialism and now post-slavery class structure; they focus on mid-Victorian British ideas one moment, and trekker political assertion and identity the next. The relations between these diverse lenses and the powerful optic of historical materialist conceptions of the mineral revolutions remain opaque.

Likewise, the articulation between the trajectory of the segregation state of early twentieth-century South Africa, and that of the high apartheid state from the 1960s – with its unprecedented efforts at social engineering and its bizarre ideological self-justifications – remains difficult to understand. In contrast to that of the 1950s, the apartheid of the 1960s cannot be understood as merely segregation by another name, to be explained by the miscellany of materialist or other analyses applied to segregation. Neither, however, do idealist accounts of the implementation of an Afrikaner grand plan hold water. Attempts to synthesize diverse approaches to the period have never approached a convincing unity.

Historical institutionalist analysis, drawing on the methods of economic history, may eventually pay dividends.[52] Materialist analysis of the mineral revolutions can avoid functionalism if the demands of capital are related to the capacities of particular concrete configurations of institutions. Such configurations were inherited from the structures of colonial society, slavery and indirect rule. Industrialization, on the back of mineral exploitation, remains a plausible transforming force. However, the post-mineral revolution trajectory of South African society was shaped by created commitments which derived from past institutional innovation.

Institutions change only incrementally. This argument has often been made by revisionists with regard to the transition between segregation and apartheid. The latter, they have argued, was a logical development given the existence of the former: apartheid was built on the foundations of segregation. While the centre of gravity in the South African economy had shifted by the Second World War, the mines remained dependent on cheap labour and the economy remained inextricably tied to mining. Yet a historical institutionalist argument goes further. The investments made in the institutional apparatus of segregation – in the legal, coercive and labour control institutions, and in the system of reserves – had developed specific institutional capacities, skilled organizations and positive network externalities which reinforced the trajectory of segregation and served to make its extension more attractive. A vast range of organizations – in public and private sector alike – had learned how to operate with rigid segregation; their systems of organization and decision were based on it, rather than on any other principle. The system of labour allocation depended upon a series of general rules which could not easily be differentially applied across sectors: the rationale for unfree labour in one sector had to be broadly consistent with the rationale for labour control in any other. All relied, moreover, on a series of executive organizations which had adapted to an environment of segregated labour.

It is not merely institutions that exhibit path dependency. Public policy decisions can, like technological investments, lay down a series of self-reinforcing mechanisms which lock future policy-makers into their preordained logic. As Pierson has persuasively argued in another context, previous public policy choices affect the contexts of contemporary choices, and serve to 'lock in' a path of policy development.[53] Policies can have the same features as technological innovations: high start-up costs; learning effects (as organizations experiment, learn from mistakes, adapt to the policy environment and develop tacit knowledge) and the adaptive ability of the human beings participating in social institutions. Segregation became embedded in the everyday experience of social life. Individual experience was structured in accordance with its rules. The extension of such a system of mutual expectation is always easier than a radical remodelling of it.

Historical institutionalist analysis may overcome some of the intellectual obstacles to a unified history of South Africa. The second of our broad sets of reasons not to expect such an end, however, lies inextricably in the nature of historical writing. Historical texts that are read beyond narrowly specialist audiences fulfil at least two kinds of condition (beyond providing a satisfactory narrative structure). They move beyond the discussion of the particular, to address wider themes within human understanding; and they respond to the concerns of an audience that is both contemporary and itself particular.

In South Africa, these conditions cannot be met. Historians' guiding questions have often been very general. Do ideas matter in history, or are events driven by material forces or human greed? Is progress a coherent notion? Can individuals change history? Are human societies systemic? Is history riven with contingency? What sense can be made of human freedom in a past that seems everywhere determined?[54] The excitement and tragedy of South African history, and the presence of so many collectivities in conflict, render these questions open to an extreme range of modulation. Equally importantly, however, South African historiography has been uniquely politicized. Historians have sought to give voice to the experiences of the hitherto ignored; they have believed themselves to be reflecting on political possibilities through the medium of historical analysis; and they have used their analytical perspectives as a badge of political commitment.

The liberal revisionist debate, in particular, was construed by quasi-Marxists as a statement about political possibility. Liberals, stressing the economic irrationality of apartheid and seeing in South African history the long-range operation of human progress, were often sanguine about the prospects of liberalization. Quasi-Marxists, by contrast, pursued an involuted functionalist argument: apartheid was the construction of the state acting in the interests of capital; the two were symbiotically interlocked. Hence, Marxists insisted, it followed that apartheid could not be dismantled unless capitalism itself was overthrown. This argument is plainly not valid, and the ease with which Marxists of the Regulation School have adapted to the end of apartheid is no surprise: a new strategy of hegemonic domination (a bourgeois democracy) is now appropriate given the fresh regime of accumulation.[55] Capitalism remains even as the apartheid state is dismantled. (The actuality of the end of the apartheid state, and the continuation of a capitalist economic system, seems decisively to prove the Marxists correct on this point.)

The expression of political difference through distinctive historical approaches remains institutionalized in South Africa. Questions of identity and matters of causality, moreover, are united with moral blame through the question of culpability. It is inevitable, and quite appropriate, that the causal and moral responsibility for the existence and actions of the apartheid state should be a central concern of historical analysis. However, this rightful concern is not just pervasive and but also largely unarticulated. No longer do liberals charge racist Afrikaners with responsibility, while Afrikaners celebrate their historical destiny. Equally, neither do Afrikaners now respond with well-worn tales of colonial brutality towards Africans, or British cruelty towards Afrikaners. English-speaking liberals no longer flagellate themselves with guilty tales of Shepstone's oppression and Milner's malice. Neither is organized African resistance ascribed an implausible and unduly meritorious role in the democratization of South Africa.

The literature is more nuanced, yet also more evasive, than such stereotypes imply. Nevertheless, guilt, blame and denial are powerful motives; and for a historian to explore them openly in South Africa is to enter a personal and political minefield.

A unified history of South Africa is unlikely to be achieved while historical writing is used as the vehicle for implicit ascriptions and disclaimers of causal and moral responsibility for the outrages that were segregation and apartheid. This, however, points us to our third broad set of reasons why South Africans are unlikely ever to bask in the glow of a shared conception of themselves as a people whose unity of present derives from a commonality of past: the sheer diversity of human experiences in both South Africa's past and its present, and the mutual incomprehension that these divides of experience and communication enforce.

E.H. Carr's famous observation that history is always written by the victors[56] is true, of course, not just in the banal sense that those who win live to tell the tale on their own terms. Across longer spans of time, some groups more than others can conceive themselves as beneficiaries of history's benevolence – the recipients of the unintended good consequences of the agency of market, empire, war and commerce. It is all too clear who the victors have been and remain in South Africa: Whites, whether English- or Afrikaans-speaking, liberal, radical or conservative. Likewise, the instance of almost all social evil associated with industrialization was shifted onto Blacks. In such circumstances, the grounds for a common appraisal of the history of South Africa in the twentieth century are simply absent. The story of Whites is at worst one of guilt and empathy; or of the need to adjust an ethic destiny to a newly circumscribed context. The story of Black South Africa is a series of reversals, defeats and tragedies, notwithstanding the belated recognition of the role of Black protests in shaping the origin, form and eventual disintegration of the apartheid state. The most powerful work in South African social history is van Onselen's *The Seed is Mine*, a testimony to both resistance and interdependence, but in the end a story of despair.[57]

POLITICAL ANALYSIS AND TWENTIETH-CENTURY SOUTH AFRICA

Three points emerge clearly from this survey of historical debates. First, comparative political analysis is strikingly underdeveloped in

South Africa when compared to the politics-rich historical literature. Even students of South Africa who are not professional historians approach political understanding through long-range historical surveys.[58] The prominence of historical analysis results in part from the role of institutional bequests in shaping current practices, but it may also reflect uncertainty about the proper role of comparative analysis in South Africa. The country appears to its students to be unique in so many ways, and especially so when viewed (incorrectly) as a dual economy – an unprecedented collision between the worlds of Europe and Africa. Acceptance that South Africa is a developing country, with an unexceptional mix of advanced and backward economic activity, and with a pattern of democratization similar to that elsewhere in the South, is obstructed by the exceptionalist theses that dominate South African political analysis.

A second area of related weakness has been the pronounced tendency towards functionalism in historically derived political analysis, and a consequent failure to focus on contingency, conflict and intention. The South African state has been analysed as a unitary actor; argument has turned on which master this state can be considered to serve. Liberal analysis have seen it as the vehicle of an imperial project or the instrument of Afrikaner oppression. Revisionists initially considered the state the servant of the capitalist class, of or fractions of that class. The state has been analysed with more subtlety over the past decade and a new focus on Black political agency has opened up potential avenues for analysis of conflict and contingency. Nonetheless, the common-sense academic template remains stubbornly functionalist. One important consequence of this has been an inability to recognize the distinctive role of fortune, contingency and circumstance; and, in particular, a falsely modest understanding of the malign role of democratic ideas and institutions in South Africa's modern history.

The third area of special weakness has been the political analysis of institutional innovation. Writing has been at its strongest when tracing continuity. South Africa's twentieth-century political history, however, has been characterized by feats of institutional creation: new systems of rule, fresh political movements, blossoming labour institutions, innovative modes of public policy and newly minted constitutional forms. The constant surprises of South African history are devalued by the flat functionalism of much historical and political analysis.

The following four chapters systematically address these weaknesses, and explore the ways in which distinctively political analysis can help to remedy them. Chapter 4 addresses the relationship between the systematic racial oppression of segregation and apartheid, and the ideas and practices associated with liberal democracy. The 'end of apartheid' is generally narrated as an uplifting tale in which the institutions of democracy supplant the authoritarian institutions of apartheid. An alternative story, common among White liberals in South Africa, sees the uniquely liberal values represented by English South Africa under apartheid as threatened by the hegemonic power of the African National Congress. This chapter draws out the points of disagreement and reaches unexpected conclusions about the potentially malign role of democracy in the modern state.

Chapter 5 turns for assistance in understanding recent changes in South African politics and society to the international fraternity of political scientists, and in particular to comparative politics. The key focus of comparative politics over the past decade has become the phenomenon labelled 'democratization'. Students of politics have tried to explain the increasing number of states around the globe that have not merely proclaimed themselves democratic – something almost universal even in the 1960s and 1970s – but that have also instituted regular multiparty elections as the instruments of popular self-government. In this chapter I investigate how much guidance comparative politics has provided for those trying to understand political change in South Africa and southern Africa as a whole.

Chapters 6 and 7 investigate how effective the specialized techniques of political science have proved in rendering comprehensible recent political change in South Africa, and in making the reality of transition less tumultuous and more benign. I investigate several species of political analyst: the constitutional engineers who have hawked their designs in South Africa over the past two decades; the specialists in political attitudes and voting behaviour who have analysed the practices of South Africa's old and new electorates; and finally the political analysts of the future, whose scenarios and risk analyses feature so prominently in the political studies departments of South African universities.

The findings of these chapters do not encourage confidence in the claims of political science to be a powerful 'policy science'. Professional political analysts have provided very little in the way of hard facts or well-grounded understanding of South African society. They have been more likely to undermine than to encourage sound political judgement. Their institutional remedies have more often than not been ill-conceived and potentially malign. And they have generated much ideological smoke and noise (under which cover conservatives have manoeuvred) while casting little light on how South African could be made less dangerous for the majority of its inhabitants. In the concluding chapter, the implications of the comprehensive failure of academic analysis of South Africa's past, present, and future politics are assessed. I show that if professional political analysis has shed little light on South Africa, then South African events have exposed many of the weaknesses within the discipline. The weaknesses of political science can be used to diagnose otherwise invisible failings in its analysis of Western liberal capitalist democracy.

4 Democracy and Apartheid

The brokers of public opinion in the Western world – its media, popular writers and political activists – propagate an astonishingly complacent conception of democracy and its benevolence. Democracy has been elevated to an almost unchallengeable ideal, woven into a tale of inexorable (if occasionally temporarily reversed) human advance, with the liberal democratic state as the institutional culmination of Western progress. This seemingly naive celebration of the forward march of an idea in fact masks considerable ambivalence in popular sentiment. Many people vote a great deal, and believe that their vote is both an effective action and a moral obligation. But abstention, cynicism and the retreat to cause group politics mark an increasing disenchantment with democratic politics. The past two decades have seen voter dealignment and a growth in anti-party sentiment in all Western states.[1] Public opinion is structured, internally consistent, persistent over time and sometimes subtle: voters recognize the constraints of political life.[2] Yet the recent trend towards unpopular leaders in Western democracies indicates a potential fragility of democracy in its heartlands, even as it is supposedly running triumphant elsewhere.[3]

Notwithstanding these concerns about democracy at home, the super-educated citizens of the West view the spread of democracy elsewhere in a rosy light. Academic analysis currently encourages these complacent and self-flattering public understandings of democracy. Liberal political science today characteristically presumes that a range of attractive consequences follow the 'democratization' of a polity. The predictive issue that political science has addressed has been whether the current wave of democracy will break and then recede, rather than the matter of the consequences that might follow from democracy.[4]

Fukuyama has famously claimed that liberal capitalist democracy expresses the full potential of the modern nation-state.[5] The predominant idiom through which academic theorists have expressed their idealization of democracy, however, has been not pseudo-Hegelianism but rather modernization theory.[6] Democratization, to liberal modernization theorists, is the final stage of a single historical process. Social structures in the modern state undergo an extended process of differentiation and specialization which culminates in the emergence of distinct political structures; these structures open the way to democracy.

Modern political thought retains a little of its traditional scepticism about the benevolence of democratic politics. It does so predominantly through studies of the conflict between investment and consumption in developing and developed countries, and especially in detailed studies of the institutionalized budgetary politics of advanced industrial states. According to some analysts, the principal–agent character of representative government, in combination with the asymmetries of information characteristic of such government, inevitably results in misled citizens.[7] Others have identified a tendency for electoral competition to promote a political business cycle, or for systematic overspending, under-investment and accompanying inflation.[8] Still others point to institutional incentives towards policies which render benefits immediate and traceable to politicians, while making costs invisible or hard to trace.[9] Today, however, these models are advanced as lessons in institutional engineering rather than as critiques of democracy.

This chapter uses the history of modern South Africa to locate systematic weaknesses in the academic literature on democracy. The first section confirms that the demise of apartheid owed little or nothing to the democratic idea in action or to 'democratization' however defined, and goes on to explore the origins of the myth of the transformative capacity of the democratic idea in South Africa. The second section explores the heuristic benefits of registering that apartheid South Africa was a representative democracy. Once recognized, the comfortable cohabitation of democracy and apartheid in post-1948 South Africa becomes problematic for liberals whose claims about the conceptual and practical tensions between democracy and apartheid prove to be without foundation. Only intellectually unjustifiable distortions of the meaning of central terms permitted the champions of democracy to argue for its benevolence. I show, by contrast, that democratic practices and apartheid were not merely compatible but mutually supporting.

The third and penultimate section argues, still more contentiously, that democratic practices were not merely symbiotically related to apartheid, but were a direct cause of the high apartheid of the 1960s. This section illustrates features of democracy that have often been written out of academic analysis. Democratic practices can render legitimate to leaders and specific publics otherwise indefensible courses of action. Attempts to secure perceived preconditions for democracy – the existence of a people or nation with a common identity, electoral institutions and a common relation to an external world – can cause immense human suffering. Democratic politics, moreover, can stimulate greed and sow confusion, and it is incompatible with the integrity of political leaders. The concluding section explores the wider implications of the relationship between democracy and its preconditions for academic understandings of the relationship between democracy and human good.

DEMOCRACY DID NOT END APARTHEID

The popular view that an oppressive system was swept away by the idea of democracy in the election in 1994 located South Africa among the wave of democratizing polities across the globe from the 1970s. Just as Eastern Europe's revolutions, in Garton Ash's words, represented 'the large scale sustained, yet supremely peaceful and self-disciplined, manifestation of social unity, the gentle crowd against the party state, which was both the hallmark and the essential democratic catalyst of change,'[10] the end of apartheid supposedly represented a triumph of human beings striving for political freedom.

Academic analysts supported this unlikely thesis by identifying the democratic idea with a process of modernization which purportedly swept apartheid away. This view, widespread among professional social scientists, sees democracy as an inevitable aspect of social change. I first use recent advances in comparative politics to show that the modernization view is not sustainable in this form. Second, I show that the demise of the apartheid state was quite distinct from democratization. Third, I examine the sources of the notion of a benevolent democratic idea. Why have publics believed an idea could be so powerful? Here, I explain the consequences of a conflation of representative with direct democracy. Intellectually moribund but politically resonant notions of collective assertion living on inside the ideological shell of Western liberal democracy have created popular confusion over democratization in South Africa and elsewhere.

Modernization approaches to democratization build on the strong relationship between regime type and economic development (usually measured by income levels):[11] the wealthier a country, the more likely it is to be a democracy. Przeworski and Limongi distinguish two ways of understanding this relationship – one 'endogenous' and the other 'exogenous'. In endogenous modernization analysis, which has dominated comparative political studies, democracy emerges as countries develop: the gradual differentiation and specialization of social structures culminates in the separate political structures that make democracy possible. Causal processes (which ultimately explain democratization) in industrialization, urbanization, education and political incorporation, cumulatively prepare the society for democratization.

Industrialization creates a need for incorporation of labour into firm and sectoral decision-making, and resulting labour unions press for the extension of the political rights necessary for their own flourishing. Wider class conflicts of interest must be neutralized through the political incorporation of working-class representatives. New social forces in civil society emerge as a counterweight to the state. The cumulative effects of urbanization and education render individuals susceptible to democratic ideas. A proliferation and privatization of information combines with increasingly sophisticated technology to render systems of coercion and direct control vulnerable.

Przeworski and Limongi demonstrate that an exogenous approach fits the facts better than this endogenous account. Dictatorships can die and democracies emerge at any level of development. Factors not dependent on development – war, economic crisis, foreign pressure, the death of key leaders and domestic political struggles – lead to the establishment of democratic regimes. The relationship between development and democracy is not explained by the conditions of initial emergence of democracy, but by the chances of a democratic regime surviving (which are higher in an affluent country). For this reason, history gradually 'accumulates' democracies and these are more numerous in wealthier countries.

Przeworski and Limongi consider countries either democratic or authoritarian, and their dichotomy brings many analytical advantages. However, this disguises one implication of their findings: if democracy is not brought about by development, but rather by crisis, war, death or insurrection, then the democratic idea has no special relationship to the demise of authoritarian regimes. The democratic idea and democratic practices within opposition movements have no special relation to the process that culminates in a democratic society.

The demise of the apartheid state, indeed, has been most persuasively explained by scholars who have focused on the long-range weaknesses of that state. These writers have made no case for the transformative power of the democratic idea. Liberal analysts of the economic irrationality of apartheid, and Marxist students of the structural crises of the South African state, emerged with something like the same explanation of the collapse of apartheid. The former pointed to apartheid's malign effects on skilled labour and its pricing, and underlined the system's inability to produce a viable domestic market for goods, and to overcome a tendency towards monopoly.[12] Regulation School Marxists argued that bourgeois liberal democracy was now the appropriate hegemonic strategy to support a regime of accumulation no longer dominated by domestic mining and agricultural interests.[13] Liberal and Marxist alike recognized the importance of trade union politics, the bureaucratic untenability of job reservation in complex labour markets, the necessity of educated, urban, resident Africans, the duplication and cost of homelands, and the burden of the ever-burgeoning security apparatus.

Other analysts registered the role of regional political turmoil and of geo-political and geo-economic change, equally independently of domestic democratic practice. The collapse of the Portuguese colonial state in the mid-1970s created two permanent bases for insurgency against the republic, and transfers of power in Rhodesia and Namibia intensified this pressure. Destabilizing neighbouring states was costly in both direct budgetary terms and indirectly in regional underdevelopment which reduced South Africa's long-term economic potential. International actors, the US Congress and the Commonwealth, placed some direct pressure on the South African regime, but the Reagan and Thatcher administrations supported the National Party reform strategy. By the late 1980s, however, the crisis of apartheid was evident and the proxy war against communism had lost its relevance. Domestically, the collapse of the USSR removed from Afrikaner ideology the anticommunist stick upon which it had leant and with which it had beaten its opponents.[14] In domestic politics, where we might hope to see the democratic idea in action, political struggles consciously motivated by 'democratic values' were the weakest in practice.[15]

The ANC's assault on the apartheid state was not justified in the name of democracy, nor was it executed by means of liberal democratic practice. Other opposition parties were not ideologically committed to liberal democracy, and the most effective struggles against apartheid were by unionized workers seeking improved living standards and by South Africans resisting influx control. Why, then, has the end of apartheid come to be so widely construed as the outcome of a popular *democratic* struggle against the oppressive, unjust and undemocratic principles that the system embodied?

One answer is that ANC myth-making and White moral evasion have reinforced idealized public and academic conceptions of democratization. After decades successfully resisting the allure of universal suffrage, South African White public opinion has equally firmly adopted an enthusiastic stance towards the idea of democracy.

Discovering that widened suffrage was inevitable, liberal Whites have followed English Victorian liberals by advancing on three fronts. First, they have championed the idiom of political rights and constitutionalism, and supported the transfer of power to a disciplined parliamentary leadership and reconstituted state bureaucracy. Second, they have maintained that the oppressed must have political power – but not too much of it until they have come to understand the limitations that fiscal prudence places on the rulers of the modern state. Third, they have given potential opponents a stake in the new political order, moving beyond South Africa's pre-1960s efforts to incorporate a 'detribalized' urban, Black middle class, and supporting economic empowerment of Blacks.[16]

Former opposition organizations have also embraced liberal democracy.[17] The ANC has tried to shroud its past, as well as its present, in the mantle of democracy despite the hierarchical and elitist origins and early decades of the ANC, its failure to align with mass protest, its isolation from worker struggles and its continuing support for nondemocratic regimes around the globe.

Key ANC constituencies – the Youth League, the Women's League and the Communist Party – have incompatible and quixotic conceptions of the democratic. Former exiles and political prisoners had little routine experience of democracy: exile spanned continents and decades in places as unamenable to liberal democracy as Lusaka, Moscow, and Peking. On Robben Island, discipline and hierarchy took precedence over collective self-government. ANC affiliates combined open debate, accountability and collective assertion with hierarchy, leadership deception and elite privilege. Only the domestic opposition of the 1980s – and especially the facilitatory leadership of the United Democratic Front and COSATU organizations – were consistent champions of democratic practice.[18]

The African National Congress was historically rooted in support for Empire, tradition and respect for White power and chiefly authority. In the 1920s and 1930s, while the Industrial and Commercial Workers' Union[19] and the Communist Party of South Africa sought popular support, the ANC supported chiefs and the aspirant African commercial class.[20] In the 1940s, as African nationalism developed among the urbanizing poor, it was trade unionism and practical day-to-day resistance to apartheid laws and influx control that achieved greatest success, while the ANC was a restraining influence in such campaigns.[21] Although the ANC performed some useful functions in gathering information and disseminating intelligence, it managed no systematic questioning of an oppressive system and made no effort to 'channel resistance towards political ends'.[22] Leaders' beliefs in progress and liberal ideals made the ANC cautious, whereas the PAC's naive Africanism permitted it to define a turning point in the history of resistance against apartheid at Sharpeville.

Only in the 1980s, as the government's 'total strategy' met with a strong response from a rejuvenated movement, did democratic practice deeply permeate ANC-affiliated organizations. The trauma of African experience after Soweto, and the growing deterioration in the economic prospects, housing, services and everyday experiences of Africans helped to create a belief in collective action. The ideological universe of the ANC, however, embraced Soviet communism just as it encompassed the liberal values of Charterism. ANC democracy was as amenable to democratic centralism in a one-party state as to the democracy of party competition and human rights. The movement still sought the destruction of existing political institutions and not their remodelling or extension.

South Africa's academic analysts have also belatedly clambered on the democratic bandwagon. Hitherto functionalist or developmental intellectuals paying little attention to democratic practice as the engine of social and political advancement,[23] today fit South African experience into comparativist accounts of democratization and everywhere trumpet the democratic ideal.

Beyond propaganda and opportunism lies a deeper confusion about democracy: whether it refers to 'direct' democracy or to 'representative' democracy, a distinction which contemporary political theory has done much to render more clear. Direct or participatory democracy is politics as the collective self-creation of a political community. Issues of common concern are collectively scrutinized and openly debated; deliberation is followed by binding decision. Contemporary experiences of direct democracy come only in local settings: small associations and committees, in which participants know one other and can collectively shape their conditions of life or work. 'Representative' democracy is the democracy of a commercial society. It is procedural, defined by institutions (notably elections) which permit some accountability of ruler to ruled. Elected representatives, themselves subject to legal and constitutional constraints, take collective decisions. As specialist political leaders, they render comprehensible the actions of the modern state to its subjects, and deploy the specialist techniques of government.

These two distinct understandings of democracy are in one way antithetical. The institutional forms of representative democracy were designed to inhibit the collective assertion of the citizenry that direct democracy champions.[24] 'The idea of the modern State was constructed', as Dunn reminds us, 'painstakingly and purposefully, above all by Jean Bodin and Thomas Hobbes, for the express purpose of denying that any given population, any people, had either the capacity or the right to act together for themselves, either independently of or against the sovereign.'[25] The populations of European states could not act with sufficient coherence and identity over time to be considered capable of self-rule. 'The idea of the modern State', Dunn considers, 'was invented precisely to repudiate the possible coherence of democratic claims to rule or even take genuinely political action', and it is thus 'democracy made safe for the modern State: democracy converted from unruly and incoherent master to docile and dependent servant'.[26]

In the twentieth century, Schumpeter has likened this distanced political accountability to the electorate's selection of an organized team of rulers from a set of reasonably similar candidates. For Schumpeter, values and interests in a modern state cannot be forged into a common rule. Human judgement is manufactured rather than generated through public deliberation. Leaders deploy associations, draw on ideology, greed and sentimentality to manufacture a purported majority will; and human conduct is shaped and coordinated by state institutions that no individual can master or even understand.[27]

Representative democracy, however, provides services for modern states' inhabitants. It allows citizens a degree of personal liberty to pursue, without hindrance of others or of the state itself, their commercial and social activities. It provides a degree of accountability, through electoral and party institutions, of rulers to ruled; and it protects a capitalist economy from the degradation of concentrated power, thus making high standards of material comfort possible for many.

The specific rationality that guides representative democracy – periodic elections, the insulation of rulers from immediate pressures of public opinion so that they may plan for the long term, the defence of 'civil society', the raising of citizen consciousness through public education – makes the system a potentially justifiable compromise with the realities of scale and complexity. However, the notion of collective deliberation and decision is more than just a depleted residue of direct democracy: it continues to animate an otherwise alien representative democracy. This ability to animate helps us to see why democracy might seem a decisive factor in the destruction of the apartheid state.

The institutions of representative democracy exclude the collective deliberation and assertion that defined ancient democracy. Representative democracy, however, echoes such properties in two ways. First, it promulgates dialogue and consensus over issues of common concern. As Revel has argued, democracy's 'practical superiority derives from the fact that it is the only system which, through trial and error, can become aware of its own mistakes and correct them.'[28] States achieve such institutional and collective learning if the polity's civil institutions are open to public debate and reflection. By means of such openness and learning, democratic states develop a kind of collective knowledge that no individual or group can command alone.

Second, representative democracy embodies an idea of collective assertion. The Schumpeterian denial of the possibility of a general rule (supported by the impossibility of deriving common interests from a set of individual's interests) is persuasive. However, it confuses collective political acts with collective administrative activities. In the ideology of liberal democracy, a political act is legitimate if it reflects the will or consensus of the sovereign authority (the people or their assembly). However, as Ricoeur has explained, if an act genuinely embodied such a full standard of consensus, it would be an *executive* act and not a political act at all. A gap must remain between act and consent if the act is to be political in nature; political consent is always reflective and retrospective.[29] Even for liberals, the legitimacy of a state cannot coherently be tied to the collective generation of its actions. Rather, it is the conviction of the ruled that they collectively control their destinies and consent to the state's actions that makes sense of its claims to act at the behest of the people.

Collective opposition to apartheid was partly responsible for the end of apartheid. These forces, however, were not successful *because* they were democratic (to the extent that they were democratic). The fact that a universal suffrage election marked the end to the struggle against apartheid does not make that end into a triumph of democracy. The conflation of two conceptions of democracy makes this illusion possible: if collective assertion is democracy and elections are democracy, then any route between the two must, it seems, represent an expression of democracy. We should remember, moreover, that apartheid was brought down by its own internal weaknesses. In different times, the end of apartheid would have been followed by a different mode of authoritarian rule and certainly not by democracy. Democratization and the end of apartheid are historically and analytically distinct episodes.

DEMOCRACY IN HARMONY WITH SEGREGATION AND EARLY APARTHEID: 1910–60

In this section, I show that democracy was quite in harmony with apartheid. South Africa after 1994 was plainly a more democratic society than it was before, since the extension of a franchise *ceteris paribus* brings into being a more democratic society. South Africa, however, has been a democracy since 1910: a democracy with a racially defined franchise, but a democracy nevertheless. From the Act of Union in 1910 to the end of the first phase of apartheid in 1960, representative democratic practices supported an increasingly systematic institutionalization of human exploitation.

My argument has two stages. First, I show that South Africa was a democratic state from 1910 and explore the confusions behind commonplace rejections of this fact. Second, I show that South Africa's lively and competitive democracy in no way generated pressure towards benevolent social change. Rather, it supported an oppressive social order that degenerated into a unique political evil. The most striking feature of this democracy was how easily compatible it proved to be with the systematic oppression of the majority of the population of the country.

Was South Africa a Democracy from 1910?

South Africa's White citizens have conceived themselves as the bearers of civilization, in politics as in economy and culture. The South African state from 1910 to 1960 was characterized by political competition within recognizable liberal institutions, and its Westminster-style elections have been analysed through election studies in the British tradition.[30] Participation has been enthusiastic and the machinery of competitive democracy has fascinated electors. Simultaneously, White South Africans were often enthusiastic about the benefits of self-government for Africans. 'Separate development' from 1960 successfully exploited the terminology of 'self-government' and 'collective self-determination' to justify the allocation of African political rights to the Bantustans. Seemingly easily interpreted as a cynical disempowerment of African inhabitants of the Republic, the homeland projects have been disturbingly difficult to condemn on the terms of liberal democracy.

The evident presence of democratic institutions and ideologies across twentieth-century South Africa has confused political analysts.

On the one hand, some elections – notably, the 1948 triumph of the National Party – have struck them as watersheds which changed national destiny. On the other hand, functionalist or developmental accounts have dominated the long-range accounts of South Africa in the twentieth century.[31] Almost all professional political analysts, in the last resort, refuse to accept that South Africa was a democracy between 1910 and 1994. The twofold reasons for this denial seem obvious. First, democracy is advertised as government by the people, thus implying a universal franchise. Second, democracy implies an equality of political rights, a rejection of oppression and an order of self-government which segregation and apartheid seemed to deny.

No society, on such criteria, can claim to be fully democratic. The creation of a democratic society is an endless pursuit, 'a demand for the opportunity to make power in our adult lives always ultimately answerable to those over whom it is exercised.... for the practical political means to replace subjugation by authority, and to do so wherever we find ourselves subject to the former.'[32] The institutional expressions of democracy will vary across times and places: the absence of an idealized 'democratic society' does not invalidate the study of democratic practices.

Many analysts have claimed that South Africa was undemocratic because it lacked a universal franchise: the right to vote was largely confined to those defined 'White'. However, the moral objection to a racial franchise is precisely that it is racially based, and not that it is not universal. South Africa's franchise was a *racist*, and racially exclusive, *democratic* franchise. This language identifies where the moral obscenity lies. Disassociating the term 'democracy' from this obscene political system conflates two objections: to South Africa's racism and to its purported lack of democracy.

Other colonial states – Australia, United States, Canada, New Zealand – were so successful at destroying native populations, and so extensively settled, that majoritarianism could bolster racial oppression. Settlers could impose racist legislation upon indigenous inhabitants not crushed by settlement and disease. In South Africa, this was never a possibility. In contrast to other parts of sub-Saharan Africa, there was a substantial African (as well as Coloured and Indian) educated middle class due to South Africa's early industrialization. South Africa's complex mixture of populations, and the equivocal political rights given to all property holders, Black or White, in the Cape, kept alive the hope of an extension of franchise. The extension of the franchise that was sought was a deepening of an existing democratic order and not a social transformation.

A universal franchise has not been a feature of the great ancient and modern democracies. Kleisthenes' Athenian democracy, the archetype of citizen self-rule, empowered a small minority and excluded women, slaves and the young. It damages the term 'democracy' to exclude this unmatched, foundational participation, while it makes perfect sense to describe this government of Athens as a democracy, but one with a limited citizenry.

If a universal franchise is a prerequisite for democracy, equal violence would be done to the archetypal modern democracy, the United States. As Gordon S. Wood argues of the American Revolution, not only 'did it largely create the United States, but it defined most of the persistent values and noblest ideals of the American people, including their commitments to equality and constitutionalism. Most importantly, the revolution created American democracy, indeed, made America (despite the contradictory persistence of slavery until the middle decade of the nineteenth century) the first people in the modern world to possess a truly democratic government and society.'[33]

The remark in parentheses indicates the tensions between 'a truly democratic government and society' and the persistence of slavery. Surely, however, Wood is correct to see in this new American government practice an example of democracy, albeit a deeply flawed one. Authors who insist that effective universal suffrage is 'perhaps the most fundamental prerequisite for a democracy'[34] are forced to place US democratization in the 1960s (by which time Argentina, say, had already become and lost its status as a democracy twice!).

Even more problematical for political analysts, the franchise was not extended to women across most of Western Europe and the United States until the period immediately before and after the First World War. These states had clearly not achieved a universal adult franchise: how could the exclusion of women be compatible with democratic values? Yet, at the same time, franchise extension plainly represented the incorporation of women into a democratic system rather than the creation of a new democratic political system.

Any franchise is exclusive: the young, and those defined in many diverse ways incapable, are denied the equality of respect that democracy promises. Perhaps most importantly of all, the franchise in any democracy excludes those who are not citizens: mere place of birth or place of officially sanctioned residence defines exclusion from any political community.

It seems that analysts categorized South Africa as non-democratic precisely because of its racial oppression, segregation and denial of human rights: the thesis that this state of affairs was caused by, or supported by, democracy was ruled out of court in advance. If one defines a society as undemocratic because of an aversion to its practices, however, one cannot advance any negative theses about the *effects* of democratic practices. One cannot, for example, suggest that democracy – a set of electoral and political practices – caused the social oppression of apartheid South Africa.

Human rights organizations, such as Freedom House, take matters further by producing indices of 'democracy' that are in fact measures of liberalism. Political rights and civil liberties are logged and converted into a quantitative measure of the extent of human freedom in a state.[35] If respect for human rights is a precondition for defining a state as democratic, however, it becomes impossible to advance any substantive negative theses about the relationship between democracy and civil rights. Analysts simply define as non-democratic any political system that they consider unappealing, thus rendering impossible any substantive statements about the significance of democracy (except positive ones).

Political analysts should choose a definition of democracy that neither does violence to ordinary language nor excludes from consideration substantive theses about the negative and positive effects of democratic practices. Such a definition must refer to a set of practices within the society and not to the characteristics of the society as a whole. In summary, we require a definition that meets the following tests: it does not confuse democratic practices with some wider democratic society; it does not do violence to ordinary usage by defining states as non-democracies in spite of their exhibition of archetypal democratic features; and it permits us to test substantive theses about the benevolence, or otherwise, of democratic practices.

Przeworski and Limongi's dichotomous classification of regimes as either democracies or authoritarian states meets all our criteria.[36] 'Democracy is a regime in which some governmental offices are filled as a consequence of contested elections',[37] with relevant offices including the Chief Executive Officer and the seats in the effective legislative body. Contestation occurs when an opposition has some chance of winning office as a consequence of elections. Countries are excluded if they have an unelected legislature or only one party.

On this definition, South Africa was evidently a democracy from the Act of Union in 1910. There was lively competition between parties;

there was frenetic electoral activity; governments changed by election; and clearly organized opposition parties existed. Chief Executives and legislative bodies had contested elections and there were clear examples of changes of regime by election. The country had an extended literature on party competition, a press which supported opposition movements, and a history of elections with significant social consequences.

Why, then, have commentators been so determined to view South Africa as an authoritarian state, which has only recently become a democracy? The key reason, I believe, is that analysts, falling in line with the ideological forces of bourgeois democracy, have been unwilling to accept that so unattractive a social order as South Africa could be admitted to the charmed circle of democratic states. Their attempt to confine the term democracy to states with a 'universal' franchise and respect for human rights defines away the questions that make the analysis of democracy interesting. In particular, it makes it impossible to ask whether democracy caused, or contributed to, the creation of a morally unattractive social order.

Segregationist South Africa as Democracy

Viewing South Africa as a democracy quite changes our understanding of its history. Since the South African state presided over segregation, it is evident that democratic practice did not prevent the continuation of systematic oppression. Democracy was plainly compatible with extended oppression: a limited franchise and the denial of human rights to the vast majority of the population were not rendered unsustainable by the demands of consistency in the application of democratic values.

In part, this compatibility reflects the indeterminacy of the system of ideas surrounding liberal democracy, and the weak conceptual relations between those ideas. 'Democracy' is quite compatible with selective citizenship, as has been demonstrated across most of the history of the idea: persons can be defined as non-citizens on grounds of age, gender, origin and race. The scales at which democracy expresses a relation between territory and political agency are arbitrary, and a part of a given territory can become a self-governing unit (to the potential benefit of inhabitants in seceding provinces, or to their evident detriment as in South Africa's homeland system). People can be characterized as lacking the qualities that make citizenship meaningful: education, civilization or property ownership. South Africa, indeed, has seen each of these arguments used to justify the exclusion of Blacks from meaningful citizenship.

Constitutional democracy did not merely permit segregation and apartheid; it was in harmony with them. The Act of Union itself, designed when British concern for the interests of natives was at a low ebb and shaped to avoid confrontation with Afrikaners after the inconclusive South African War, embodied African exclusion as a deliberate political action. Educated African opinion had favoured continued lobbying of the British Parliament for an extension of the Cape franchise. The blatant unconcern with which the Act was prosecuted demonstrated that the democratic constitution's creation was itself a political act with powerful ramifications for included and excluded alike.

Aside from the constitution itself, and pre-dating it, poor Whites' capacity to vote gave them access to power that even wealthy Blacks lacked. Closed compounds, introduced by De Beers for the control of convict labour, and later extended for use with all diamond workers by the increasingly monopolistic mining companies, offered clear advantages to those companies, whether workers were Black or White. Smuggling could be limited; workers could be directly controlled (so hampering unionization or worker militancy); and the companies could secure extra profits from the sale of accommodation and food. In 1886, however, White workers electorally rejected company candidates, an option closed to Africans. 'As a result', according to Worden, 'the compounds were implemented for Black migrant workers alone.'[38] Access to the ballot box enjoyed by White men did not create racism; but unequal access did cause a deepening of the boundaries of emerging segregation. Likewise, by the turn of the century, the right to vote encouraged political leaders to provide relief to the White urban poor, especially on the Rand. While the Afrikaner poor could reward political leaders for the provision of relief work, Blacks could shape no such incentive structure to their benefit.[39]

The labour framework that was put in place by mining houses and the state from the 1890s maintained reserve areas, limited the proletarianization of African workers and crushed African labour organizations and their attempts to increase wages.[40] White workers in mining, steel and railroads advanced their interests more successfully, and had their labour subsidized directly through industrial organizations.[41] But electoral power was also crucial. After the Second World War, many White workers supported the HNP policy of expanded job reservation, the splitting of mixed unions and a more elaborate framework to limit African workers' urbanization.[42]

For liberals, as Greenberg emphasizes, 'the elaboration of the racial order and the development of the State racial apparatus in this period proceeded under the ascendancy of commercial farmers'.[43] As the largest single bloc in Parliament (and, even more so, in the governing parties) the concerns of commercial farmers became the key issues for the state. Commercial farmers, through their electoral dominance, were to promote the social distance, and hierarchy that were to characterize relations between European and African thereafter.[44] Racial domination thereafter 'drew heavily on ideas nurtured in the precapitalist countryside and articulated by commercial farmers during the transition to capitalist agriculture' – ideas that could not have been turned into practice as they were had it not been for the transmission devices of democracy.

The banal truth is that democratic elections can help intolerant electors to impose their beliefs on others, and to secure their interests at the expense of those others through the state. Elections notoriously benefit extremes in a range of circumstances. Numerous and backward Afrikaners could dominate a first-past-the-post electoral system which favoured rural constituencies, giving a boost to segregationist practice and ideology. The idea that South Africa was a democracy, moreover, allowed English and African apologists for segregation to excuse their participation. A system that permitted all relevant (adult, educated, civilized) citizens to participate carried legitimate authority – regardless of the legislation that it encouraged or endorsed. The ANC, indeed, was hamstrung by its commitment to an extension of the franchise. ANC quiescence was guaranteed by the need to accept the rules of democracy: agreement over the limits of legitimate opposition, and consensus about the boundaries of political obligation, confined the ANC elite and forced it to look for 'constitutional' advances where no such were available.

The election of 1948 displayed a number of the least attractive features of democracy all at once: fortune, populism, fear, unreason, prejudice and manipulation all played major roles. Between 1948 and 1960, however, democratic practices were largely facilitative: elections reinforced a collectively binding series of decisions that a majority of the White population (and an overwhelming majority of the populations as a whole) would have resisted. The key causes of early apartheid lay in the logic of segregation. Nevertheless, democracy made their implementation easier, and paved the way for the bizarre change of direction in the 1960s.

I have explained in chapter 2 why 1948 should not figure as a watershed in South African history. The apartheid of 1948–60 was segregation by another name. These 12 years, however, did see the meeting of certain preconditions for apartheid by an elected government in a constitutional democracy. The 1948 HNP victory was a remarkable political triumph of coalition building in adverse circumstances. In the 1930s South Africa saw not just segregation but a politics of class and regional division. White workers, farmers and petty bourgeoisie had clear class interests regardless of whether they spoke Afrikaans or English, and these interests were reflected in voting behaviour. Regional divisions, moreover, kept the Afrikaners of the Cape apart from their new ethnic kin in the former Boer republics.

Afrikaner identity, the fulcrum of mobilization, comprised an ill-defined language, a few short decades of myth-making and cultural education, a grudge against the English (but not one that the HNP could exploit) and the slogan of apartheid and the fear it represented. Only representative democracy could have achieved such a dramatic transformation of fortune while retaining legitimacy in the eyes of the losers. The machinery of the state had been seized by a self-conscious ethnic alliance with the woeful power to enforce its fantasies on a territory, and with the full legitimacy of democratic practice behind it.

The election win was far from decisive: 40 per cent of Afrikaners voted for the United Party, and it was the protest vote of English speakers that helped the HNP to its 39 per cent of the vote. Translated into a narrow national victory (by means of weighted rural and peri-urban constituencies) the NP actually campaigned on few national issues: anti-Indian land controls were important in Natal, Vaal and Orange Free State farmers developed doubts about the United Party, and only Smuts' failure to reassure Whites about Black labour was a trans-national phenomenon.

Once in power, however, the liberal democratic myth of the majority right to govern permitted a massive shift in control. English-speaking bureaucrats, soldiers and state employees were sidelined by reliable Afrikaners, with key posts going to Broederbond members (with their ideological commitment to separatism). The electoral system itself was manipulated to reduce the impact of immigrant English speakers and eliminate that of Coloureds.

The democratic triumph of the NP brought with it a wave of new segregationist and supremacist legislation, including the Natives

Resettlement Act of 1954 which began large-scale removals, the Group Areas Act of 1950 which separated residential areas across the country and the Population Registration Act of 1950 which provided the necessary framework of racial and ethnic classification. Extensions of influx control, labour bureaux and the pass laws accompanied 'petty apartheid' measures, against 'mixed marriages' and in support of segregated social, educational and cultural amenities and public institutions.

Thus the democratic method of selecting chief executive and legislature produced a range of alarming consequences. It most decidedly failed as a force for moderation, protection of human dignity or recognition of minimal standards of human decency, acting rather as a mechanism through which a minority mobilized ethnicity into a force for evil. Democracy was more than in harmony with the system of segregation and early apartheid: it was a resource upon which segregationists drew, and which helped them both to construct and to implement their vision of a remade social order.

DEMOCRACY AS CAUSE OF HIGH APARTHEID: 1960–

What was High Apartheid?

The work of Posel and others has firmly established that the 'second phase' of apartheid, from around 1960, was quite distinct in character from the first.[45] It was the combination of three factors – moral outrage at petty apartheid, the slogan of 'apartheid' itself and the myth of the 'grand plan' implemented by the National Party from 1948 – that led to the conventional and misleading periodization of the apartheid era from 1948 through to the early 1990s.[46] High apartheid, from 1960, ran counter to trends in post-colonial Africa. It defied the logic of modernization as it enforced labour controls upon the workforce of an economy increasingly dominated by manufacturing, and no longer centred on mines and agriculture. It was prosecuted in the face of concerted opposition. The distinctiveness of 'high apartheid' is established in part by its context, in part by its content and policy, and in part by the discontinuities it represented in terms of state structure.

The context of high apartheid from 1960 was dominated by decolonization. Harold Macmillan's 'Winds of Change' speech, and systematic attack on segregation in the southern states of the US, turned disapproval into condemnation. The content of high apartheid policy and legislation was a stunning departure. While 1950s legislation systematically oppressed Blacks, the 1960s and 1970s were marked by extraordinary experiments in state creation and social engineering. The Republic of South Africa determined to generate eight (and later ten) Bantu homelands. These were designed to become self-governing, and later independent states; by 1970 homeland citizenship had been imposed on all Africans. Independence was declared for Transkei in 1976, for Boputhatswana in 1977, Venda in 1979 and Ciskei in 1981.[47]

Two features of high apartheid illustrate most clearly its revolutionary nature. The first was the scale of forced human displacement. Whereas the Group Areas Act of 1950 had largely urban implications and mostly extended and reinforced existing patterns of segregation, the policy of separate development led to a multitude of removals of Africans – tenant farmers, freeholders and squatters alike – from rural areas designated White. Between 1960 and 1983, around 3.5 million people were forcibly relocated under group areas and separate development legislation.[48]

Second, high apartheid was a period of the deliberate creation of tribalism in the African population of South Africa. Outsiders, in the form of missionaries and anthropologists, had defined tribal entities and created formally distinct languages out of a series of closely related dialects and languages. 'Tribes' had always been understood and reshaped by Whites in accordance with their own interests and their understandings of tribal affiliation. South Africa's multiple processes of conquest, industrialization and quasi-proletarianization through the migrant labour system, however, undermined the potential for political tribalization. In the 1960s, de-tribalization – the idea that Africans or an African elite needed to be gradually introduced to civilization in the cities and weaned off their dependence on primordial attachments – was abandoned for an aggressive programme of re-tribalization. Ethnicity was a key organizing concept in the new apartheid, as every person was to be assigned an ethnic designation and a corresponding political citizenship.[49]

High apartheid was also discontinuous from segregation and early apartheid in terms of state structure. While the policies of the 1950s had been grounded in pragmatism, policy from the late 1950s began to reflect the ground that had been gained by Broederbond hardliners within the state. The Native Affairs Department became a state within a state targeted at destruction of the Black proletariat and reversal of its growth. Every African, whatever his or her place of birth, was to be defined as the permanent resident and later citizen of an ethnically defined homeland. While the urban labour preference policy was maintained, quotas and a newly aggressive resettlement policy were added to the state's armoury. Between 1960 and 1970, the Bantustan population increased by almost 1 million while the number of Africans in urban areas actually fell by 200,000.[50]

Such extraordinary experiments in social engineering and state creation had been contemplated a decade earlier when the National Party came to power. Early apartheid from 1948 to 1960, however, was merely segregation by another name. To seek an explanation for the imposition of high apartheid from 1960 is to ask what it was that caused this distinctive social experiment. I argue that democracy was responsible.

The Meaning of Causation

Our dominant image of causation is the relationship of causes and effects in the mechanical sciences. When trying to explain how some state of social affairs came into being, however, the relevant causes and effects are hard to identify. When we say that an event or a state of affairs was caused by an event or an act, we never mean to identify (and neither could we identify) the complete set of causal conditions which brought about that state of affairs. Rather, we isolate particular causes as the relevant ones. These are likely to be the conditions that have changed, rather than remaining unnoticed as background conditions. As Hart and Honore explain in their analyses of the notion of cause in the law, a cause is likely to be an event or act that is especially visible, or that is the last of the set of conditions required to bring about a change.[51]

Equally significant, we normally trace 'causes and effects' in order to ascribe responsibility for events. Indeed, we often place the notions together, talking about causal and moral responsibility for an outcome or a state of affairs. In seeking to ascribe responsibility, we are usually looking for some party that we can coherently consider to be the site of agency. When ascribing moral responsibility for an event or state of affairs, we almost always seek a human agent as that site. Moral responsibility is almost always attached to an intention or set of intentions, as well as to the moral character of an agent. Yet, it is also a social and cultural phenomenon: the proper behaviour to be expected of an agent, in terms of which his or her behaviour is appraised, is socially defined.

However, while our languages of moral appraisal are drawn almost entirely from local situations and relationships, the notions of causal and moral responsibility are also applied to events and processes at great scale and over considerable stretches of time. Shame for past national deeds, for example, indicates an ability to identify closely with the complex and past and present actions of a collectivity with which one considers oneself constitutively affiliated. In South Africa much historical and political writing has been concerned with the matter of causal and moral responsibility for segregation and apartheid, although this has taken the form of an implicit series of questions rather than an open research agenda. As I explained in chapter 2, the materialist analysis of segregation dissipated some of the energy of this debate by ascribing responsibility to the systematic properties of the capitalist mode of production. If segregation was in some sense an inevitable response to the demands of capital, the ascription of blame becomes difficult (though, of course, not impossible).[52] Segregation, moreover, was a phenomenon that was not exclusive to South Africa, and comparative analysis of the southern states of America and South Africa served to diffuse moral opprobrium by contextualizing the experiences of Black South Africans.[53]

Within liberal English history and Afrikaner academic history a submerged debate continues about the relationship between the moral character of the British and the Afrikaners, and the difference these characters made to the South African state under segregation. Segregation, however, is rarely understood as simply, or even predominantly, an expression of Boer racism. Neither is it understood as simply a product of Imperial exploitation and cruelty.[54]

The focus of these debates has been on the period of high apartheid. Historical distance from the segregationist era has produced detachment from particular actors, and a clearer sense of how those actors were themselves creations of circumstance. As events move into the distance, they come to seem more fully determined: less the result of choices made by particular persons and more the result of the weight of causal forces in combination. Additionally, materialist analysis of segregation has been powerful, and it has become hard to ignore the logics of labour demand and control in post-mineral revolution South Africa.

High apartheid, by contrast, seems less easily explained through materialist analysis. Quasi-Marxist explanations for the extension of labour control across the economy run against much evidence: manufacturing and services were predominantly and progressively disadvantaged by the skill shortages and market inadequacy that was a consequence of segregation. Many liberals trace high apartheid to the frontier prejudices of the Boer, but now in command of a powerful state. More nuanced studies have examined the impact of the inheritance of slavery, the internal structure of the state, the consequences of the political agency of African societies and the practices of the colonial powers in early twentieth-century Natal.[55]

Among these many diverse avenues of enquiry there has been little attempt to assess the role of democratic practice in this vibrantly democratic state. In the next two sections, I argue in two ways that democratic practices were direct causes of high apartheid. First, I argue directly for the malevolent consequences of elections in delivering to Afrikaner Nationalists the control of the state. Second, I argue that complex conceptual and imaginative relations in the ideology of liberal democracy had a direct causative role in the creation of high apartheid. Relationships between Whites' notions of agency, self-government and territory were expressed in the programme of separate development. In my conclusion, I consider the implications of the South African case for our understanding of liberal democracy, arguing that this instance of economic dependence and political independence was not so unusual as it has seemed.

Elections and the Causes of High Apartheid

The causes of high apartheid must be sought in the differences between conditions in 1948 and those a decade later. Posel has shown that the apparatus of high apartheid – the homelands, industrial decentralization, population removals – were not part of a continuous and cumulative process that began in the 1950s. Rather they represented a new phase of apartheid, an attempt to remedy past failures.[56] In the early 1950s, the Native Affairs Department (NAD) had accepted that economic integration was unavoidable; policies that did not recognize this fact were regarded as impractical (even as the electoral arithmetic forced NP leaders to do something rapid and conspicuous to reduce White fears of Africans in urban areas). Yet, by 1960, the now renamed Bantu Affairs Department (BAD) had reversed this position – and in far less propitious circumstances in which dependence on African labour was far deeper and African urbanization yet more entrenched.

Posel offers four suggestions for this change of direction, each of which is persuasive in its own right as a cause of high apartheid. First, resistance in the form of anti-pass campaigns and industrial disputes, and then in an escalation of violence after Sharpeville, rekindled Afrikaner concerns about the viability of controlled urbanization. As Lazar suggests, this resistance seemed a part of the continental, or even global, trend towards nationalist anti-colonialism and demanded institutional responses.[57] Second, realignments within BAD, and in particular the growing strength of the Broederbond within it, allowed the marginalization of the reformist lobby. The South African Agricultural Union (SAAU), a strong opponent of rigorous apartheid, was infiltrated and then controlled by the Bond. Thirdly, the government found what it believed to be a way of circumventing local authority opposition to influx control. A newly centralized apparatus offered the prospect of dispensing with local mechanisms altogether.

Fourth, and decisively, the NP formally secured an electoral ascendancy that freed its leaders from fear of defeat. The electoral system continued to be a first-past-the-post one, with a continued advantage built in for the party's rural power base. But it was only in 1958 that the NP won a majority of the vote. 'State power in South Africa', as Beinart emphasizes, 'came to be dominated by a group of Whites who used the term nation narrowly to mean an ethnically defined segment of about 12 per cent of the population.'[58] Within the political party elected by those 12 per cent, the ascendancy was gained by a powerful grouping with a clear ideological programme which ran counter to the interests and expressed wishes of the country's industrial and commercial elites. The role of democracy went beyond the illegitimate imposition of minority rule, however. The influence of the ideas associated with liberal democracy proved to have a decisive role in shaping high apartheid.

Conceptual Relations in the Causation of High Apartheid

Liberal commentators have explained the development of high apartheid in a way that protects the democratic idea from criticism. They have seen the project of separate development – in which each and every inhabitant of South Africa was reassigned a homeland on the basis of an ascribed ethnic identity – as an imposition of a racist ideology over which the fig leaf of self-government was belatedly placed. However, it seems just as plausible to view the Bantustans of the 1960s and 1970s as an expression of democratic principles and as a natural outcome of the unfolding of the ideology of liberal democracy within South Africa's Afrikaner elite.

Legassick has shown how nineteenth-century liberal ideas lent themselves naturally to the support of segregation, quoting Mill's considerations on conquest:

> If the smaller nationality is supposed to be the more advanced in improvement, is able to overcome the greater... there is often a gain to civilization; but the conquerors and the conquered cannot in this case live together under the same free institutions. The absorption of the conquerors in the less advanced people would be an evil; these must be governed as subjects, and the state of things is either a benefit or a misfortune according as the subjugated people have or have not reached the state in which it is an injury not to be under a free government, and according as the conquerors do or do not use their superiority in a manner calculated to fit in a conquered for a higher state of improvement.[59]

Legassick also quotes James Bryce as follows: 'To toss the gift of political power into the lap of a multitude of persons who are not only ignorant, but in mind children rather than men, is not to confer a boon, but to inflict an injury.'[60]

As Plumb has pointed out, after the loss of American possessions, the idea of colonies and their inhabitants as children gave a sense of purpose to Britain's strategic manipulations, so rendering them fit for the consumption of a moralistic public. The analogy 'gave a sense of moral wisdom, and moral purpose, to economic and strategic conditions, which in their nakedness would have been incompatible for a nation, which, on increasing drafts of religion and reform, was to become intoxicated with the idea of its own moral superiority.'[61]

This was not merely the expression of a sensitive utilitarian sentiment, a civilized impulse or a smug and moralistic sense of superiority. It also followed from the need inherent in the liberal democratic system of ideas to define the citizen. If government by the people is to be coherent, the people must be identified: those ineligible to participate as citizens must be defined out of consideration.

Hierarchy, the champions of liberal democracy assert, is ultimately incompatible with the democratic idea. A system of government within which citizens are classified according to race and ethnicity could never survive the unfolding of the democratic idea. Even where such inconsistency has become politicized, however, there are many ways in which hierarchy and subjugation can be rendered compatible with democracy. Democratic ideology did not lead to the incorporation of the whole population within a single political community in South

Africa. Rather, the democratic resolution to the problem of racial hierarchy in South Africa was separate development.

Representative democracy relies for its coherence on a correspondence between a collectivity, a territory and a mode of agency. Collectivity is represented by the idea of a nation or a people with shared understandings, identity or traditions and a common moral life.[62] Territory and agency are each represented in the modern state: a clearly demarcated territorial entity and a field of agency for the modern state. This state, conceived as a unitary actor able to express the will of the citizens, acts upon and within the field of the territorial state and is counterposed to other states beyond its borders.[63]

The division between the 'inside' and the 'outside' of the modern political community is stark. Connolly summarizes Walzer's conception of the territorial boundary as follows:

> Inside the wall of walls, there is the rich, warm world of we, community, primary goods, membership, internal understandings, our morality, meanings, distributive mechanisms, mechanisms of state security, democratic accountability, obligations and obediences. On the other side, there are alternative worlds of strangers, danger, external principles, uncertain obligations of mutual aid and inconceivable moralities.[64]

The stability, security and economic prowess of a nation all depend, in Connolly's eyes, on its internal legitimacy; the nation is at home with itself only if it governs itself. It can only be an actor if it is 'legitimate', and such legitimacy derives from the attitudes of the people to their own collective coherence and way of life. Thus, the three elements of the modern state are mutually reinforcing. It must have a citizenry with a sense of shared membership, identity and mutual understanding to sustain its legitimacy, and it must be tied to a territory that is both a metaphorical 'home' to its people and that corresponds in extent to the state's power to extract resources.

How does this illuminate the debates leading to the creation of high apartheid? The Fagan Commission, set up by the UP government to investigate the control of natives, argued in 1946 that there was no incompatibility between partial segregation and the viability of the South African state. African urbanization, further urban industrialization and a permanent and growing presence of Africans in the cities were 'facts which have to be faced as such'.[65] Nonetheless, permanent urbanization was quite compatible with the permanent withholding of political rights for Africans: thoroughgoing political integration was not the only alternative available to 'total segregation'.

This reflected the views of South African business and White agriculture. Each saw their dependence on Black labour as inescapable; and the latter was opposed at that time to any increase in the size of the reserves, a necessary measure for supporters of total segregation.[66] The drive to high apartheid, therefore, did not come from the pragmatics of economic management; nor did it follow from a fear of racial mixing. Rather, it was driven by the logics of self-government in the modern state.

The South African Bureau of Racial Affairs (SABRA) was from 1947 the central intellectual organization of the Afrikaner Broederbond. It was within SABRA that the concept of total segregation was elaborated and the half-measures of controlled integration were declared untenable. SABRA argued for a complete – if phased and gradual – withdrawal of African labour from White business. With the support of Afrikaner intellectuals, teachers, lawyers, workers, the church and some business circles,[67] the Broederbond and its SABRA vehicle advanced an unremitting campaign for complete segregation. At the heart of the Bond's argument was a demand for 'self-determination' of Whites; this was the key initial assumption of SABRA thought.[68] This notion of *self*-determination contains within it the key interrelated demands of democratic rule, rule by the people: a definition of the people; a territory within which they are to rule; and a mechanism through which their collective will can be expressed. Self-determination is necessarily an exclusive notion (no matter how insistently it is promoted by democrats as an inclusive one). Non-participants must be excluded: and this may be done either territorially or through a controlled franchise which defines criteria for membership of the political community.

The mystificatory separation of the political from the economic within liberal democratic ideology helped resolve Afrikaner leaders' problems. Exclusion from citizenship, or its displacement to homelands, was quite compatible with participation in the economy of South Africa.

The idea of culture also helped transcend the divide between repression and assimilation. The notion of distinctive 'native mentalities' provided a 'relativistic' vehicle for segregationism. Unlike the scientific racism of inferior and superior cultures, or the notion of 'civilizing the natives', each of which embodied a hierarchy of domination open to challenge, the idea of separate cultures provided an unmatched opportunity to weld the ideology of self-government with that of science. General Smuts in his 1929 Oxford lectures could famously announce a new policy 'to foster an indigenous native culture or system of cultures and to cease to force the African into alien European moulds'.[69] The Native Economic Commission of 1932 confidently used the existence of 'tribe', each possessed of a mentality, propensity to violence and 'cattle complex', as a justification for an increase in the size of reserves as areas to contain them.[70]

The relations between collectivity, territory and mode of action in democratic ideology helped support the Afrikaner separatist project. Many Afrikaner intellectuals and religious authorities considered racial nationalist groups were the primary categories of social division: Afrikaner self-realization was their goal. The seizure of the state should help Afrikaners to subordinate capitalism to their needs and to suppress class division where it threatened their identity. Separate development permitted formal equality between peoples to go hand in hand with a conscious project of exploitation.

One great inspiration for high apartheid was the process of decolonization that was sweeping the African continent. Apartheid could be understood by its architects as a process of 'internal decolonization', an idea especially resonant following the independence of Botswana, Lesotho and Swaziland – three states which Afrikaner ideologues had hoped to incorporate into the Union. While the Promotion of Bantu Self-Government Act of 1959 contained pseudo-Africanist extensions of traditional authority and customary law, self-government has not been so different to the self-determination beloved by democrats. External domination was to be replaced with rule by the people of a territory. Moreover, this was not to be an imposed 'European' conception of democratic government, but an African mode of self-government.

The 1955 Tomlinson Commission's claims that funding was required to make the reserves into viable mini-states – claims vehemently rejected by Hendrik Verwoerd – were irrelevant to this process. Perhaps these states were to be economically interdependent with South Africa; perhaps they were dependent upon South Africa to an extraordinary degree. But no less was true of Swaziland or Lesotho; and what state in the modern international economy – beyond the great national economies of Japan and the US – could claim to achieve more than the 'political independence with economic interdependence or simple dependence' – the formula which best describes the homelands' predicament.

We have hitherto paid little attention to the role of electoral opposition to the programme of high apartheid and to the use of constitutional methods of protest to oppose it. Critics might point to Prime Minister Strydom's statement to the House of Assembly in 1956:

> We as a government can only announce a policy and try to apply what is practicable and what will therefore be accepted by the country and by the majority of the electorate as they come to understand the implications of it and are then prepared to lend support to it. For that reason, as we have repeatedly stated very clearly in the past, we cannot in present circumstances propagate or apply a policy of total territorial apartheid.[71]

On this view, the ideologues of the Broederbond were propagating a total apartheid that was impractical, economically irrational and abhorrent to the electorate. The electoral method was a bar to the imposition of this sectional policy.

To the degree that potential electoral resistance was important in 1956, however, it was no longer so by 1958! This highlights rather than diminishes the truth that elections placed in power and then entrenched a government that was propagating the policy of apartheid. The ease with which White South Africans accommodated themselves to this settlement, and the extent to which English-speaking Whites fell in behind the Afrikaner National Party as the policy was implemented, demonstrate further the ability of the language and symbols of democracy to facilitate systematic exploitation.

The machinery of self-government for the homelands was designed to ease domestic qualms and not merely to secure international acquiescence. In fact, no overseas state recognized the homelands. Within South Africa, however, the independence of these states was widely supported as a fiction. To observe that contempt was expressed by White South Africans about the collaborationist and bureaucratic elites of the homelands is to miss the point; just such contempt was expressed by them about the governments and ruling elites of internationally recognized southern African states. Here again, White South Africa was not widely at variance with international liberal democratic opinion in the OECD zone. African states were now self-governing, and were therefore responsible for their own inability to secure reasonable living conditions for their citizens.

Other critics might object that racism or tribalism, rather than self-rule, was the fundamental intellectual support for separate development. This, however, is to overlook the central role that ethnicity and nationality play in the otherwise arbitrary definition of identity in liberal-democratic theories of self-government. Belief in permanent tribalism in Africa reflected the efforts of Afrikaner anthropologists, but also mirrored Afrikaners' ethnic self-conception. Afrikaner and English alike continued to conceive the Boer republics, the Cape and Natal as distinct in character; and the reserves froze into place another reminder of pre-Union South Africa. Given the violence of unification, Afrikaners were surely simply less mystified than most Western citizens, recognizing the arbitrariness of state creation and how it results from the imposition of external state power.

Total apartheid was the ideal that made practical segregation legitimate. Without the belief that self-government for all lay at the end of the road, apartheid's evident oppressiveness would have been unjustifiable. The legitimacy conferred by the ideal of self-government – a restored harmony between ethnicity, agency and territory – rendered acceptable to Whites an evident denial of political rights. For the collaborationist classes, their role as leaders of their people likewise made legitimate their oppression of their own quasi-citizens. The exercise of unlegitimated power is problematic for any ruling class. If subjects do not believe that they have some voice or stake in the social order, they can prove costly passive or active obstacles to the achievement of leaders' interests. Representative democracy, whatever benefits it may bring in particular historical settings, can at times justify oppression and exploitation to its perpetrators and encourage passive acquiescence among its observers and even among its victims.

RAMIFICATIONS: NEGATIVE RESPONSIBILITY AND THE DYNAMIC OF DEMOCRACY

In this chapter we have debunked the widespread myth that democracy ended apartheid. The global spread of democratic ideas and practices did not cause the collapse of the apartheid state. Apartheid's end has been most persuasively explained by structural economic changes in combination with a range of international factors. Academic opinion has reproduced the myth of a benevolent wave of democratization.

We then examined the role of democracy in twentieth-century South Africa and identified two distinct ways of approaching democracy. To see democracy as an outcome of struggle is to view it as a recognition by rulers that citizens must be accorded political and civil rights if they are to consent to be ruled. It also reflects the degree to which the franchise has been extended and political participation encouraged. To view democracy as cause, by contrast, directs our gaze to the consequences (intended and otherwise) of democratic practice. Despite some analyses of the benevolent and malign affects of democratic practice, and the institutional design that can encourage the former rather than the latter, academic analysts have too often used the evasion that a society is not 'democratic enough' to be a real democracy to explain its malign properties. Western political thought contains powerful criticisms of democracy as a method of rule, which Dunn has summarized as follows:

> The vividly competitive character of democratic political choice favours and reinforces greed and spite at the expense of self-restraint and mutual understanding [;] within democratic decision-making, rhetoric, or prior economic or political resources, exert markedly greater causal force than justice and the truth about the matter in hand [;] circumstances of democratic collaboration generate confusion (if not mutual deception) at the expense of clarity [; and] the life of a democratic politician involves an inherently degrading subjection of personal judgement to hopes and fears about the prospective popularity of being seen to choose in one way rather than another.[72]

Taking a detached perspective on South African society from 1910, I have argued that South Africa was a democracy, albeit a democracy with a limited franchise. Exploring the consequences of its political practices, I first showed that representative democracy was quite in harmony with the elaboration of segregation and early apartheid. I went on to advance the thesis that democracy caused apartheid. 'Democracy' here referred to the use of competitive elections for the selection of legislature and chief executive; 'causation' was identified as ascribed human responsibility for social outcomes; and the apartheid that is of most interest is the high apartheid from 1960 – the phase of apartheid otherwise least explicable and certainly most cruel.

Democracy caused high apartheid first by electoral means. It pushed governments to favour White workers' interests over those of Africans. Competitive elections later handed the infrastructural powers of the state to a small and determined minority with an ideological project. Second, the need to create the preconditions for Afrikaner self-government, or democratic rule, could only be met by separate development. Afrikaner elites, put in place by democratic elections, chose to create the preconditions for self-government. In order to do so, they had to make use of liberal democracy's mystificatory separation of politics from economics to perpetuate economic integration while denying political integration.

The democratic notion of self-government was a prop to the National Party, and helped to secure its project electorally in the face of powerful industrial and commercial opposition. Liberal democratic ideology related ideas of territory, membership of community and agency; these ideas could be expressed in South Africa in the 1960s only by creating new territorial units and institutional forms with matching 'ethnic' affiliations.

South Africa offers a window onto the experiences of all liberal democratic states. In particular, one troubling feature of Afrikaner defences of apartheid – and of the difficulty liberal critics have in undermining them – becomes clearer. Afrikaners were using the languages of liberal democracy quite conventionally in their defence of the evils of high apartheid. The notion of self-determination has been the common sense of liberal internationalism. As Frederick Cooper remarks, 'global acceptance of self-determination as the ultimate value in international politics has often occluded discussion of the content of that sovereignty'.[73] In South Africa, as elsewhere, the 'objective' basis for the division of peoples into distinct 'nations' was easily constructed with the materials of academic anthropology and linguistics, and from the easily woven narratives of 'national history'. Intellectual and political leaders could always be found to attest to the reality of an identity and to the collective moral life it represented. The cant of collective identity was not a South African invention; nor was the bizarre fusion of such identities with territories and states.

Afrikaners, likewise, could not easily be condemned for creating dependent territories, or for giving political independence without the economic self-sufficiency or state capacity to make this independence meaningful. Post colonial states are everywhere bereft of the capacities that might render sovereignty meaningful.[74] There are few states in the world, moreover, that can claim economic self-sufficiency, and none in sub-Saharan Africa comes close to the credible claim of control over its own destiny.

Democracy does not just create domestic responsibilities, it discharges external ones. The Republic of South Africa could impose homeland citizenship on all Black South Africans in 1971 only because the international ideology of liberal democracy rested on precisely such an externally defined exclusion. Self-determination brings with it responsibility for self. For states which simply lacked the means of creating for their citizens a tolerable standard of living, or for sustaining life at all, the declaration of self-determination is mostly a declaration of the other's non-responsibility. Others are no longer responsible for the travails of a self-governing state's citizens: this is now their own affair.

5 Analysing Democratic Transitions

This chapter has three key purposes. First, I explore the strengths and weaknesses of the academic literature on democratization and examine the three major schools of thought represented within it. Second, I show how the history of democratization has shaped the literature which analyses it. Third, I demonstrate the systematic weaknesses of this analysis for understanding political change in southern and South Africa. My focus is on the role of external actors in sub-Saharan Africa and analysts' failure to take seriously the experiences of African states. Africans have not merely suffered the imposition of external forces; they have had their history ignored by professional analysts of political transition.

THREE APPROACHES TO DEMOCRATIZATION

The idea of democracy is unusual in articulating the academic sub-disciplines of political theory and comparative politics. It is equally special in representing a shared preoccupation of practical politicians, citizens and professional analysts. Political theorists have reflected on the moral and political character of democratic systems of government, while citizens have found the idea of democratic rule both attractive and powerful. Comparative political scientists have tried to explain the successes of democratic practice in the modern world. They have had their minds concentrated by the spread of democratic institutions to many parts of the globe in the past 20 years. In 1975, almost 70 per cent of the countries of the world could be confidently classified as authoritarian; by the end of 1995, only about a quarter could be so classified, the rest all having held some form of competitive election and instituted formal civil and political rights.[1]

Huntingdon has famously described this as the 'third wave' of democratization.[2] The first wave, according to Huntingdon, occurred between 1828 and 1926, and included the United States, Britain, France, overseas British dominions and a number of European states. A 'reverse wave', from 1922 and 1942, saw states such as Italy, German, and Argentina reverting to authoritarian rule. The shorter second wave commenced during the Second World War and had ended by the early 1960s. In this wave, West Germany, Italy, Japan, India and Israel among others became democracies. Decolonization at the same time created a mini-wave of new democracies in former colonial states. Huntingdon identifies a short reverse wave, from 1958 to 1975, in which several states (predominantly African and South American) reverted to non-democratic rule. Between 1974 and today comes Huntingdon's 'third wave', the most impressive of all, bringing a remarkable number and range of democratizations in three regions. In Latin America, only one in ten states remained authoritarian by 1995 (from seven in ten in 1975). In Eastern Europe, where all states were 'authoritarian' in 1975, four out of five were engaging in democratization by 1995. Lastly, in sub-Saharan Africa, two out of every three states were partial or full democracies by 1995, whereas authoritarianism was dominant or even overwhelming in 1975.[3]

Political science has a range of approaches to the definition and analysis of democratization. These can be reduced to three categories, albeit at the cost of doing some violence to recent attempts to synthesize them. All three broad theoretical approaches pre-date the 'third wave'. The first two have a tendency to determinism, and can be categorized as 'modernization' and 'structural' approaches. The third, which has derived increasing authority from changes since 1989, is an 'agency' approach. In the following brief overview, I illustrate the attractiveness of these approaches prior to assessing their respective usefulness for understanding change in South and southern Africa.

Modernization Perspectives

Diamond sums up the modernization approach as follows: 'The more well to do the people of a country, on average, the more likely they will favour, achieve, and maintain a democratic system for their country.'[4] Modernization approaches to democratization are directly grounded in quantitative evidence, and are intuitively persuasive on first viewing. They also provide gloomy reading for analysts of democracy in southern Africa. That the achievement and maintenance of a democratic system is in some way related to levels of per capita income or levels of 'development' is the core thesis in the modernization approach to explaining democratization.

The notion that democracy is related to economic development was first advanced by Seymour Martin Lipset in 1959, but the nature of the relationship is still much contested.[5]

Crude modernization theorists advance a direct and causal relationship between 'modernization' – the social, political and economic processes associated with 'development' – and democratization. Causal chains of industrialization, urbanization, education, communication, mobilization and political incorporation culminate in a society ripe for democracy.[6] An authoritarian state, subject to social processes of modernization, experiences the differentiation and specialization of social, economic and political subsystems. Social structure becomes complex, with professional groups emerging and new ranges of skilled employees. Labour organization becomes increasingly important in an economy increasingly interdependent and so more easily disrupted by sectoral- or firm-based industrial disputes. Technological change requires the dispersal of knowledge, and communications become necessarily less susceptible to centralization.

Lipset argues that education, and higher education in particular, makes democracy not only viable (as citizens become capable of reasoned electoral choices) but also necessary, as the educated, with their longer political horizons and greater strategic grasp, make determined efforts to promulgate opposition and seize political power. The vast range of institutions labelled 'civil society' expands in scope. Wealth grows with development of the economy. These causal sequences comprise a process of development which culminates in democratization.

The strength of the quantitative relationship between measures of economic development and measures of democracy has made this thesis sometimes seem unassailable. As Przeworski and Limongi have recently demonstrated, however, two quite distinct reasons can be advanced to account for the clear relationship between per capita income and the incidence of democratic regimes. The first 'endogenous' explanation is the one with which we are now familiar. Democracy is more likely to emerge as a country develops economically. Przeworski and Limongi distinguish this endogenous thesis from a second exogenous one which supposes that democracies 'may be established independently of economic development but may be more likely to survive in developed countries'.[7] Przeworski and Limongi show that the evidence best fits this exogenous account. 'History gradually accumulates wealthy democracies, since every time a dictatorship happens to die in an affluent country, democracy is there to stay.'[8] Democracy, on this account, survives if a country is 'modern', but it is not necessarily a 'product of modernization'.[9]

These authors demonstrate that transitions do not occur when authoritarian regimes reach higher levels of development.[10] The likelihood of transition rises up to about $6000 per capita income, but above that level dictatorships stabilize as the countries become more affluent. As predicted by Huntingdon,[11] the evidence illustrates a 'bell-shaped pattern of instability',[12] showing that 'the causal power of economic development in bringing dictatorships down appears paltry'.[13]

The survival of democracy, however, increases 'monotonically' with per capita income. It is difficult to see why this should be so. In rich countries, Przeworski and Limongi speculate, the gain from winning all rather than part of national income may be less significant for a dictator, and the damage done to the economy harder to repair. In poorer countries, by contrast, destroyed capital stock is more easily rebuilt, and the rewards of holding all possible wealth are greater.[14]

Structural Perspectives

The second of our three broad perspectives on democratization can be traced back to the work of Barrington Moore.[15] Moore's account is historical: he asks why, in the transformation of seventeenth-century agrarian societies into modern industrial states, some states became liberal democracies, while others became fascist or communist. Moore traces three 'routes to the modern world': the path of 'bourgeois revolution' – the combination of capitalism with parliamentary democracy after a series of revolutions (England, France, United States); the path of conservative revolutions from above, culminating in fascism (Germany and Japan); and the communist past, with its origins among the revolutions of the peasants (Russia and China).[16]

Moore argues that the paths taken by these three types of state depended on the precise historical circumstances they faced – that 'the historical preconditions of each major political species differ sharply from the others'.[17] A unique constellation of historical factors in particular early Catholic societies led to the emergence of liberal democracy. Moore's thesis has supported the view that democratic transitions in the West, dependent on a specific set of historical circumstances, cannot be replicated. For his particular historical cases, Moore identifies the 'main conditions that have apparently been most important for the development of democracy', and these include the following features: the absence of too powerful a Crown or too independent a landed aristocracy; a turn towards appropriate forms of commercial agriculture; the prevention of an aristocrat–bourgeoisie coalition against peasants and workers; and a revolutionary break with the past.[18]

Moore's stress on the importance of class structure in the development of political systems has influenced recent structural approaches. Rueschemeyer, Stephens and Stephens'[19] attempt to develop an answer to the question posed by Lipset ('How can the relationship between levels of economic development and democracy be explained?'), while rejecting functionalist assumptions of modernization theory, draws on the historical-structural approach pioneered by Moore. They concentrate, however, on a period of decades rather than centuries; on the urban working class rather than the bourgeoisie; and they add trans-national power relations to Moore's predominantly domestic analysis. Democracy is an aspect of struggles for political equality, and three relations are key to the playing out of such struggles: class balances and coalitions; the nature of the state apparatus; and the trans-national power relations in play at any time.

These authors agree with Moore that large landlords are the most entrenched opponents of democratization (threatened as they are by a loss of labour). Where large landlords have been especially powerful, democratic prospects have indeed been weak. They also consider, however, that the bourgeoisie is an unlikely champion (or even supporter) of democratization. Owners, traders and commercial bankers have often opposed the destruction of liberal democratic movements, but their role has varied with the alignment of other classes, the power of the state and trans-national actors. But it is the urban working class, in whose interest democracy most obviously works, who represent its key proponents. While the bourgeoisie have supported representative constitutional government, but have opposed lower-class inclusion, the middle classes have held an ambiguous role, desiring their own inclusion in government structures but viewing the working class uneasily as an unwelcome but necessary ally.

If the nature of class relations and coalitions is pivotal, almost as important, on their account, is the role of 'civil society' as a counterweight to state power. Rueschemeyer et al. also pay great attention to the nature of state power. A state recognized as 'universal' – separated from particular class interests – has been, they claim, a prerequisite for democracy. An autonomous state organized in the interests of a military or security apparatus cannot provide for democratization. Rueschemeyer et al. also argue for the potential importance of trans-national power, in particular as it influences class interests and the position of the state.

Structural approaches of these kinds are united by their insistence that 'a country's historical trajectory towards liberal democracy or some other political form is finally shaped by changing structures of class, state and trans-national power driven by a particular history of capitalist development'.[20]

The Agency Perspective

The modernization and historical sociological approaches are dominated by metaphors of structure and system. Democratization is produced by inexorable forces – be these the causal chains comprising development of a modern society (with the urbanization, education and industrialization that go along with this) or the historical pathways down which states are propelled by a range of class, structural, state and trans-national forces. Such perspectives leave little room for human agency, a feature that became problematic from the mid-1970s as democratization appeared on political agendas across the world. 'The protagonists in the struggles for democracy could not and did not believe that the fate of their countries would be determined either by current levels of development or by the distant past. They maintained that, albeit within constraints, democratization was an outcome of actions, not just of conditions'.[21]

Analysis of actors and their strategies in the explanation of democratization can be traced to the work of Rustow who famously rejected the 'functional curiosity' of Lipset and focused on 'how a democracy comes into being in the first place'.[22] Rustow's approach is based on a linear model of the origins of democracy: national unification and prolonged political struggle are followed by a 'historical moment' at which compromise is reached; habituation ensues, in which bargains become embedded. Rustow's emphasis on the centrality of social conflict and elite initiative has marked much of the recent literature on transitions.[23] The transition approach highlights the role of political elites, treating social and economic structures as at most a context of decision, or as a structure of opportunities and constraints. Opportunities are created by processes of liberalization that allow regime and opposition to enter into conflict and argument. Such liberalization itself results from economic failure or military disaster, or from the so-called paradox of success, by which elites wish to gain the benefits of domestic and international legitimacy, and view themselves as strong enough to secure victory under democratic conditions.

Transition analysts characteristically distinguish 'transition' to democracy from consolidation and tend to use procedural definitions of democracy. The struggle for democracy is always subject to reversal:

at any point elite negotiation can collapse or external shocks undermine negotiated settlement. Political leadership, moreover, and the skills of interim rulers, can cement or undermine democratic practices. The path towards consolidation (usually defined in terms of the second or reverse transfer of control) is always a hazardous one and requires the skills of human actors committed to democracy. Mass publics also play a role. Popular support, while not usually openly pro-democratic, contains pro-democratic segments, and usually a majority that views a new democratic regime as preferable to the old authoritarian one.

HISTORY AND ANALYSIS

In the next sections, I explain why these approaches to democratization must themselves be understood historically, as creations of particular institutions in specific historical circumstances. I then go on, by means of banal chronology and identification of bias, to show why democratization analysis is inappropriate to understanding (and guiding) political change in southern Africa.

Chronology and Model Development

The analysis of democratization has been dominated by professional political scientists employing the 'comparative method'. Comparison is inevitably problematic, especially in the case of democratization. The search for generalization across cases is always in tension with respect for the particular: given the very small number of cases, and the inordinate complexity of the processes of democratization (where entire social and political systems and their international relations are being transformed) comparative approaches to democratization are necessarily difficult to accomplish.

For our purposes, two weaknesses of comparative political analysis are particularly important. First, as we shall see, analysis of democratization affects the behaviour of political actors. It modifies the expectations and strategies of opposition leaders, affects the perceptions (and actions) of economic agents and influences international actors in their encouragement or imposition of courses of action upon weak developing country elites. In sub-Saharan Africa, the intervention of international actors, and therefore the importance of professional intellectual constructions in analysing political change, has been especially important.

Second, the comparative method has been backward-looking, drawing on evidence from existing cases of democratizing or democratic states. The body of evidence against which theses about democratization can be tested is constantly modified in an era of rapid political change. The institutional and intellectual processes through which contemporary events feed back into theory-building can therefore be decisive in determining the power of political science analysis. I shall argue that small and weak states are generally the victims of prescription; whereas more powerful states' experiences generate rethinking of democratization analysis itself. Third wave transitions led to retrospective adjustment of academic analysis and to the prevalence of transition approaches at the expense of structural and modernization accounts. Events in southern Europe, Latin America and Eastern Europe have each, by turns, forced major rethinking of conventional wisdom. African democratization, by contrast, belated and externally engineered, has been treated as a marginal case or an anomaly.

Modernization and structural approaches seemed tremendously powerful in the late 1960s. The trend in the South, as each would predict, seemed to be towards the entrenchment of authoritarian rule. In much of sub-Saharan Africa and the Middle East, one-party states had been instituted in place of rapidly collapsing postcolonial structures. In South-East Asia, quasi-communist national liberation movements seemed unlikely to move towards liberal democratic government. In Latin America, military dictatorships appeared entrenched as a regime type.[24]

The southern European transitions from 1974-6, in Greece, Portugal and Spain – shattered rigid structural and modernization accounts. Deterministic renderings of processes of social and political change, in particular, came to seem singularly inappropriate. Military conflict, the death of important leaders and colonial war triggered democratization, and all three countries were led towards democracy by a new generation of modernizing politicians, anxious to integrate their states into a wider pan-European project of unity and disenchanted with the anticommunism of the Cold War period.[25]

Even more damaging for deterministic accounts was the influence that the southern European transitions exerted over Spanish and Portuguese spheres of political influence in Latin America. Whitehead suggests that just as the Spanish civil war had helped to polarize Latin American ideologies between Marxism and militant Catholicism, so democratic systems caused Latin American elites to reconsider hitherto strongly felt antagonisms.[26] International factors played a further crucial role in Latin America. The Carter administration's 'human rights' agenda, a regular theme in US foreign policy thereafter, and a reduction of Cold War communist hysteria, contributed to reduced US support for authoritarian regimes (although not in sub-Saharan Africa at this stage).

Despite commonalities in external conditions, the democratic transitions of the 1980s 'took multiple routes and passed through a series of stages'.[27] Liberalizers within ruling elites were often responsible for initial changes, buttressing their own positions and attempting to defuse opposition by means of limited liberalization. Liberalization, however, tended to develop a momentum of its own, as a series of 'improvisations under pressure' led the authoritarian coalition and temperate opposition towards negotiation. Eventually an agreement, or 'pact', would permit open contestation for public office with no preordained victor. 'If the voters, rather than the incumbents, controlled the final outcome of this contestation, then the transition could be called democratic.'[28] Przeworski has emphasized that one must see democratization as 'a process of... institutionalizing uncertainty'.[29] In a democracy, 'outcomes of the political process are to some extent indeterminate with regard to the positions which participants occupy in all social relations, including the relations of production and the political institutions.'[30]

The transitions of southern Europe and then Latin America led to a recasting of the conventional analytical frameworks for understanding democratization, and in turn generated something like a new consensus as to how these should be best understood. This new common sense – embodied in the O'Donnell–Schmitter–Whitehead volumes – saw a set of actors engaged in strategic interplay rather than as a set of external determinations.

The structural approach pioneered by Moore was undermined by changes in the nature of democratization and its rapid proliferation. Moore's account of the emergence of political forms in the modern world can be conceived as an actor-centred approach: the agrarian class structure of the nineteenth century, and the consequent behaviour of class actors, explained regime types in the twentieth century. Moore's argument that liberal democracy in the US, Britain and France was produced by particular historical constellations within early capitalism remains powerful. However, the rapidity with which democratization followed democratization from the mid 1970s onwards, and the degree to which deliberate intention shaped events, demonstrated that Moore's analysis was not appropriate to all contemporary cases. Structuralist accounts were modified by Rueschemeyer et al. to incorporate the relationships between state and civil society, and to incorporate the trans-national factors lacking from Moore's analysis.

Modernization accounts underwent a more gradual change of emphasis in response to these events. In their sophisticated form, of course, they were never deterministic. Lipset stresses that he is examining the social 'requisites', and not prerequisites for democracy, and that he is doing so in a probabilistic manner: 'Socio-economic correlations are merely associational, and do not necessarily indicate causes.'[31] He argues that 'whether democracy succeeds or fails continues to depend significantly on the choices, behaviours and decisions of political leaders and groups.'[32] Lipset's classic account of the modernization approach reminds us, according to Leftwich, that 'he was not talking so much about the causes or conditions of democratisation as the *conditions for its survival*'.[33] Modernization theorists correspondingly found room to accept historical contingency and international economic and political factors as influences on the pace and nature of democratization. These factors could affect its timing, advancing or delaying a transition for which the requisites may be in place.[34] Modernization theory came through democratic transitions up to the late 1980s virtually unchallenged.

The democratic reforms initiated in the late 1980s in Central and Eastern Europe, by contrast, were an earthquake. They suddenly challenged the framework of analysis propounded by democratization theorists of different schools over the previous 20 years. The superficial resemblance between certain Central European transitions and some earlier southern European ones – the space for negotiation created by liberalization, the existence of elite pacts familiar to southern American specialists and the role of the member states of the European Union in promoting and encouraging each – initially allowed analysts to incorporate experiences of Poland and Hungary into existing theories. There was no escape, however, from the fundamentally different nature of the democratization process in Eastern and Central Europe. Whitehead notes that these transitions 'occurred very rapidly and were bunched together within a few months. The "contagion" affect was much more powerful and direct than elsewhere.'[35] More significantly, perhaps, the decisive decisions in the case of Central and Eastern Europe were taken in Moscow. It does not seem unjust to the domestic actors involved to say that theirs was an influencing role and not a deciding one. The initiative to dismantle the Soviet Union (whatever the intended limitations on its consequences) was scarcely a result of the efforts of the democratic opposition in the states that were to benefit from it. The key initial factor in the end of communist rule was the reduced ambition of the Soviet leadership in the light of extended military weakness and economic stagnation.

In sum, political change in the former Soviet bloc presented a new scale of challenges to analysts of democracy. If analysis was to illuminate democratization as a phenomenon, it had to account for all cases. Analysts of democratization reworked their explanatory tools in the light of Eastern and Central European experiences.

Modernization approaches initially seemed vindicated by events. After all, the socially and economically developed countries in Eastern Europe were the first to democratize.[36] However, there was little within modernization approaches to explain why this might hold true in these countries. 'As in the earlier literature, current accounts leave the translation of economic forces into democratic and political institutions largely unexplained. The correlation is a persuasive one on an intuitive and broad empirical basis but it remains imprecise in its more specific implications.'[37]

Structural accounts hoped to fill this lacuna. In particular, the rise of Solidarity was identified as indicative of the importance of class structure. Socialist industrialization, on this view, changed the balance of class forces and the nature of potential class coalitions. 'By 1980', Lewis points out, 'the Communist system in eastern Europe had produced a large working class which no longer had the opportunities for social mobility and occupational advancement available to the first generation of socialist workers.'[38]

Transition approaches, however, inevitably predominated in explanations of democratization in Eastern Europe. The effects of divisions within political elites were particularly carefully traced. Behind the accounts of leadership choice and elite strategy, however, lay the failure of the Soviet imperial project, an external factor that has such weight that transition approaches, with their domestic focus, have been unable satisfactorily to incorporate.

The major approaches to democratization are creatures of the processes they are supposed to explain. Their resilience in the face of changing events required mutual accommodation between schools. As Leftwich has argued, 'it is both easy and tempting – but wrong – to exaggerate the differences or to overestimate the confidence or claims' of approaches to democratization.[39] In evidence, Leftwich cites

Lipset's disavowal of determinism, and Rueschemeyer et al.'s respect for modernization approaches. While their focus is on 'the economic power base of elites, and the strength of civil society, the balance of class power and the political articulation of civil society', they nonetheless admit that these factors 'were originally shaped by the structure of the economy and the state'.[40] These structures are in some sense at least products of economic development and social change. Purveyors of transition accounts, likewise, often observe that their focus on elite politics rests on assumptions about wider economic development and the nature of social structure (which they reinterpret as the constituencies of political leaders).

Potter notes that

> scholars working with these different theoretical approaches have found that the empirical evidence related to democratisation in any country is so complex and multi-faceted that no one theoretical approach completely captures that complexity and explains it satisfactorily. Certain ideas and modes of analysis from one approach may work well on aspects of the story; other aspects may be captured more effectively by using another approach.[41]

This does, indeed, capture the new spirit of sociability between different schools of analysis.[42] It also points up weaknesses of such mutual tolerance. Assumptions about social change and human behaviour that are not consistent across approaches are used in an eclectic manner. We are offered elaborate related positions that remain ultimately inconsistent.

The limitations of 'democratic transitions' as objects of enquiry are confirmed by a second aspect of the accommodation between approaches: a turn to 'consolidation'. Przeworski and Limongi's remarkable article on modernization approaches magnificently demonstrates the need for this shift of focus, but also highlights disappointment with democratic transition accounts. By showing that history accumulates democracies in wealthier countries (rather than democracy being developed in a privileged way within them) the authors do indeed demonstrate that 'the emergence of democracy is not a by-product of economic development. Democracy is or is not established by political actors pursuing their goals, and it can be initiated at any level of development. Only once it is established do economic constraints play a role: the chances for the survival of democracy are greater when the country is richer.'[43] However, this renders the question of consolidation far more important an explanandum than transition, rather than the mere adjunct to it that it is often taken to be.

Leftwich likewise, after a discussion of the inconclusive nature of debates between approaches, considers that 'whatever the democratization route' a critical question follows: 'What conditions will sustain the new democracies? In short, we must shift the focus of attention from the *processes of democratization* to the *conditions for its consolidation*.'[44] This shift of focus carries disappointment: it robs attempts to explain transition of content. Only when democracy has been consolidated will we be able to reflect back on its significance. This displaces problematic aspects of democratization to the future, as Leftwich's summary of conditions likely to promote consolidation indicates:

> Democratic consolidation seems more likely... (a) when the polity has geographical, constitutional and political legitimacy; (b) when there is agreement about the rules of the political game and the parties abide by them; (c) where opposing groups agree on policy restraint; (d) where there are low or declining levels of poverty; (e) and where ethnic, cultural and religious cleavages are not deep and uncompromising.[45] This amounts to a definition of democracy together with theses about poverty and some potentially circular statements about gross cleavages.[46]

PUTTING AFRICA IN ITS PLACE

Bracketing Africa Out

Democratization in sub-Saharan Africa has come at the very end of the 'third wave'. The analytical apparatus that emerged from efforts to match theory with evidence in a time of great historical change was created before the recent series of elections in Africa. That apparatus bears the mark of adjustment to the experiences of Southern Europe, Latin America, the Far East, and Eastern and Central Europe; but it arrived ready formed in sub-Saharan Africa, and has not been modified to take account of experiences there.

Some African scholars consider such a failing, results from entrapment within a conceptual framework of 'binary opposites'. Modernization theory, on this view, conceptualizes a society as either modern/industrial or as pre-modern/pre-industrial; Marxist theory views a society as either capitalist or as pre-capitalist; dependency theorists view society as exemplifying development or under-development. In each case, the 'lead term' – 'modern', 'capitalist', 'development' – is accorded all analytical value. The negative term is merely residual.[47] The failure of the state to follow the trajectory laid down in the model is treated as a deviation that is best understood in terms of what it is *not*, rather than being understood in itself. Such a theory tells us only what a deviating society is not; moreover, it forces us to accept a mythologized (Western) understanding of the positive term.[48]

This critique is misplaced because it allows no conditions to render comparative political analysis legitimate. Any model must begin somewhere, and no model can incorporate the lessons of cases to which it is not yet been brought. In general terms, democratization analysis is an activity of Western political science, shaped by Western audiences and preoccupations. But the notion of the West itself needs deconstruction, especially in the light of the category's lack of specificity of scope. African states' problem is less intellectual than political: power asymmetries allow outsiders to define African states as deviant, and so to prescribe remedial public policy for them, thereby undermining domestic political authority and bringing unintended social consequences.

This expression of power relations is not hindered by the analytic machinery political science has developed. The democratization literature circumvents the experiences of sub-Saharan Africa in part because it contains no genuine generalizations about 'democratization'. Modernization theorists have almost nothing to say about the processes bringing about democratic transitions. On consolidation they offer only the most general (and depressing) information for southern Africa's rulers. It is for this reason that modernization theorists have seen democratization in sub-Saharan Africa as a fly in the ointment: the poor states of the South should not have become democracies at all. Analysts predict that democracy will not be consolidated (thus restoring the correlation between development and democracy that these states temporarily threaten).

Structural and transition approaches are even less helpful for those trying to make sense of sub-Saharan Africa. Class formation has been weak (or, in South Africa, where quasi-proletarianization in a migrant labour system developed with the gold mines, of an exceptional kind). There is no large urban proletariat, no commercial or agricultural class and no effective middle class. This leaves structural analysts pessimistic. Weak 'state classes' have depended for survival on control over statist economic levers making democratic contestation an unattractive (zero-sum) game. Transition theorists have failed to adapt their models of elite compromise to African states. Factors elsewhere important in successful transition are absent in South Africa: steady economic growth, a pre-existing national community and religious and ethnic homogeneity.

Since approaches to democratization have failed to engage with sub-Saharan African experience, they can provide little guide to events. Rather than revising their models in the light of events, comparativists have responded in three ways: they have supported a marginalization of African experience as exceptional; they have re-engineered facts to fit pre-existing models; and they have turned models into blatantly prescriptive constructions, to be used to make African states more like those which have successfully democratized. Political science has been the servant of the external engineers of democracy in Southern Africa.

External Imposition and Internal Preoccupations

The facts of democratization in Africa are startling. Since the late 1980s, embedded national leaders have been displaced, elections have led to changes in executives and open political competition has been widespread. By 1995, multi-party systems could be found in more than three-quarters of African states. Moreover, in 13 states changes of government through the ballot box had actually occurred. 'By 1995', as Wiseman has observed, 'the classic single party system, which has for so long been [Africa's] most common form of civilian rule, could be observed nowhere.'[49]

As Young has noted of democratization in sub-Saharan Africa, '[a]lthough no doubt we require a fuller historical distance to reach proper assessment, the recent wave of democratisation is largely externally engineered.'[50] Yet analysts have mostly denied the importance of external engineering and tried to render events compatible with pre-existing models of democratization. Democratization analysis has been historically domestic in focus, with scholars belatedly incorporating external factors. Commentators often attribute change to internal factors where this runs contrary to their own analysis.[51]

Arguments for the primary significance of internal factors are unpersuasive. African political elites have almost all accepted since decolonization that Western political institutions were not merely attractive to gain international recognition but were in fact the best institutions to construct.[52] 'Where elections have been suspended in

Africa', as Young points out, 'it has rarely, if ever, been because of coherent objections to their legitimacy as such'.[53] External proponents of democracy are therefore pushing against an open door.

Considering internal pressures for democratization, analysts often argue that authoritarian regimes face a 'crisis of legitimacy'.[54] The record of political oppression and economic failure, according to such commentators, renders such states vulnerable to democratic opposition. On some accounts, 'civil society' is invoked as an agency of opposition, with churches, trade unions and an increasingly independent media attacking incumbent regimes.[55] Wiseman even argues that 'demonstration effects' from Eastern Europe 'emboldened pro-democracy activists' and 'weakened the confidence of many autocratic leaders'.[56]

The two most important activities contributing to the success of a regime are its capacity for military self-defence and its ability to promote economic development. Each of these activities occurs in an international rather than a purely domestic realm. It has been unusual in the twentieth century for regimes to be overthrown by purely domestic enemies. Economic success likewise relies on the creation of conditions which facilitate collaboration and the import of skills and technologies, rather than merely improving domestic productivity directly. As Dunn remarked in the wake of 1989, one cannot dispute 'the need to see democratic success and failure in a context of ceaseless geo-political struggle, military, territorial and ideological'.[57]

African states, moreover, are particularly vulnerable to international military, financial and ideological pressure. They often lack the most rudimentary ability to manage and compensate for the impact of external actors and forces. The reasons for this vulnerability include limited state infrastructural capacity (an ability to control a territory through reliable logistical command over its resources) and the absence of a viable national currency, literacy and national communications.[58] African vulnerability has also been guaranteed by the destruction of pre-colonial institutional and cultural forms in politics; the destruction of pre-colonial institutional forms in agriculture and the lack of any alternative basis for economic self-development; the destruction of existing political institutions and the failure of the colonial state to create the conditions for new institutions; and the vicious cycles of weakness in the economy in debt crisis and in human capital creation.

The external engineering of democracy in Africa has had several sources. The end of the Cold War made it possible for Western patrons to abandon unattractive client states. The Soviet Union was obliged to withdraw almost entirely from its African commitments. This removed from African elites the possibility of manipulating the superpowers to their advantage. As Whitehead argues, 'western donors no longer had much interest in providing further aid to client regimes whose corruption and mismanagement seemed inexpungible. The resulting western demand for "democracy" could prove, in various cases, just an excuse for budget cutting.'[59]

Multilateral Western agencies underwent a sea change in thinking about the relationship between government styles and economic development. In the 1960s, many analysts claimed that economic development and democracy were in tension in poor countries. Such views, based on abstract models of competition for resources within democracies, supported Galenson's claim that 'the more democratic a government is...the greater the diversion of resources from investment to consumption', and De Schweinitz's assertion that developing countries 'must limit democratic participation in political affairs' if they are to grow.[60] To secure development, resources directed to investment had to be increased in the face of a consumption-favouring electorate. 1980s doctrine reversed the common sense of previous decades by arguing for a relationship between 'good governance' and economic advance.[61] The heavily indebted and aid-dependent states of sub-Saharan Africa have had little option other than to fall into line with the demands of their credit brokers. Overseas expertise has worked with various models of African politics, moving from the condemnation of democracy in very poor states to its fairly warm embrace. The damage done by such swings in analysis has been considerable.[62]

The relations between political system and economic performance are obscure. An authoritarian government may be best placed to impose certain kinds of shock treatment associated with the creation of market economies from scratch (as in Eastern Europe) or with the imposition of programmes of 'structural adjustment'. However, in the former case broader coalitions have to be built for the economic reforms to take benevolent effect. In the latter, already weak states may not survive the adjustment they must themselves undergo as their leaders find clientelistic structures harder to maintain.[63]

Analysts underplay the direct coercion and violence involved in 'external factors'. Southern Africa endured externally promoted civil wars; the end of deliberate destabilization was a necessary condition for democratization. Many African states, moreover, have had democracy imposed upon them directly, with the threat of state collapse as the only alternative on offer.[64]

The distinction between internal and external is hard to sustain where states lack the basic attributes of stateness. Any contribution to democracy (which by definition is domestic) must in some sense have domestic effects! Commentators can therefore overestimate the importance of the 'internal' for three reasons. The first main reason for the presence and prevalence of the internal/external distinction lies in the nation-state focus of modern political science. Internalizing the characteristic images and metaphors of the age of the industrial nation state, political science has viewed politics as the unfolding of the internal logic of the state. The causal processes that permit explanation were often internal to such states. Analysis of contemporary transitions in quite distinct circumstances has followed this pattern. The objects of study have remained states, reflecting how fully comparative politics idealizes its objects of comparison (notwithstanding recent attempts to move to regional or sub-national units of comparison).

Secondly, it has suited almost all external actors and internal powerbrokers in southern African politics to portray democratization as an outcome of the virtuous struggle of domestic actors. Victorious leaders want to erase predecessors' claims to have been 'fathers of the nation' by arguing that the people (and the churches, unions and civil society) raised them to their exalted positions. Officials of international agencies have likewise (and somewhat self-deceptively) seen their role as the empowerment of domestic actors. Western governments have remained properly modest about their role in events.[65] Elites negotiating new political dispensations have used models of the domestic causes of democratization to help impose settlements on domestic interests. In one fascinating example, the South African corporate sector sponsored scenario exercises in which the decisions of domestic actors play the key role. In practice such scenario studies were (and remain) the vehicles of business and state prescription, used by leaders to demonstrate the advantages of compromise.

Third, some academic commentators do not wish to rob Africans of historical agency by describing events in Africa as determined by outsiders.[66] The ability of the inhabitants of African societies collectively to take control of their own destinies, however, is profoundly weak quite independently of the beliefs of Western analysts.[67]

CONCLUSIONS

This chapter has developed three key themes. First, I offered an overview of the academic literature on democratization, identifying three broad approaches to what has been taken to be a cumulative global phenomenon: modernization approaches, structural historical perspectives, and approaches that stress the role of political elites in the transition process.

Second, I assessed the strengths and failings of the literature for understanding and promoting benevolent change in southern Africa, advancing two important propositions: that the literature must itself be understood historically, as a collective endeavour to make sense of the emergence of democratic regimes; and that academic debate has influenced expectations and so politics. Early models, stressing domestic factors, have remained influential despite their failure to explain political change in Eastern Europe and sub-Saharan Africa. All share a bias in favour of structural and domestic factors, sheltered behind an incoherent distinction between internal and external. Compromises between different schools of thought, moreover, have fused inconsistent assumption into incoherent models. Furthermore, scholars have ignored African experience, treating the continent's distinctive politics as anomalous.

Finally, I assessed the usefulness of this literature for understanding political change in sub-Saharan Africa. Accounts based on domestic factors prove quite untenable, given that political change has been externally engineered to an unprecedented extent. The domestic focus of analysis has been sustained because it is in nobody's interest to challenge it. External actors would lose legitimacy by admitting to causal responsibility for events. Domestic activists gain credibility from their purported actions. Academic analysts have remained trapped in the assumptions of a political science establishment whose audience resides elsewhere. The models they borrow were built out of different historical experiences and are pervaded by the politics of the states from which they were drawn.

The next two chapters show how the failure of comparative politics has gone beyond this one field. Interventions by political scientists in modern South Africa have been policy-influencing by design. Professional academic analysts have advised South African governments on appropriate courses of action, with their scientific professionalism and the Western origins of their prescriptions as supports. So far we have seen political science as inept; in the next chapter we view it as malign.

6 Political Science and the End of Apartheid

INTRODUCTION

Comparative political studies have contributed little to political actors' understandings of the causes of 'democratization' in Africa, and still less to their ability to assess and improve the prospects of continued and deepened democratic rule. Democratic transition and consolidation analysis, however, has not represented the entirety of efforts by political scientists in modern South Africa. In the next two chapters I examine four other areas in which political analysts have made major contributions. First, and in this chapter, I explore how they have constructed narratives of political change, attempting to turn bewildering events into a coherent sequence of causes and effects which seem intuitively and logically to follow one from the other. Such narratives have been a key source for journalists and politicians alike, but have also been used as elements of the detailed transition analysis that has increasingly displaced general models of democratization.

Chapter 7 explores three further fields of work. First, political scientists have engaged in 'constitutional engineering'. South Africa has been the subject of many detailed studies in constitutional design across many decades and these have drawn on (and manipulated) the work of political and legal-constitutional analysts from South Africa and abroad. Second, political scientists have sought to influence the design of more narrowly electoral systems and to advise on the necessary conditions for free and fair elections to take place. In order to perform this important work, they have had to engage with thorny problems: in particular, how to explain the significance of elections to the citizens of modern states, and how to explore the relationships between social structure, political attitudes and voting behaviour. Third, political science has engaged in various attempts to read the future and to influence it. In particular, domestic political analysts have contributed to political risk assessments and scenario-building exercises, the latter designed to create structured sets of possible futures as guides to action for decision-makers. Less glamorous areas of policy science – future-oriented public administration and basic public policy development – have also received attention from political analysts.

The conclusions I reach about the effectiveness of professional analysis in each of these domains are depressing. However, my intention is most certainly not to castigate commentators for their almost comprehensive lack of success in their work. I depend on the capabilities of professional academic analysts to identify the failings of their colleagues (even if perspicacity has largely been achieved in the face of, rather than because of, professional techniques). My focus, rather, will be on the weaknesses of political science as a discipline.

MAKING SENSE OF SEEMING CHAOS: NARRATIVES OF CHANGE

At first sight, there is no reason to expect political scientists to possess special skills in the creation of political narratives. Indeed, the aspiration of political science to detachment should commit it to counter-intuitive analysis rather than to plausibility. As Unger argues, the investigation of surprises – events running contrary to expectation – is likely to yield most intellectual dividends.[1] While many comparativists continue to write single-author and single-country monographs, particularly early in their careers, and these necessarily possess a narrative structure, their organizing categories are usually features demonstrated by a national polity in common with, or in contrast to, other polities. While a historian can privilege the integrity of narrative, a political scientist should not organize even a single-country monograph around a compelling or persuasive account of how events follow one another.

Most comparative political scientists, moreover, are explicitly concerned to deny that a particular case offers an unrepeatable combination of historically unique causes and effects. Furthermore, with the revolution in availability of aggregate data, comparativists often approach the analysis of national (or sub-national) units about whose specific characteristics and day-to-day politics – not to mention culture, language or even location – they may know next to nothing.

The purported intellectual advantages of detachment and counter-suggestibility have only unevenly affected the practices of political scientists. Many comparativists have placed very heavy weight on the selection of cases for comparison. Reflection on the notion of incommensurability and the need to be sure of data quality have persuaded some investigators to reduce the number of case studies drastically, and to deepen their knowledge of each. Such knowledge has also increased analysts' ability to use wider variables – concerned, for example, with sequence or with memory – thus making still less attractive a wide array of cases.

The idea that political scientists should trace the behaviour of key actors in specific circumstances has been supported by recent developments in the analysis of transitions from authoritarian rule. The consequences of elite strategy before and during transition attract increasing attention. Such investigations have demanded narrative skills, since plausible causal chains must be constructed from fragmentary and uncertain evidence. Impressive attempts to generalize about the implications of who is governing in the interim period between authoritarian and democratic rule, and how they govern, inevitably rely on sensitivity to the perceptions of local actors and the context within which they understand themselves to act.[2] The actions of political elites are shaped by social reality and political opportunity, and by the perceptions of each held by historically located actors.

Academic analysts also possess specialist skills and training which might be expected to help them in the construction of well-informed accounts of events. Disinterested, they will not (it is hoped) adopt partisan perspectives or become carried away by the emotions associated with political success and failure. With their understanding of changing social structure, and their grasp of the interrelations between political strategies, they might be expected to achieve a measure of detachment. With their skills in information retrieval and access, moreover, they can be expected to display an impressive level of knowledge about actors' perspectives and the unintended consequences of actions.

In South Africa, however, it cannot be said that political scientists achieved any special degree of success in predicting events or explaining developments. Indeed, among professional analysts it was those least persuaded of the benefits of the comparative method who were the most perceptive readers of events. Mostly overwrought narratives, and sometimes hysterical ones, predicted calamity, revolution or civil war with dreary regularity. In a range of situations, academic analysts fell back on 'common-sense' categories of classification which had no proper place in an advanced intellectual armoury. In particular, notions of violence, 'mass politics', ethnic fratricide and 'chaos' or 'social disorder' were applied as organizing categories by South African and visitor alike. The intellectual tools of comparative politics were often deployed to confirm intuition and prejudice rather than to discipline analysts and direct research to counter-intuitive results.

Political scientists' collapse of intellectual discipline is highlighted by both the relative detachment of historical analysts, and by what we now know from insiders of the process of transition.[3] Detached historical analysis has proved powerful in part because extra-political context is vital. Long-range and plainly international developments shaped the circumstances within which the end of apartheid and the negotiation of a democratic settlement took place. Economic nationalism became decreasingly viable across the 1970s and 1980s as international financial movements and floating exchange rates defeated state defences. The importance of technology transfer and international collaboration for modern industry redoubled these pressures.[4] Theorists of economic deregulation advanced, and eventually made inescapable, a set of neoclassical policy programmes that were fundamentally at odds with the foundations of apartheid. Domestically, the South African state had long faced a structural crisis. Influx control institutions, never very effective in operation, began to crumble, and urban Black populations to grow rapidly. The effects of South Africa's longstanding productive investment crisis (with low-quality investment barely replacing capital stock) began to kick in sharply.[5]

Decisive shifts, as I argued in chapter 5, have been mistakenly classified 'domestic' by many political analysts. The economic collapse of the Soviet bloc and its aid projects massively reduced the interest of the United States and other Western powers in their client regimes in Southern Africa. The US began to press for rapid progress to end conflict in Namibia and Angola. The many simultaneous experiments in democracy around southern Africa show how general were the pressures at work. The requirements of economic growth, inward investment and international political legitimacy all pointed the same way. In South Africa, in combination with the stagnation of the economy, the collapse of labour control, and urbanization, these pressures made collaboration between the ANC and the government a very great likelihood rather than an unexpected miracle.

A simple account of this kind makes the key parties' arrival at the negotiating table quite unsurprising, and in South Africa there was very little doubt about who the key parties would be. The prospects of a negotiated settlement, moreover, would seem to have been exceptionally bright. There were, after all, few identifiable ideological divides between the Afrikaner leaders of the NP and the leaders of the ANC. Statist and South African nationalist, pragmatic about economic policy-making and public policy, each was evidently capable of compromise and sophisticated negotiation. The ANC looked at all stages to be a disciplined and moderate organization. Despite the diverse experiences of exile, imprisonment and domestic struggle through the United Democratic Front, the ANC attracted loyalty and showed an almost absurd commitment to correct procedure and accountability. The National Party at no stage had serious doubts about the reliability and integrity of the military and (with some exceptions) the security apparatus. There was no possibility of state disintegration or coup; and, notwithstanding the conflict in Natal, there was no possibility of a state destabilizing civil war. The means of state coercion remained overwhelming.

The negotiation process itself reflects the powerful forces for settlement. Kader Asmal's account of negotiation[6] is striking for its focus on continuity and process. It explores elite strategy – the purported focus of transition analysis – and all but ignores the day-to-day turmoil of political struggle which has obsessed political scientists. Asmal points to the immense economic and international pressures that led even P.W. Botha to begin contacts with Nelson Mandela in mid-1987. F.W. de Klerk's release of Walter Sisulu and others, and his relaxation of controls on political activity in 1989, are developed as natural corollaries to this recognition. February 1990 brought de Klerk's decisive legalization of organizations, multiple unbannings and selected releases of detainees, followed rapidly by the return of exiles, the lifting of the State of Emergency and an increased frequency of meetings between the ANC and government.

On Asmal's calm account, the concentrated and extensive negotiations of 1991 ended at Christmas with a reasonably unproblematic statement of joint commitment to negotiation (through the Convention for a Democratic South Africa). CODESA incorporated 18 political groups each of which agreed to the goals of an 'undivided' South Africa, a bill of rights, a multi-party system, constitutional government, separation of powers, civil liberties, and specified freedoms to be enjoyed by all citizens.[7] In contrast to most political analysts, Asmal makes clear the cumulative nature of the negotiating process and the degree of consensus it embodied.

1992 was a year of temporary stalemate within the negotiating process. The CODESA working party on constitutional principles found itself unable to advance, especially on the size of majorities required to achieve control in the elected constitution-making body. As Asmal indicates, however, the withdrawal of the ANC was not the dangerous risk that many analysts made it out to be. 'From then on the process was particularly well-managed.... By setting the agenda in terms of realistic steps [the management committee of negotiations] managed to avert unnecessary blockages and to create a sense of confidence that there was continuing forward movement.'[8]

By March 1993, all 26 negotiating parties were back in public debate in the multi-party negotiating process. 'Consensus' was the basis on which talks were deemed to be based, although this rapidly became established as 'sufficient consensus'. The core of the negotiations was the ANC–National Party combination. As Johnston has remarked, ANC–NP negotiations were 'helped by the assumption on both sides that "sufficient consensus" meant consensus between themselves'.[9] As early as April 1993, the Negotiating Council had resolved to create technical committees to explore solutions to problems in the fields of violence, discriminatory legislation, the media, the electoral commission, human rights, constitutional issues and the Transitional Executive Council (or TEC), which was to take over executive functions in the run-up to the election.

By September 1993, the Constitution of South Africa (known usually as the transitional or interim constitution) had been enacted and legislation on the conduct of a 'free and fair election' passed. At the insistence of the NP, moreover, everything had been enacted by existing institutions – as clear an indication as there could be of the degree of extraordinary control over events achieved by the key negotiating parties. It was the TEC, under powers constitutionally granted to it, that agreed with the government to amendments on provincial powers which cemented the Inkatha Freedom Party's participation in the election.

Asmal's account is not merely one of a cumulative and controlled process of negotiation. In explaining the reasons for the success of the negotiations, Asmal draws notice to the immense attention to detail displayed in the drafting of the interim constitution: powers and rules were precisely specified and much of the document read like a detailed contract rather than a framework of general rules. The TEC – the alternative cabinet, which was to be the ultimate executive authority in the run-up to the election – was regulated by precise and detailed statutes. Further transitional arrangements were equally carefully defined, including the demand that the final constitution be passed by May 1996 and that it be formulated in accordance with the 34 'Constitutional Principles' (with adjudication powers of the Constitutional Court carefully defined).

The chronology and conditions of creation of the final constitution provided a tidy solution to an entrenched difference between the key negotiating parties. While the NP was always in favour of drafting the full constitution before the first election, the ANC and the Pan Africanist Congress (PAC) wanted the election to create an assembly with the power to write a constitution from scratch. The inclusion of compulsory respect for Constitutional Principles – together with the safeguards offered by the principle of consensual decision-making, a government of national unity and the constitutional court – permitted de Klerk to carry his constituency into an agreement that plainly favoured the ANC. The ANC's additional concessions – the sunset clauses and pension protection for a vast range of state and security force employees – were a fairly direct bribe to present incumbents to abandon the claims of their descendants. (Guarantees of politicians' pensions – effectively direct transfers of monies into the pockets of individual leaders of the NP – were perhaps the most shameless of the measures.)

Asmal identifies some legal-constitutional changes as important to success. He believes that the overthrowing of the idea of 'parliamentary sovereignty' – itself inherited from British legal thought – rendered less threatening the idea of majority rule. Confidence was cemented by the elevation of the constitution to a new status as supreme law of the land and by the expanded role of judicial review. A number of 'fundamental rights', moreover, were inscribed in the constitution, thus placing them beyond the reach of parliamentary power; property rights, in particular, were given firm and visible expression.

Perhaps more important in practice, the negotiators developed both an inclusive formula for parliamentary elections – one that guaranteed the privileges of parliamentary membership to the elite within even the smallest parties – with all manner of ingenious curbs on majority assertion. Inclusion was achieved by means of a broadly proportional electoral system without the cut-off for very low votes that characterizes most such systems. One seat was allocated for every 0.25 per cent of the vote. In the event, this proved most important in guaranteeing for the very visible Democratic Party and PAC a number of seats in Parliament despite their tiny vote shares. These parties contained both key political figures and the potential to become important political forces in later elections.

The curbs on majority power were unobtrusive – as we shall see later, political scientists had championed a range of grandiose and imprudent constraints which canny ANC negotiators avoided – and used a range of special majorities, parliamentary procedures and cabinet rules. A multi-party executive was guaranteed for a period; fundamental rights were defined; the potential use of emergency powers was restricted; courts with new review powers were set up; new offices, including the Public Protector, the Human Rights Commissioners and the Financial and Fiscal Commission, were developed. Asmal notes that the 'line between fair and equitable protection of the interests of those not represented in government and the hobbling of a government with a clear popular mandate must be finely drawn'[10] – an issue that has always been at the heart of liberal democratic political thought. However, the decisions reached were the product of extended horse-trading rather than of academic deliberation.

Both the broader forces leading towards negotiation, and the negotiation process itself, were marked by incremental change, open and evident pressure towards negotiation, meticulous stage-by-stage advance and the systematic (and fairly unproblematic) exclusion of extremists. In these circumstances, the analysis of some political scientists seems quite extraordinary. A very substantial number of professional academic accounts suggested that the processes of negotiation and transition were highly vulnerable and that their outcome was open to doubt.

SOUTH AFRICA IN TRANSITION: A VOLATILE STATE?

Political analysts' alarmist understandings of the negotiating process originated in the weaknesses of political science as a discipline, but also in the immense complexity and unfamiliarity of the politics they were trying to understand. South Africa's political institutions and movements were familiar only in caricature; when they began to behave in unfamiliar ways, it transpired they were virtually impenetrable to conventional instruments of investigation. The South African state was predominantly an Afrikaner state, shaped from the 1950s by the Broederbond with its commitment to secrecy and loyalty. It was influenced by a set of immensely wealthy and powerful concentrated capital-holding corporations, themselves opaque to observers; and it was dominated, first, from the 1960s, by a state-within-a-state concerned with the control of labour; and, second, from the early 1980s, by a security state-within-a-state.[11]

The political movements vying for power and influence in the run-up to negotiations were formed into disparate coalitions, united by strategy rather than by fundamental commonality of interests. Almost all political movements were involved in instrumental mobilizations around racial, ethnic or class issues, or in the generation of mass political action. It served the interests of negotiating elites to keep their supporters at the margins of apparent central control (a process they portrayed as desperate attempts to rein in militant followers). The NP relied not just on the rhetoric of disinvestment and White flight to bolster its negotiating position, but also on the spectre of far right secessionism, violence and disorder. For this reason, the NP welcomed the presence of the Afrikaner Weerstandsbeweging (AWB) in confirming its own moderate status. Although the Conservative Party and the (agricultural and military) Afrikaner Volksfront (AVF) were more serious threats to the NP, it recognized that an electorate motivated by race was always likely to return to the fold to cast its ballots.[12]

The ANC, for its part, has seemed to academic analysts a broad political movement of immense complexity. In 1964, the ANC organization within South Africa had been virtually destroyed, and its existence thereafter was predominantly as an exile movement, with its leadership in Lusaka and its guerrilla army in Angola. (By the end of the 1980s, there were up to 15,000 ANC members in Angola, Tanzania and Zambia.) The experiences of exile had potentially complex ramifications: many ANC activists received training and education in Scandinavia and Western Europe; others in Eastern Europe, the Soviet Union or China. ANC leaders' first-hand observation of postcolonial African states, especially Tanzania, left a legacy that was difficult for analysts to read.

The national leadership of the ANC was famously imprisoned for three decades on Robben Island. The leaders, inevitably isolated from events, and even isolated from younger transitory residents on the island itself, had a unique and impenetrable political education. They were, moreover, to emerge into a South Africa that had changed almost beyond recognition.

If the relationship between Robben Islanders and exiles was uncertain, that between both and activists under the United Democratic Front (UDF) umbrella seemed potentially fraught with difficulty. In 1980, there was almost no organized opposition within South Africa. Between 1980 and 1991, however, Lodge argues that the key to understanding Black political movements was 'the resurrection of legal mass political organisation as the main dynamic of Black resistance'.[13] Black political movements increasingly organized themselves under the banner of the UDF from 1983. Bolstered by recession from 1982, and the unemployment and debt that came with it, and given space by government liberalization that was designed to replace direct coercion with state authority,[14] the UDF united student groups, youth congresses, civic associations, women's organizations, church societies and trade unions. The more than 700 affiliates of the UDF were, according to Lodge, 'ideologically diverse, united only in their opposition to the government'.[15]

Commentators have indeed failed thus far to identify much coherence in the activities of UDF affiliates. In most settings, three groups were central to political activity: civic associations (locally elected representative bodies and the centres of community debate), women's groups and youth congresses. Schoolchildren sometimes played an important role and, on occasion, the participation of populist trade unions in community struggles added weight. However, with the exception of the unions, each of these key groups, with their massive regional, functional, organizational and political diversity, lay outside the range of conventional professional political analysis.

The role of 'youth' in the UDF is an exemplar of this weakness. Lodge notes that 'without doubt it was the youth – university students, schoolchildren and unemployed young people who provided the cutting edge of political radicalism in the 1980s.'[16] Yet we possess virtually no convincing analysis of youth politics and its significance. As Seekings has argued, professional approaches to youth politics have either demonized or celebrated its participants without providing any steady analysis of motivation, organization, achievement and potential. Academic analysis fed an extraordinary paranoia among White South Africans and fuelled their fear of 'the townships'.[17] Just as 'the townships' had become, for Whites, a metaphysical category – not referring to any time and place, but to a concatenation of images and fears – so their inhabitants became to many professional analysts an elemental and uncontrollable threat.

If youth were largely demonized, women's, civic and church politics were largely passed over in political analysis. Women's organizations' role in political opposition has been on the margins of political science, a specialist interest rather than an integrated enquiry. There have been many studies of particular protests organized by women – against the extension of passes to women and in opposition to the banning of traditional women's enterprises, particularly in brewing and township entertainment.[18] There have also been attempts to derive more general conclusions about the significance of women's social and political organizations in contemporary South Africa.[19] But there has been little attempt to explain the significance of women's organizations, and in particular the ANC Women's League, in contemporary politics. While the ANCWL is one of the key organized constituencies within the ANC, the nature of its influence is highly untransparent, and the articulation between the ideology of gender equality that suffuses much of the ANC and the particular and respected claims to influence of the ANCWL is unclear.

Civic associations, especially important in the politics of the Western and Eastern Cape in the 1980s, remain a murky unknown to most political analysts, their behaviour characterized in the most general terms. At the heart of the UDF's struggles, the organizational pivots for consumer and school boycotts, and the creators of 'people's institutions', civics were both pervasive and yet particular. The foundation of a national 'representative' body for civics, the South Africa National Civics Organization, has added another unreadable agent into the ANC leadership's political world. To the degree that political analysts recognize the influence of women, youth and civic associations, they tend to conceive these as categories of actor in the metaphysical township of the White South African imagination.

Still less attention is paid to the politics of rural and homeland South Africa. There have been very few powerful studies of homelands, perhaps the most difficult practical objects of institutional analysis in apartheid South Africa.[20] The potential for political mobilization in rural and homeland areas has always looked too slight and too little grounded in recognizable political institutions to be registered by political analysis. Social anthropologists, by contrast, have recognized that viable systems of understanding and action in such oppressive environments need not be labelled 'political' to have political significance.[21]

The contrast is striking when one examines categories familiar to Western European political analysis – in particular, the growth of organized labour. The role of trade unions has been better documented and integrated into political analysis than any other kind of politics. A series of impressive if partial studies have documented the rapid rise of trade unionism over the 1980s, and highlighted the nature and import of divisions within the pro-ANC union federation, the Confederation of South African Trade Unions (COSATU). The nature and import of unions affiliated with other political movements, and of White-only unions, are also well documented and impressively analysed.[22]

If analysts were familiar enough, on the face of it, with the ANC-affiliated unions, they returned once again to the dark when exploring the influence represented by the South African Communist Party in those same unions – and directly within the ANC. This party was very difficult to investigate because of its illegal status, its tradition of secrecy, the impenetrable theoretical morass into which it was drawn by the intersection between race and class in South Africa, and its seeming adherence to an exceeding literal version of the official line from Moscow. SACP cadres were not encouraged to disclose their membership of the party, even when it was legal to do so and even after the leadership's decision to join in a three-way 'tripartite alliance' with the ANC and COSATU.

All of this was a recipe for intellectual disaster. It was fairly clear who the central actors should be in South Africa's political drama. The ANC, its supporters and its affiliates were the objects of professional analysis of the opposition. Yet each of the elements that went to make up the strange organism that was the ANC presented numerous imponderables, each of which demanded problematic preliminary investigation. The mysteries of women's, youth, civic and church politics defied analysis; unions, communists, exiles and the imprisoned each seemed comprehensible (if distant) on their own, but their sudden throwing together in a new political environment opened bewildering possibilities. The regional peculiarities of Natal (with its Indian Congress and the Inkatha Freedom Party) and of the Western Cape (with its Coloured politics and its multitude of civics) added to the murky stew. Hidden and poorly understood intellectual systems swirled in the depths of this soup. Africanism, communism, socialism, Black Consciousness, charterism and the influences of decades in diverse exiles – each left academics bewildered.[23]

Black politics outside the ANC's gravitational field in the UDF was still harder, if anything, to comprehend. The Pan Africanist Congress (PAC) had no open presence in South Africa at the start of the 1980s. Its strength, particularly in the Cape, was a matter of much speculation, and only its poor showing in the election of 1994 confirmed for certain that its traditionalist programme had reduced it to second-rank status. If the PAC was something of an unknown quantity, the Azanian People's Organization was all too familiar to academics and intellectuals. The National Forum launched in 1983, a loose association of groups but primarily the vehicle for AZAPO's ambitions, represented the considerable ideological diversity that the label Black Consciousness could cover.[24] Some authors have attributed extraordinary influence to Black Consciousness ideas and organization; but all Black

Consciousness and Africanist organizations remained small, organizationally weak and of little demonstrable influence on political opposition. It may be that the 'anti-White' rhetoric of Black Consciousness had greatest impact on the young White students, intellectuals and activists towards whom it was (essentially benignly) directed, and they later came to record and to celebrate it. The cultural organizations upon which Black Consciousness traditions were erected may have had a more circumscribed and particular role within Black politics than was imagined by university activists.

Black South Africa also contained political movements firmly allied to the right, of which the Inkatha Freedom Party was by far the most important. Conservative in ideology, advancing ethnicity, traditional authority and reformist capitalism, Inkatha controlled a massive system of patronage and employment, a trade union federation of its own, and high levels of support among a large (if territorially concentrated) constituency. Its control over jobs, school curriculums and propaganda, together with its effective servicing of its supporters' immediate interests, gave it considerable independence and capacity for self-defence. The unpredictability of the IFP from the perspective of political analysts lay first in the intentions of its leadership, as symbolized by the indecision, megalomania and intellectual disarray of its leader, and in the ever-present tensions between Chief Gatstia Buthelezi's coterie of advisers and royal authority in KwaZulu. Uncertainty also surrounded the levels of political support enjoyed by the party – an uncertainty risible surveys and the election result in 1994 did little to resolve. Other homelands had viable, if less well-supported, ideologies of self-justification, but none was sufficiently robust to survive the process of transition largely intact.

One feature of the negotiating process in Natal was the instrumental use of violence by the government, the IFP and the ANC in support of their negotiating efforts. Such instrumental violence was also found in the PWV region. Regardless of its political uses, violence and the perception of violence, came to be important in shaping academic analysis, so exposing weaknesses in the conduct of political research. Many political analysts considered that 'Black-on-Black violence' was an unproblematic category of classification. Unsurprisingly, therefore, they produced racialized explanations. In particular, assumptions about the inherently conflictual relations between different tribes (prudishly renamed 'ethnicities') were the (usually unspoken) presuppositions brought to analysis. Even where such assumptions were resisted, perceptions of violence and danger further distorted analysts' preconceptions about the nature of 'township politics'. I have argued that accounts of 'the townships' were collections of images unattached to any particular location or time. Violence was both an ascribed ingredient of township politics, and also, for (usually White) researchers, an eventually almost absolute deterrent to research into the realities of political life.

Intellectually, political analysts registered the strength of moral orders contained within South Africa's townships: the demands of survival in an economy of low and sporadic incomes inevitably imply very strong mutual obligations. Yet, 'the townships' were violent and so could not be investigated. Because they were uninvestigated, they could be viewed as 'chaotic' and 'disorderly', ruled by 'the youth', the homes of disorder and ungovernability. Such speculative analysis was encouraged by the genuine complexity of township politics. Households, social networks and kinship categories were fluid and hard to organize intellectually. 'Identities' and political affiliations were multifarious and of uncertain texture. The imposed institutions of local government were often preposterous in their actions and claims to legitimacy. The inhabitants of South Africa's townships were strenuously renegotiating their own social and moral relationships, thus temporarily removing the signposts professional analysts might otherwise have used to trace their political dynamics.

Professional accounts of South Africa's negotiating and transition process were written in these extraordinarily difficult circumstances. While the multiplicity of unfamiliar processes and political movements prohibited confident and comprehensive attempts to explain events and predict developments, they also provided a resource. Political analysts found a world of possibility in front of them: they could draw upon and support all manner of modes of analysis in constructing their narratives of transition. While they were in practice often overlapping, I have distinguished below three kinds of analysis that were widespread during South Africa's transition to democracy. The first and most important was the venerable tradition of 'first and third worldism' which was permeated with the idea that South Africa contained a first (White) world and a third (African) one. This was (and remains) the key organizing principle of South African social science. The other reinforcing modes of analysis were those of Africanists; and those of comparative politics specialists from the US and Europe, together with the scenario merchants from South Africa's own academic community. Each style of interpretation was misleading on its own; as they were rewoven together in popular and media debate, they created a perverse and negative vision of South Africa's prospects.

THREE WORLDS: DEVELOPMENTAL, AFRICANIST AND COMPARATIVIST

First and Third Worldism

The first distinct intellectual framework for approaching contemporary South Africa remains pervasive across its social and political sciences. This is more than just an intellectual framework: it is a projection of the common-sense world of White urban South Africans that is used to structure information. Behind it lies a tradition of social thought encompassing Victorian understandings of civilization and postwar notions of development. We have seen how liberals maintained a very clear conception of two worlds living side by side (a conception challenged intellectually by revisionists who maintained that the affluence of Whites was interrelated with the poverty of Blacks). Liberals viewed South Africa as a European territorial entity superimposed upon a borderless African continent. The spread of settlement through the eighteenth and nineteenth centuries represented a European dynamic infused into a static African social world; only gradually could the African be introduced to, and perhaps incorporated to some extent into, the international civilization of the European.

The notion of South Africa as a territory containing two distinct worlds shows few signs of decay. The 'first and third world' idea is used routinely by White South Africans attempting to explain their predicament to foreigners or to Black South Africans. The first world, in this vision, is represented by freeways, modern hospitals, suburbia, rationality (and rugby); the third by teeming townships, poverty, superstition, ethnicity (and football). In politics, the first world has enjoyed political rights, issue-based voting and Western political institutions; the third has achieved only patronage, clientelism, tribalism and violence. In economics, the first world has resembled Western European states: industrialized, with consumer affluence, advanced technology, commerce and finance. The third has been characterized by subsistence agriculture, migrant labour and devastatingly low productivity.

This way of conceiving the relationships between predefined groups is pervasive in White public opinion. (This does not reflect any special intellectual or moral failing on the part of South African Whites: the rationalization of structured inequality is a preoccupation of the privileged everywhere.) The mechanisms by means of which apartheid institutions enforced the exploitation of Black South Africans, moreover, provided Whites with overwhelming evidence that these assumptions were indeed correct. Were not Africans living in rural reserves and squatter camps, unskilled, unemployed, poor? And the welfare state that virtually eliminated the truly poor Afrikaner likewise helped create a wealthy White reality out of a prejudice.

The faulty intellectual understanding of a fundamentally divided social world helped perpetuate a false conception of the distinct nature of humanity on each side of the divide, and a faulty perspective on the public policies that might relieve the 'sufferings' of those in the 'third world'. This has been most striking in the field of 'development'. As McCarthy has explained, 'the South African economy differs little from other third world economies.... in having a dominant modern industrial sector side by side with large, less productive traditional and informal sectors.'[25] It is apartheid, with its unique ability to hide poverty from the affluent observer, that has reinforced the notion of two worlds, and made possible generations of inappropriate analyses of 'development' and 'uplift'. This has served to misdirect policymakers' attention away from the alleviation of poverty and inequality in an integrated economy.

In politics, South African commentators continue to apply different standards of political rationality to different groups in accordance with their 'world' of habitation. Whites respond to argument and form intentions. They are capable of rational argument. Indians and Coloureds (especially urban Coloureds) have advanced abilities but not the fully developed cognitive capacity of Europeans. Africans, however, lack even the most rudimentary capacities for participation in liberal-democratic politics. Their political life is constituted by group reactions to collective experiences, mediated through primitive categories. They have mass expectations and they engage in mass politics; their political affiliations are primarily ethnic and secondarily racial; they act under the sway of primitive religious and traditionalist thought; and they are capable of violence and unpredictability, as their 'high expectations' are thwarted by the realities of western economics and political rationality.[26]

Such implicit conceptions of rationality no doubt continue to guide much public policy. They seem, moreover, to be perpetuated by the institutions of South African research funding. The availability of funding to conduct research into the nature of South African society has come from few sources and been channelled to a small number of academics. These analysts have almost all taken prior racial cleavages and differential racial rationalities as the bases of their research, a relation between power and knowledge to which we will have to return.[27]

Survey analysis has been confined to Whites until recently, and electoral analysis trapped within a descriptive tradition.[28] Survey data on individuals' political attitudes were unavailable until the media commissioned polls in the 1970s. Even today, the only pan-South African survey of political attitudes is conducted by the Human Sciences Research Council, a parastatal once concerned with improving the implementation of apartheid. It continues to use the racial classifications of apartheid in its research; and it continues to apply questions designed for particular 'population groups'.

There was no tradition of empirical research to give pause to political analysts as they reached automatically for familiar racial categories. Research simply reproduced those categories and so helped to sustain them. Little investigation into Black politics (other than Black Consciousness and student politics) was conducted in the major universities until the 1980s. The lack of any apparatus for thinking about Black politics was reflected, when such research became unavoidable, in the use of the vague terminology of the 'militant youth', the 'lost generation' and the 'underclass' (terms predominantly derived from foreign contexts) in conjunction with unspecific processes such as 'spirals of violence', 'unrest', and 'ungovernability'. It was no wonder many commentators drew upon the language of 'Black-on-Black' violence. This seemed to discharge them from their scholarly responsibilities by providing a ready-made explanation for conflict in the nature of African society.[29]

Africanism and Political Analysis

A second influence on political analysis has been the emergence of African studies as a distinctive field of scholarship in the North, and the consequent bolstering of a distinctive Africanist style of political narrative. We observed in chapter 2 that the evolving discipline of African history had been important in introducing to South African historiography a proper respect for the dynamics of African political systems prior to colonisation, during the unification of the South African state, and through to its contemporary politics. There have, however, been less intellectually benign spillovers from 'Africanist' approaches to South Africa.

The investigation of African political systems is today driven by one fundamental question: what has gone wrong in Africa? The failure of Africa can be framed illuminatingly as both a relative and an absolute one. In relative terms, it is the contemporary relative prosperity of states elsewhere in the world that used to compare in prospects with successful African states that has been most striking. Who today would equate the prospects of, say, Ghana and South Korea, as seemed possible in the 1950s? In absolute terms, it is the stagnation or fall in real incomes across the continent for two decades, together with political instability and collapsing state capacity, that best testifies to substantial political failure.

In response to these failings, there has been a proliferation of writings on the African state over the past decade. Mamdani has persuasively suggested that this literature can be divided into two 'tendencies'. The first 'modernist' group of authors, often labelled 'Eurocentric' by critics, locates Africa's problems in its 'civil society'. The state has failed to penetrate African society and therefore remains a hostage to it. The second group of 'communitarian' authors are self-consciously Africanist. They place Africa's communities and their histories at the centre of politics, and argue that these communities (and society more widely) have failed to hold the African state to account, and have therefore fallen prey to it.[30] Each of these opposed positions potentially reinforces first and third worldism in South African political analysis, since each relies upon the notion of a generic African state form. This notion is inevitably counterposed to the Afrikaner state and its successor.

Mamdani's proposed way of moving beyond the modernist: communitarian antithesis is to focus on mechanisms of 'indirect rule' by means of which colonial powers enforced their authority. Under indirect rule land remained communal or 'customary', a degree of institutional autonomy was maintained at local level, and tribal leadership was selectively imposed, reconstructed or created. In Mamdani's view, indirect rule was the characteristic form of colonial rule across Africa and helps explain the distinctiveness of the politics of the continent: 'The form of rule shaped the form of revolt against it. Indirect rule at once both reinforced ethnically bound institutions of control and led to their explosion from within. Ethnicity (tribalism) thus came to be simultaneously the form of colonial control... and the form of revolt against it.'[31]

Mamdani insists that indirect rule represents the key to the 'specificity of African experience', and that it should 'establish the historical legitimacy of Africa as a unit of analysis'. He proposes that South Africa, far from being an exception, was an exemplar of these processes. Apartheid 'idealized' the form of rule dubbed 'association' by the French and 'indirect rule' by the British; it was, indeed, 'the generic form of the colonial state in Africa'.[32] The implications of this currently fashionable analysis for the study of South African politics have been malign. Mamdani's argument suggests that a democratization that does not (somehow) root out the structures of indirect rule will be 'both superficial and explosive'. Free and fair elections cannot remove the 'decentralized despotism' that marks all postcolonial African politics.[33]

Mamdani asserts that Africans cannot transcend but only attack the (imposed) institutions they inherit. This analysis seems arbitrarily to imprison Africans in their past.[34] Moreover, it also ignores the special conditions to be found in South Africa. Nineteenth-century wars of dispossession, mass population displacement and enforced changes in social organization undermined the communal land control Mamdani identifies as crucial to indirect rule. The mineral revolutions transformed social structure in late nineteenth- and early twentieth-century South Africa; and proletarianized and urbanized South Africans, with their sophisticated urban intellectual and political cultures, have been capable of remarkably detached understandings of exploitative social institutions. South Africa's rebellion against apartheid was not in any way confined to a war against institutions equivalent to 'indirect rule', even if these institutions did indeed bear the brunt of direct protest. Opposition to apartheid was also often self-consciously anti-ethnic, political, urban, unionized and ideological.

Comparative Politics

A third influential style of analysis has been comparative politics, practised in the United States as the third (and junior) of the subdisciplines comprising political science and in Western Europe, Latin America and some of Asia as a distinct field of political analysis.[35] American comparativists working on South Africa were traditionally preoccupied with the presence of systematic segregation and with the light that this practice might shed on the American South.[36] More recently, however, South Africa has been especially attractive as an example of a state in transition to democracy. The new comparativists brought with them assumptions about how social change should properly be explained which proved especially infelicitous in South Africa. Many of these assumptions were residues of the golden age of comparative politics in the 1960s, when general theory was ambitiously advanced. On the one hand, Western (and especially North American) states were assumed to be the end point in a linear process of social evolution, a point to which South Africa must be proceeding by means of development (including political development). On the other hand, South Africa seemed to lack many of the bases for social order that marked, especially, the United States: overlapping cleavage patterns, an aggregative party system and a powerful but constrained state.

The discovery that South Africa lacked these accepted 'preconditions' for political order has alarmed many contemporary analysts. Cleavage patterns were the decisive difficulty for some: Sisk, for example, organized his entire analysis of South African transition around the notion that South Africa is a 'deeply divided society'. 'South Africa', he argued, 'is a test case of the possibility of negotiated settlements in societies deeply divided by racial, ethnic, religious, or other forms of ascriptively based conflict.'[37] South Africa, equally, seemed to lack a potential party system that might lead to the happy alternation of government and opposition. Likewise, the country lacked a state with the 'universal character' that Hegel identified as necessary to its survival.

We shall follow below how these prejudgements affected some North American political scientists' prescriptions for constitutional design, and their prognoses for the country's future. However, these problems were not confined to American scholars. European comparativists applied their own traditions to equally poor effect. Schmitter describes the procedure of early European comparativists thus: 'Basically, they took the case they knew best (usually the one in which they lived and taught), summarized it, and generalized its characteristics to other settings.'[38] One venerable comparativist, Lijphart, was especially influential in South Africa. Generalizing from the cases of the Netherlands and Belgium, he has famously argued that segmented pluralism allows an alternative route to social stability and political order. Consensus-generating and minority-protecting variants of democracy, in such situations, can achieve what majoritarian systems cannot. When Lijphart turned to South Africa, he displayed an extraordinarily casual attitude towards South African political reality.

Deep-seated tribal or ethnic distinctions were freely attributed in seeming ignorance or rejection of the substantial scholarly (and especially historical) literatures which had been written precisely to caution against this error.

While unwilling initially to commit themselves to any explanation of the nature of ethnicity – rather being concerned with the reality of deep social cleavages and the means by which they might be controlled – comparativists borrowed the vocabulary and imagery of Victorian analysts of tribal society and their descendants. Simplistic racial and apartheid state categories were reproduced as facts. Lijphart argued that, far from being 'homogeneous communities', Black and White are each 'divided into a number of ethnic groups'. Black South Africa, indeed, 'is made up of Africans, Coloureds and Asians, and the Africans are further divided into several ethnic groups, the largest of which are the Zulus and the Xhosas'.[39] Such groups were ascribed a Victorian propensity to conflict. These baleful assumptions rendered some comparativists' contributions to the negotiating process worse than useless.

A majority of South Africa's home-grown comparativists were assembled into two great camps, advancing either quasi-Marxist polemic or conservative scenarios. As we saw in chapter 3, 'radical' scholars viewed capitalism and apartheid as mutually interrelated. They considered, moreover, that the latter could not be dissembled without the overthrow of the former, so close was their interdependence and mutual reinforcement. Revolutionary rhetoric abounded, only belatedly to be tempered by the scientism of 'regulation theory'.[40]

Scenarios, usually collaborations involving conservative academic political scientists as well as economists, businessmen and lawyers, were the central contribution of South Africa's domestic political analysts to transition. Scenarios, visible to White and Black decision-makers alike, had one inescapable feature: they presented a range of alternative hypothetical trajectories, at least one of which was a scare scenario – an appalling outcome brought about by the faulty reasoning of actors or by the game theoretic complexity of the situations they faced together. Disaster potential is intrinsic to a scenario: it is the possibility of a disastrous outcome that drives actors prudently to reconsider their strategies. Scenarios thus disseminated dismal projections that were highly implausible. Their repeated invocation made realistic debate less rather than more likely. Rather than adopting prudent strategies, domestic actors adopted defensive ones which had the potential to be self-defeating. The winners in these games of chicken were scenarios' corporate sponsors.

A PROVISIONAL CONCLUSION: MUTUALLY REINFORCING MYTHS

These discrete styles of analysis were intellectually supported by different sets of assumptions, and they were generated and advanced by distinct collections of scholars in South Africa, Western Europe and North America. They were not, however, merely self-sustaining intellectual worlds. They achieved a degree of mutual awareness, and then interpenetration, which served to reinforce the worst misconceptions of each. Their point of greatest agreement was their area of greatest error: each suggested that there existed within South Africa, perhaps within its 'radical' youth in its metaphysical townships, some threat of violent and state-destabilizing social disorder, and one that might threaten the very integrity of the South African state. On this vision, moreover, there existed the threat of civil war in South Africa at large: Black South Africans, freed from the shackles of the apartheid state, would mobilize against each other in ethnic conflict, and against White South Africans in a greedy (or simply inexplicable) frenzy to satisfy their 'high expectations'. Mutually reinforcing predictions of disaster merged into a shadowy threat which professional observers saw hanging over the negotiating process.

7 The Failure of Political Science

INTRODUCTORY

We saw in chapter 6 how different schools of professional political analysis propagated distinctive but mutually reinforcing falsehoods. Unique features of South African society created by apartheid sustained these misconceptions. The turbulence within the South African academy, in particular, often led visiting specialists astray. 'Liberal' host institutions, undergoing the ordeal of full racial integration, were the sites of much protest and even more revolutionary rhetoric. South African social scientists have been extremely self-conscious about their intellectual affiliations, with marxist credentials and a belief in the interdependence of capitalism and apartheid prominent in their canon. Conservative academics' scaremongering reinforced radicals' trumpeting of the revolution to come. For visitors, the collapse of the apartheid state seemed to promise (or threaten) revolutionary upheaval. For such outsiders, the marxist analysis of one academic was as bemusing as another's conservative pseudo-science – but each pointed to a frightening future.

The naturalization of racial division was almost complete. Racial categorizations of human beings that visitors brought with them from their own societies were everywhere deepened. Visitors, moreover, were denied the experiences that might have challenged their preconceptions about the racialized and radicalized nature of Black South African society. The social engineering of apartheid left most of the residential areas of the country effectively out of reach for visitors (except in ritual township tours, which were more likely to reinforce than to break down misconceptions). Domestic analysts' strange idioms ('going into the townships'), and an absence of local power studies, further distanced these alien spaces.[1]

The absence of background knowledge may have encouraged the building of generalizations on the shaky basis of anecdotal testimony. Perhaps because the ascription of group properties and constitutive identity are commonplace, the claims of students and political activists about the political attitudes of Africans, and especially African youth, were taken at face value – despite the social exclusivity and political self-selectivity of those testifying. This reliance on testimony extends through political analysis and the media: exiles and people resident for 30 years in prison are assumed to have knowledge of the attitudes of quite distinct social strata with experiences they cannot possibly share – presumably solely because they too are 'Africans'. Where social forces militate so strongly against effective political analysis, practitioners must depend on their professional procedures to avoid systematic error. This chapter explores three areas of political scientists' work – 'constitutional engineering', electoral system and 'free and fair election' design, and policy studies – to demonstrate the weaknesses of these safeguards.

CONSTITUTIONAL ENGINEERING

The making of constitutions is a specialist occupation of a species of constitutional lawyer, but also of a type of political scientist. Each constitution is its own thing, the product of specific circumstances and often of extraordinary political pressures; the role played by political science is often small. But there have been times and places, and South Africa in the postwar period has been one, when such analysts have played a decisive part in defining the kinds of constitutional arrangements that would be 'technically' the most appropriate.

In the recent history of South Africa, the constitutional engineers Lijphart and his followers have been especially influential.[2] These scholars have conceived South Africa as an ethnically riven society whose politics centre on ethnic identities: ethnicity pre-empts the rational individuality that is the (supposed) foundation for liberal politics; and political institutions must be designed to compensate for an absence of the preconditions for successful liberalism. They affirm that ethnicity or 'tribalism' is the key source of political danger in South Africa and that institutional solutions can ameliorate this danger.

This work is merely the latest example of the conventional priority attached to race in South African constitutional design. The first constitution of the Union of South Africa in 1910 provided for White and Black South Africans a perfect introduction to the dangers of constitutional government. Reflecting existing dispositions of power, it deprived Blacks of any real hope of shaping their own destiny and of participating with Whites in a single system of political authority. (It was, of course, also a constitution in the liberal democratic tradition.)

Perhaps the greatest South African leader, General J.C. Smuts, who went on to become a statesman of international standing and a founder of the League of Nations, introduced culture and nationality to this formula. He was a believer in the principles of freedom, justice and equality, and in the fundamental rights of all human beings (except for certain colonized peoples). He famously did not believe that African institutions should be pressed into an alien mould. In his 1929 Rhodes Memorial Lectures in Oxford, Smuts argued that 'The British Empire does not stand for the assimilation of its peoples into a common type; it does not stand for standardization, but for the fullest freest development of its peoples along their own specific lines.'[3] The National Party pursued this philosophy, if less high-mindedly, after it achieved its narrow success in 1948. Initial constitutional reforms were evidently self-serving. It moved rapidly to secure its electoral advantage by enfranchising White Namibians, ending the Cape property franchise and halting Indian parliamentary representation (instituted only in 1946). The 1950 Suppression of Communism Act was drafted so as to permit the designation of almost any person or organization as communist by the Minister of Justice. Later decades saw constitutional reform become a more direct instrument of control: the creation of Bantustan self-government; the deepening controls over political activity; and growing censorship: each of these was a form of quite proper constitutional reform.

Whereas homeland independence could be portrayed as an aspect of African decolonization – 'internal colonization' carried out by a benevolent and self-reducing republic – attempts to incorporate Indian and Coloured South Africans into a single constitutional framework with Whites (while ultimately denying them genuine power) seemed initially to lack precedent. The tricameral constitution has been misleadingly described as a way of 'sharing power without losing control'.[4] It did not in fact involve any genuine power-sharing. The design of institutions was driven by the size of population groups. A three-chamber parliament, based on the Population Registration Act, provided separate representation for Whites, Coloureds, and Indians (with 178 White, 85 Coloured and 45 Indian representatives). In matters of 'own affairs' – health, education, and welfare – each chamber had some freedom to set spending priorities within predetermined ceilings. 'General' affairs – those pertaining to all groups – were to be decided by a 'multiracial' cabinet drawn from the three chambers: taxation, foreign affairs, defence, law and order, commerce and African affairs were all to be determined 'jointly' in this way.

This new system was designed not merely to reorder executive power, but vastly to expand the power of the core executive. The president was now to be elected by the parliament (by an electorate of 50 White, 25 Coloured, and 13 Indian MPs) and he was to appoint cabinet ministers, dissolve parliament and rule as to which areas of policy were to count as 'own' or 'general'. The overall responsibility for African affairs lay with the president. He also had the power to refer any legislation opposed by one chamber to a White dominated President's Council. All of this allowed a White president, with control of the White chamber, to impose decisions by means of his automatic majority in the Council.

This, obviously, was not a subtle constitutional reform. Its effects on the opposition were striking: Sisk rightly notes that 'the new constitution precipitated the widespread domestic and subsequent international revolt against the South African government in the mid-1980s. Opponents of the system realized that the government was prepared to adjust minority domination but not abolish it.'[5] It also, however, introduced White South Africans to the possibilities offered by constitutional engineering. Many international constitutional experts seemed only too willing to provide the regime with internationally approved blueprints for further 'reform'.[6] Two frameworks were most widely promoted by overseas experts in the 1970s and 1980s: consociational democracy, based on 'consensus' and largely the initiative of the National Party; and a federal solution designed to protect territorial spheres of partial autonomy, the approach of the Inkatha Freedom Party.

We have seen that comparativists were willing to attribute to South Africa 'deep social cleavages' without investigating the nature of such purported divides. Lijphart's confidently proposed reforms carried weight because of his international renown and despite his seeming failure to carry out basic secondary research into South African society. For Lijphart, consociational democracy is a form of democracy to be found in countries 'deeply divided into distinct religious, ethnic, racial, or regional segments'.[7] The purported fact of social cleavage is more important to Lijphart than the quality, nature or significance of the division – a hangover from comparativists' early attempts to generate general theses about social division and political order. Lijphart identifies two features as the keys to existing consociational successes. First, they involve a 'grand coalition' in which there is shared decision-making by representatives of all segments where the matter is one of common concern. Second, there is 'segmental autonomy' on all other issues – on what apartheid engineers would call 'own affairs'.

Two further features of consociational democracy are secondary: proportionality and a minority veto. The notion of a minority veto over all significant decisions affecting that minority was evidently an added bonus for South Africa's White constitutionalists; the proportionality principle was less welcome in its implication of proportional representation for non-Whites and equality of allocation of resources and civil service posts. However, as with equality, so with proportionality: some ethnic groups' proportional allocations of jobs and money may be expected to be more proportional than those of others. Lijphart's features, moreover, are not prescriptions: consociationalism, on his account, is an 'ideal type' and real systems can expect to incorporate a number of abnormal features.[8]

Given the tidy formulations that they accomplished in the 1983 constitution – with Whites retaining control of a purportedly democratic system by means of all manner of quasi-consociational conjuring tricks – the full-blooded consociational option struck many Whites as a least worst option. Indeed, 'liberals' such as Helen Suzman were almost as likely as homeland leaders and conservatives such as chief Buthelezi and Lawrence Schlemmer to favour quasi-consociational solutions.[9] Consociationalism held four major problems, however, in South Africa: it was unlikely to work on the terms its analysts proposed for it; it failed to incorporate quite enough defences of privilege to satisfy Whites; it was rejected by most Black opinion; and it threatened to create the very problem it was advanced to solve.

South Africa did not meet the conditions for success that consociational theorists had identified in the method elsewhere. The 'segments' were ideally to be of roughly equal size with no single majority segment dominant. However, it has never been clear how South Africa can be characterized as a 'divided society'. Its racial, ethnic, linguistic, religious, political and regional divides are too multifarious and cross-cutting to be reduced to discrete categories. Afrikaner anthropologists, to be sure, considered the Republic contained Africans who were Zulu, Xhosa, Tswana, Venda or Pedi. However, this division into ethnicities has never been acceptable to the majority of those so classified or to the reputable analysts of South African history. The only two ethnic parties in the 1994 election, moreover, achieved less than 50 per cent of their target 'ethnic' support and managed to accumulate between them just 13 per cent of the poll.[10] Furthermore, Afrikaner and English were reduced to European for political purposes; Africans, by contrast, were divided into meaningless pseudo-ethnic fragments.

There was some sign of overarching loyalty to South Africa, a second condition favouring consociational success. Beyond that, however, all was negative. There were too many segments to make consensus easy (with 3–5 as the ideal); the population overall was too large; there was no perception of foreign threat to unite diverse groups; there was little tradition of political accommodation; and, perhaps most importantly, South Africa did not enjoy the high levels of socio-economic equality that consociational advocates themselves saw as a crucial condition for its likely success.[11] That the obvious failure of South Africa to meet conditions favourable to consociationalism did not alarm its advocates may indicate that their attention was wandering to narrower questions of tribalism. Engaged in debates with South African academics and policy-makers, and offering testimony to state-sponsored reform investigations, they became preoccupied with the pseudo-problem of inter-tribal conflict that had been so laboriously elaborated by conservative academics.[12] Lijphart even managed the following extraordinary prediction about the dangers that would follow the removal of Afrikaner control. While 'South Africa's ethnic cleavages are currently muted by the feelings of Black solidarity in opposition to White minority rule, they are *bound to reassert themselves* in a situation of universal suffrage and free electoral competition.'[13]

Consociationalism's second central flaw was that it failed to satisfy the ambitions of conservative Whites. The principle of proportionality could hardly be excluded altogether; and yet South Africa was so unequal that attempts to redistribute jobs and resources would inevitably cut deeply into White, and especially Afrikaner, systems of welfare support and job reservation. These systems, which had propelled Afrikaners into near equality with English speakers by the 1980s, were central to the National Party's electoral coalition. Many White South Africans, moreover, did not seem amenable even to formal equality of respect at elite level. Elite cooperation was unlikely to assuage conflict and represent a source of moderation while Afrikaners understood their destiny in grandiose historical terms.

Like all politics in this state, the claims of the White right were partly territorial; but the dispersion of Afrikaners (as well as their historical dependence on Black labour and contemporary urban indolence) made a territorial separatist solution inconceivable. Forced removals had combined with the pass laws to make African-ascribed ethnicity and imputed homeland citizenship conceivable bases for a combination of federal with consociational principles; but Afrikaners were concentrated only in the PWV region, and even there they were a small minority of the population as a whole. Nevertheless, whatever the objections from the conservative right, consociational proposals provided Whites' best hope of blocking a major transformation in the distribution of wealth and power in South Africa, and for this reason the proposals, for all their intellectual incoherence, may have had a benign unintended consequence: they drew the NP into negotiations, the outcome of which, if known in advance, would have led its leaders to baulk. Consociational proposals tempted the White elite into negotiations they were never to control.

Consociational solutions were never going to be implemented for a more important reason: the depth of opposition among Black South Africans. Comparativists, hosted by parastatals and academic institutions, may have failed to register the strength of this opposition (or discounted it in the face of the investigations of the Human Sciences Research Council and the Buthelezi Commission). There was, however, no possibility that Black political leaders active within South Africa in the 1980s would accept any constitutional settlement that entrenched apartheid categories. NP propagandists could produce little more than the acquiescence of some homeland leaders and captive Black elites already participating in the tricameral system. Evidence, as ever, is scarce, but the non-participation of the overwhelming majority of those designated Indian and Coloured in this system demonstrated *prima facie* resistance to its basic principles. The case among Africans seems equally clear: ethnic divisions simply did not represent substantial cleavages in Black South African society.[14] This was not merely a result of South Africa's history of population displacement, land alienation, urbanization and proletarianization across the nineteenth and twentieth centuries: it was also a direct response to the use of ethnic categories to justify and enforce apartheid.

Western analysts often shared with White South Africans an unlikely embrace of ethno-cultural essentialism, and seemingly could not help but treat ethnicity as prior to, and pre-emptive of, other forms of identity – and indeed of any form of human individuality. Many commentators learned intellectually that ethnicity could not rightly be understood in essentialist terms, but rather had to be understood as contextual, fluid and in part the creation of political agents (which included the Bantu Affairs Department). Their arguments, nevertheless, collapsed repeatedly into crude ethnic apriorism. The idea that an identity could be fixed was rejected intellectually by almost all analysts; yet they still wanted to retain the idea of a deeply and inherently divided society.[15]

The intellectual heart of consociationalism was always rotten. Its proponents predicated their prescriptions on the claim that there was no majority group in South Africa. No matter what historical and political experiences they have shared, whatever they may believe, and no matter how often they may assert doctrines quite to the contrary (Black Consciousness, non-racialism, pan-nationalism), Blacks are in reality divided into fairly small ethnic groups in accordance with the categorizations of the apartheid state. However, at the same time, there is a threat of majority domination (which justifies the resort to consociationalism in the first instance). This, it transpires, is the threat that the Black majority will seize power from the White minority and monopolize it. As MacDonald notes,

> if these abuses are caused by the majority, then surely a majority must exist, potentially if not actually; and if it does exist, the presumption that South Africa is composed entirely of minorities must be inoperative and the conclusions that follow from that prescription... must be reassessed.... Otherwise an absence (the majority) explains a presence (majority domination).[16]

The dangers of consociational proposals lie in their making ethnicity salient – indeed, inescapable – in political competition. As Welsh has noted, ethnicity's major stimulus in Africa has 'derived from the introduction of competitive politics' which can easily politicize differences of language and culture.[17] Consociational proposals may perhaps help contain politicised ethnicity when it already exists; but they seem certain to stimulate such politicization where it is not already a significant aspect of political competition.

In a society as unequal as South Africa, moreover, proposals that enforce ethnic labelling threaten to turn class conflicts into ethnic ones. 'Successful' consociational states have tended to exhibit very low levels of inequality, distributed within, rather than between, ethnic groups. South Africa's 'ethnic groups' divide into rich and poor; and the rich would inevitably use their minority powers to resist redistribution, an obstruction that would be registered in ethnic terms. 'Moderation' and 'stability', the watchwords of consociational thinkers, are all very well. But that 'which is being stabilised... and thus conserved', as MacDonald emphasizes, 'is in part the very society formed under apartheid.... Moderation, therefore, begins where apartheid left off.'[18] Where a society perceived as racially exploitative is 'stabilized', according to a formula rejected by most of its citizens, this is a recipe for less long-term stability rather than more.

Consociational specialists were used by government negotiators for their own purposes, rather than providing impartial advice as they presumably imagined. The NP, after all, was capable of ingenious constitutional manipulation all on its own. Its trumpeted reliance on the recommendations of foreign experts never led to an overturning of the party's orthodoxies. The echo of global political scientific expertise in dissembling government tracts was striking, as in this passage from the Minister for Constitutional Development in 1990: 'In divided societies such as South Africa, inter-ethnic parties are virtually unknown.... It follows that simple majority rule in divided societies will result in permanent rules and in permanent opposition parties.'[19] One legacy of political science's positivist heritage is that analysts conceive themselves to be set apart from the relations of power they are analysing. This sense is reinforced if they are overseas, in a poor state that is benefiting from their 'technical' expertise. The experience of comparativists in South Africa suggests that the interests they themselves serve should properly comprise a substantial aspect of their reflection and scholarship (and not merely represent an afterthought).

These experiences also suggest a commonality between consociational and communitarian theory. Each is most satisfying when addressed in general terms to the preconditions for social order between diverse 'segments' of a divided society, and to the conditions that must hold for the notion of the modern self to be coherent. Each, however, makes unfounded claims to be able to locate and define, quite unproblematically, the content of particular, actually existing constitutive identities or communities. There was an assumption, unimpeded by knowledge of those to whom the categories were applied, that these labels did have referents. In South Africa, consociationalists were willing to accept the guidance in this regard of local state functionaries.

MAKING ELECTIONS WORK

South Africa's 1994 election enjoyed unprecedented and extraordinary attention from the first world's media. Much of this was tedious recycling of images. Conservative commentators celebrated a multitude of smiling natives in an 'uhuru' election.[20] White liberals and gawking foreigners lauded long and 'multi-racial' queues. Even the best funded and most liberal of analysts shared four preoccupations with conservatives: queues, patience, heat and high expectations. 'Voters queued patiently for hours, often in hot and cramped conditions, many forced to return the second and some even the third election day, all determined to express their collective relief and expectations at the end of apartheid.'[21] It is churlish to complain about these patronizing commentaries, but their omnipresence is telling. Black South Africans are unfamiliar with neither hot weather, nor with grotesquely extended queuing; and their working hours and distance from places of work (when they have it) make rising before dawn a necessity and not a special event. Moreover, Blacks' employment (on election days as on public holidays) in White areas makes 'multi-racial queuing' unsurprising. (There were few, if any, international journalists on hand in Lebowa or Venda to record the absence of multi-racial queues.) Just as the motives and expectations of voters were obvious to Norwegian election observers, so one American political scientist was moved to observe that 'Black and White lined up together to inaugurate a new democracy. The mood was festive; the act of voting was a liberation from the chains of oppression for Black South Africans and began to lift the mantle of guilt for Whites.'[22]

Such effusions are symptoms of the elusive power that elections still possess for the Western political imagination. Elections are the central routinized public events in any modern polity. As Young points out, they are virtually unavoidable given the twin imperatives of large numbers of citizens and egalitarian doctrines.[23] The former rules out the conduct of public business in open meetings; and the latter renders inconceivable the advancement of personal characteristics (from heredity, to divine right to excellence) as sufficient entitlement to rule. But the prominence of elections reflects also their widespread appeal: even where ruling elites fail to respect rules of fairness and impartiality in electoral practices, it is elections that they feel they must manipulate (even when they can and do determine the result by fiat). The human significance of electoral choice, especially in the face of the overwhelming evidence of the individual's impotence in modern elections, remains elusive. The opacity of electoral politics is common to North and South. The South African election – and the manner in which it was analysed by academics and received by international publics – can help us to identify some of their most obscure aspects.

Political scientists have amassed much useful information on the effects of elections. Much of this has been organized under the rubrics of 'legitimation'. The notion of legitimacy in political theory has referred to the idea that the (legal) authority of a political order can be worthy of popular moral recognition. 'Legitimation', by contrast, has, since Max Weber, been a category of sociological analysis. It has referred to the capacity of a state to generate belief in the legitimacy of its rule among mass publics (rather than among the intellectual analysts of state legitimacy). Theoretical and legal analysts have focused on the problem of the modern state's capacity to rule justly and to maintain peace in a potentially (or necessarily) fractious society; or on an implicit contract between citizens which might morally ground the state's rule. Sociological analysts, by contrast, have used the notion of legitimation in a number of (slippery) ways, but always with scepticism about the coherence of the notion of obligation. The state has mostly been seen either as parasitic upon society, or as the instrument of class domination. It is the consent of subjects to this evidently unjust state of affairs that constitutes legitimation.

Elections have been considered legitimizing events in two ways. First, they have been seen as rituals by means of which the form of the state itself is rendered legitimate, regardless of the activities of any particular regime. In an electoral democracy, ultimate responsibility for outcomes is shouldered by electors in public discourse: they are the collectivity that has authorized their rulers to do wrong (or good) and that will judge them on their achievements. This is 'legitimation' rather than 'legitimacy', because of the mystified nature of the purported relationship between actual rulers (elite) and responsible collectivity (electors). Second, elections can be considered as legitimating of particular regimes. Such legitimation does not rest on any perceived ability fundamentally to change the nature of the social order. Rather, it rests on the perception that voters, within a given social order, have the (potential) power, through elections, to change the composition of ruling elites and the policies they promulgate.

This second usage is more sociologically plausible, in the sense that it better fits voters' professed understandings of the potential of their electoral power. But is also scarcely related at all to political authority. The replacement of one set of crooks by another – a plausible characterization of electoral politics from the perspective of the jaded elector – does not render any system of government 'legitimate' or morally worthy; and changes in the composition of elites can be immensely divisive – by class or by ethnic group. Multi-party systems in Africa in particular may be credited with the potential to create or exacerbate politicized ethnicity; by so doing, they can undermine the authority of the political order as a whole.

While 'legitimacy' and 'legitimation' have dominated the jurisprudence and sociology of electoral systems, they have not surprisingly provided little purchase on the popular significance of elections. Resting on the very modern view that 'legitimate' governments are those chosen by, and hence responsible to, their people, these views evade the realities of modern social life. 'Legitimacy', as Lonsdale has put it, 'is the universal aspiration of rulers, their occupational delusion, their search for power.' Reliance by the state on force is expensive and generates resistance, evasion and resignation on the part of the populace. 'By claiming responsibility rulers have hoped, literally, to convert that force into power, to carry society with them rather than always fighting against it. In other words, effective power can scarcely avoid submitting itself to some test of accountability.'[24]

Lonsdale exactly identifies the relationship between state power and popular aspiration that gives electoral politics its significance. People struggle everywhere to establish for themselves a right to be taken into account, economically and politically. The inherently conflictual nature of society makes it impossible for rulers to govern 'exclusively in their chief supporters' class interest'; and this means that 'to share out power is in a very real sense to create it. The contested accountability of power appears to be essential to its productivity.'[25] For this reason, rulers need to permit some negotiable freedom to their subjects. But those subjects are always aware of the unnegotiably constrained nature of that potential freedom, and their demands for and participation in electoral politics are always combinations of asserted self-worth with severely limited ambition.[26]

Elections have further significance for electors. In the West, cultural traits have been broadly homogeneous across electorates and stable systems of majority (and sometimes consociational) rule have postdated the creation of nation-states. Systems of representation, moreover, prefigured mass party organizations. In such situations, elections are reminders of the existence of a nation, of its unity as a political community, and of the unity of a state's authority. More elusively, elections remind citizens of the scale of modern politics in a world in which metaphors of personal agency, drawn from local settings, are the commonplaces of political debate. In African states, elections can serve as an assertion of these same facts of nation-building (or its absence) and of the scale and complexity of national political life.

The right to vote cannot therefore be understood directly as a symbol of equality. It draws attention to and reminds of inequality. The social divisions of industrial society were built into the foundations of mass democratic politics in the West. In Africa, political rights were conferred on Africans by departing colonial powers just as these nascent nations became acutely aware of their own internal divisions.[27] Elections, moreover, are explicit expressions of desire, from the weak to the strong. They are claims to equality, but also recognitions of its absence in routine politics. They are in this sense achievements: recognitions by the more powerful of the right of the somewhat weaker to an institutionalized participation in the decisions that affect their lives. Democracy in this sense is an outcome, and an achievement of struggle.

Electoral democracy is also a cause: participation in elections has effects, in terms of the composition of elites, the importance of social division, the content of public policy and the social outcomes of state actions. Democracy-as-effect and democracy-as-cause are tightly, if untransparently, related: for it is the consequences that can follow from voting that make the right to participate a symbol of respect (and achievement); and it is the accordance of respect that generates the otherwise irrational obligation that motivates participation in an election.

The instrumental irrationality of electoral participation seems evident. It is not merely that it is more likely that the voter will be run over by a bus on the way to the polling station than for her vote to make a difference to the outcome of an election.[28] It is also that the benefits of voting are most closely tied to personal rather than collective consequences. Personal integrity is enhanced by the need to decide in the face of personal uncertainty, contradictory inclinations and aspirations; gains in personal moral and cognitive capacity follow from engagement in electoral politics.

It is equally plain that instrumental accounts that focus on policy-making outcomes are very hard to construct. While analysts have demonstrated some relationship between voters' perceptions of economic policy-making success and their support for political leaders, the nature of this relationship remains opaque. In particular, the complexity and intractability of economic policy-making debates makes it hard to view the relationship as an expression of rationality.[29]

Some analysts have gone further. Young, for example, while rightly identifying the double standards of analysts who seek to apply to Africans yardsticks of rational behaviour that Western electorates have never approached, states that 'the emancipated citizen/voter has proved to be a chimera.' He quotes Dryzek that voters 'have proved ignorant and intolerant. They pay scant attention to the political issues of the day, vote under the sway of psychological forces outside their control and generally lack the virtues thought... necessary in a democratic citizenry.'[30]

The difficulties academic analysts have faced have stemmed in part from the impossibility of the task they have set themselves and in part from a confusion of analytical apparatus with reality. Their task – predicting and explaining the political affiliations and voting practices of citizens – would only be truly tractable if voters had easily determinable interests and projects. The confusion of model with reality has been a common failing of social science. Two models of human behaviour have dominated studies of political affiliation: identification models and rational choice models. Neither is founded in plausible assumptions about human behaviour. The first, an analogy with the processes by means of which infants respond to figures of authority, has inevitably best fitted sceptical readings of the political intelligence of citizens. The second, equally unsurprisingly, has been advanced as prescriptive as well as descriptive. (Those who most resemble academic analysts have registered as those closest to rational behaviour.)[31]

The analysis of political attitudes and voting behaviour is as difficult in South Africa as in the US or the UK, and only limited resources have been devoted to it. South African researchers, however, have made use of voter models in a distinctive way: they have applied different models to different racial groups without explicit justification. Taylor and Orkin's pathbreaking analysis of the racialization of South African social science has exposed the way in which assumptions about race and ethnicity have undermined 'mainstream' social science in South Africa.[32] The presumed fact of ethnic division has shaped survey questions and the collation of findings; and selective and manipulative choices in questions and answers have been used to organize results. Taylor and Orkin argue that these practices amount to 'inscription' rather than description, in that racial and ethnic categories are used so as to uphold the advantages of the powerful and privileged.

The consequences of the assumption that priority should be accorded to ethnic and racial categories can be most clearly seen in the most widely disseminated (and best funded) study of political attitudes and the 1994 election in South Africa, Johnson and Schlemmer's *Launching Democracy in South Africa*. This book has aroused a lively debate, but perhaps for the wrong reasons. It presents the findings of a major opinion research project, for which the Institute for Multi-Party Democracy (IMD) received funding from USAID and Westminster Foundation for Democracy as well as the South African corporate sector, and which Yale University has now graced with its imprimatur. Controversy has centred on allegations of bias against the African National Congress; Shula Marks's comments on 'the almost visceral hostility to the ANC which seeps insidiously through the text' stung R.W. Johnson, who headed the study, into deriding Marks's personal and scholarly commitment.

Whether the book has a partisan agenda is not an irrelevant issue, and one to which we shall have to return. However, while the text is full of throw-away lines, these are almost endearingly transparent: as when, for example, Johnson and his co-editor Schlemmer confide that 'Xhosa' respondents were 'staggeringly' less independent-minded than 'Zulus.'[33] More important, perhaps, is the reliability and value of the opinion surveys themselves. After all, very little survey research has been conducted into political attitudes in South Africa, and this project included two nationwide polls (of 4,000 and 2,000 voters respectively) as well as two large-scale surveys in the three most populous regions.

The need for systematic survey research is especially urgent because much of the data on political attitudes that has been collected to date in opinion polls and market research (on which the present text occasionally draws) is of such poor quality. Statistics have been collected in extraordinary ways in South Africa, especially when Black communities are surveyed. Samples taken in African areas have been based on crude estimates of population. Large assumptions about ethnic identity and social structure have been made, often highly inappropriate to the social fluidity and geographical mobility of individuals and households. Survey designers lack relevant languages and understanding of interview context. Black university students and middle-aged ladies from churches – two of the most morally and physically intimidating categories of township residents – are the usual interviewers, producing inevitable distortion.

While money was presumably not a major problem in this project, it is hard to assess how far the IMD surveys improve on their ancestors. The pages seem at first sight to contain masses of useful survey information and analysis and a profusion of tables and charts, but on investigation these prove to be mostly misleading and unserviceable. Sampling techniques are not explained other than to say that samples were 'stratified' (we are not told how: by income? by age? by rural versus urban residence? or solely by race?). Although they are described as 'random probability' samples, significance levels are not given for the correlations asserted. The omission of any breakdown of data by sex, let alone any account of gender issues in survey design and interpretation, is particularly unhelpful. ('Women' do pop up once, mysteriously, as more likely than men to support higher taxes on alcohol and cigarettes – 'doubtless because they drink and smoke less', the authors helpfully supply.[34])

Finally, the survey designs and interview methods are seldom explained. Nowhere are the actual questions posed reprinted in full, and systematic discussion of potential sources of bias and inaccuracy is strikingly absent. Unless, that is, one counts Chris de Kock's brief aside on the limitations of telephone surveys, 'which of course do not reach people at the lower socioeconomic levels'[35] and hence, he wants to argue, underestimate levels of IFP support compared to house-to-house surveys. However, other survey instruments, as he neglects to add, may equally under-represent certain groups, such as poor and rural people, women or youth. Political bias is not the issue. Any author using statistics can be carried away by the desire to confirm her intuitions, and along the way it is all too easy to overlook inadequacy or bias in a sample, to write questions that answer themselves, or to select insufficiently stringent tests of significance. Careful interrogation of method and interpretation on the part of the reader is the only safeguard, and Johnson and Schlemmer do not provide their audience with the resources necessary for such oversight.

Although ethnicity (as opposed to income, age, gender or any other factor) is the only analytic category employed in most of the book, how ethnic ascriptions were made is apparently too obvious to require any explanation. As conventional South African practice is glossed by de Kock, 'the positions and roles of the four population groups – Whites as the wielders of power, Africans as the subordinate group mobilised for resistance and coloureds and Indians as marginalised groups – meant that the questions put to one group were not always relevant to the others'.[36] De Kock weakly argues that 'the decision was made to treat the various population groups separately for the purposes of this analysis, especially since the legacy of apartheid is that population group (race) remains a major explanatory variable.'

Racial categories loom so large in our editors' minds that individuals are ascribed characteristics on the basis of aggregated survey results. Exploring political tolerance by means of questions on permissible political activity of opponents in a neighbourhood, for example,

Johnson discovers high proportions of all 'groups' offer responses that seem intolerant – but with a slightly higher proportion of Coloured than Indian or White respondents giving responses deemed intolerant. No effort is made to analyse the data other than by racial category. Moreover, rather than seeing that the data suggest that 'fewer Coloureds than Indians were tolerant' – an interpretation which opens up interesting questions such as which ones and why? – Johnson insists that 'Coloureds were less tolerant' than Indians.[37] Elsewhere, we are similarly told that Indians and Coloureds are relatively cautious, Africans are especially intolerant and that Inkatha supporters are timid.

When it suits their argument, contributors all too quickly assume that responses reflect reality. Johnson and Paulus Zulu, for example, report that '24 per cent of Whites and 20 per cent of Coloureds said their views had changed' over a given three-month period, and they contrast this with the fixed views of Africans. A professional analyst might investigate the self-conceptions of different voters and try to explain why some conceive of themselves as rational choosers in an electoral market (given the evident reality of political identification). Johnson, by contrast seems to believe that such a market exists, and seems in this way to ignore the findings of political sociology. This perception is confirmed by the authors' statement that 'African voters gave the impression of having made one big choice – of their party – and of then orienting all other attitudes around that'[38] – once again a seeming indicator of absence of self-deceit.

Indeed, the validation of the surveys and of the election itself is accomplished by means of a tidy circular argument. Our editors seem happy to see their pre-election voting intention surveys used as evidence in judging whether the election itself was free or fair – particularly in KwaZulu-Natal. At the same time, however, the fact that election results broadly matched their polls is used as a justification for trusting the poll data themselves: 'The results of the surveys... certainly appear to be sufficiently valid to offer representative insights as regards other aspects of the responses of voters.'[39] This unsatisfactory procedure both substitutes for adequate analysis of electoral procedures – on which we are offered anecdotes and a couple of personal interviews with interested parties – and casts an inappropriately rosy light over the project's own research.

Only the Western Cape study evades the survey quagmire. Aware that voter attitudes to policies and leaders are secondary phenomena in any polity, with voters tending to have 'previously established "identifications" with parties, usually based on socialization and evaluations of past party performance', Robert Mattes and his team do not have to fill page after page demonstrating that exactly this is true of African voters. Those wondering how a province with a minority of White voters could return the National Party, the party of apartheid, to power will find persuasive answers here, and along the way will discover a mass of fascinating information about sources of political information, political tolerance, and the unexpectedly limited role of religion and language in the voting patterns of Coloured electors. Most importantly, however, the authors go beyond the crude categorization of all respondents by racial group, and interrogate the notion that the election was an 'ethnic census'. They recognize that 'if the importance of race emanated from the role given to it by apartheid, one might have expected the election to pit the coloured and Black victims of apartheid equally against their former White oppressors', and look for the ways in which race, through its determining effect on social location under apartheid, might have 'shaped the larger class structures, economic incentives and life chances which themselves might more directly relate to voting behaviour'.[40] Sophisticated analyses of this kind should have been delivered in other regions.

Other than in this chapter, conclusions drawn on the basis of surveys nearly always go beyond those which results can really justify. De Kock responds to his own question: 'What message is conveyed by the sociopolitical trends of the past decade?' with the recommendation that the

> government of National Unity – and any subsequent government – will at all times have to ensure an optimal balance between freedom and order... [and]... therefore has to bear in mind that order without freedom (a dictatorship, for example), while obviously highly undesirable, is possible; but that freedom without order is impossible, for freedom without order would result in a Hobbesian "war of all against all", in which only the strongest is free.[41]

The inhabitants of poor Hobbes' state of nature make few appearances, perhaps because an international audience might not catch on to its intended referent; but also because it advances a conception of African society that runs counter to the concept of 'mobilized community'. According to Johnson, this concept is the key to understanding his second extended preoccupation: the absence of freedom in the African vote.

The reader is briefed early on in a section on 'The National Party's Lost African Vote' about a slippage of potential African support for the National Party which is purportedly 'the key to the entire election'.[42] Johnson makes some noise about violence and intimidation – themes that deserve more serious treatment given their role in the election – but his intention is plainly to reflect more profoundly on the nature of African society and individuality. 'All told', he hazards, 'one had the impression that Africans, particularly those in an urban context, were subject to a great battery of pressures emanating from many different parts of the social structure, while their non-African counterparts experienced significant (and far less) pressure only from friends, colleagues, family members and politicians.' This is not a matter of open intimidation. Indeed, surveys 'left no doubt that the approaching election was viewed in a quite special way, with a mood of excitement, even euphoria, apparent among many African (and some Indian and coloured) voters.' Later surveys even identified 'African euphoria' or 'the state of elation we have come to regard as typical of a "liberation" or "uhuru" election'.[43] Johnson's case, rather, turns on the elusive existential quality that he sees in non-African electoral choice.

This matter is best introduced through Gotz's and Shaw's chapter on 'Choice and First-Time Voters in Gauteng'. They believe 'real democratic choice is a liberating act of self-analysis and expression of personal will behind an effective veil of anonymity' and this raises the problem that 'if subjects' identities are formed within an over-determining social context, is it not possible that this context might impose certain attributes that would secretly constrain those subjects when they come to exercise democratic choice?' They suggest a stark dichotomy.

> Were voters pure and passive products of their social situation, compelled to mark the ballot paper in a particular way by the daunting constraints imposed by their communal context? Or did they instead carry their social situation into the ballot box in an eminently critical and creative manner by shrugging off the determinism of their society and history and choosing autonomously?[44]

This combination of potted philosophy with flattery of the electoral choices of the civilized peoples characterizes many Western commentaries on the election, and Gotz and Shaw perhaps should not be castigated for following them.

Johnson, however, is clear about what he is saying. 'The possibility of privatised space and individualistic behaviour is simply less than it is within the more atomised and suburban lifestyles of the non-African communities.'[45] Indeed, community mobilization is a condition under which community members are mobilised by means of multiple pressures within an extremely dense environment, that density being both physical (as in the crowded confines of a squatter camp, township or favela) and social (with a closely surrounding network of street, area and party committees, church and trade union groups, civic associations, relatives, and so on).

'Individuals', indeed, 'are subjected to such massive and continuous pressures to take one particular direction that they are both coerced into taking it and yet are also happy to take it, in some sense the decision is also voluntary.' Thus not only do outsiders find it hard to know if a choice was voluntary, 'the individuals might not be sure themselves'.[46] Africans are not only incapable of existential choice in the ballot box, but do not even realize that this is the case.

The editors build on their model of African society to castigate Africans for not learning the lessons of Thatcherism. Leading questions fail to elicit a clamour for redistribution policies: given the opportunity to select the three most important problems before the government, unemployment was mentioned by 60 per cent, housing by 55 per cent, education by 34 per cent and lack of water by 25 per cent, but only around 2 per cent mentioned 'reducing the gap between rich and poor' as among the key three issues, and a similar number land reform. 'On this evidence the more radical and redistributive policies being urged by the ANC left had little popular backing.' At the same time, the editors uncover a 'culture of entitlement' and support for 'tax-and-spend policies' in respondents' selection of jobs, housing, education and water over foreign investment, low inflation and stable taxes as priorities for government. Indeed, 74 per cent of Africans wanted more spent on health, education and housing even if that 'means extra taxes for everyone' – what the authors describe as 'a comfort for ANC radicals'. 'African opinion did not explicitly favour redistributive measures, but it did so implicitly, perhaps even unconsciously.'[47]

Such arguments bring us back to the question of the political biases embedded in the book, and especially in the chapters by Johnson. Over the past five years, Johnson has acquired some notoriety from broadsides against the ANC, exposes of the secret cabal of Indian communists who really run it and dire predictions of a slide into civil war ('during the suffering to come South Africa will be the land of the politically correct and the dead') or (when that failed to materialize) a steady march towards authoritarian rule. Although he here relinquishes the persona of journalistic gadfly for that of political scientist with clipboard, connoisseurs of Johnsonian reasoning will recognize several classic examples of his inimitable style of analysis. Narrating the political background of the 1980s, Johnson and Schlemmer construct in one paragraph a bizarre chain of causality which seems to hold the leader of the ANC-aligned Confederation of South African Trade Unions responsible for years of bitter violence:

> The COSATU president... launched a bitter attack on Chief Buthelezi at the COSATU founding congress in Durban; with this the implicit opposition between the UDF and Buthelezi's Inkatha movement took a new turn. Predictably, an Inkatha trade union federation... was soon formed to oppose COSATU. Bitter fighting between the two sides became entrenched, particularly in the killing fields of KwaZulu-Natal. By the time of the 1994 election more than 10,000 had died in this conflict.[48]

More dubious still is Johnson's and Schlemmer's determination to ignore evidence that 'Black-on-Black violence' was in part mobilized by state security forces (the so-called 'Third Force' thesis). The existence of police hit squads following commands issued at high levels; the training of Inkatha killers by the military; and the use of decommissioned soldiers to massacre train passengers have all now been documented. Recently released cabinet notes from post-Soweto 1976 record Jimmy Kruger, Minister of Justice, arguing that 'the police must perhaps act more drastically to bring about more deaths'.[49] Johnson's and Schlemmer's insistence on 'ethnic' identity as the touchstone of political conflict between Africans, and hence an implied cause of their alleged incapacity to adopt genuinely democratic habits of tolerance and freedom of conscience, looks increasingly indefensible.

In the past, Johnson's talent for incensing his enemies has sometimes been valuably directed at the myth and humbug produced by the current party of government. Survey research, however, is not the right vehicle for such an exercise. When Johnson and Schlemmer categorize affirmative action and 'rejection of White role models' as 'radical' views, prescribe that holding government primarily responsible for improving standards of living is incompatible with 'a healthy democratic political culture', explain that urban communities' aspirations for better housing reflect elemental emotions rather than justifiable political demands, or use acceptance of the uncontroversial truth [sic] 'that most popular needs can only be met through rapid economic growth' as a standard of political rationality,[50] they not only insult their readers, they also do not enhance the reputations of the project's backers. USAID and the Westminster Foundation are among the institutions that, by investing aid funds, have also lent international credibility to the project. Yale University Press has not helped matters by publishing the research in its current form.

Johnson and Schlemmer's work represents merely the most widely disseminated study of the election and that with the greatest weight of support within South Africa's social science establishment. As Orkin and Taylor have demonstrated so persuasively, the relationships between quantitative sociological and political science research and powerful interests are extraordinarily close in South Africa. A small coterie of academics has secured a near-monopoly of funding from key parastatal and corporate sponsors; they have been involved in the major regionally focused reformist projects (especially in KwaZulu and Natal); and they have enjoyed the patronage and publishing access of the Human Sciences Research Council and the South African Institute of Race Relations.[51]

As Taylor and Orkin indicate, however, the role of what they describe as racial and ethnic 'common sense' has been crucial. It has been all too easy to convince professional analysts to adopt a primordialist or essentialist view of ethnicity; and they have been still more willing to accept somewhat more complex, but ultimately unfounded, analyses of racial and ethnic consciousness as latent potentials.[52] International colleagues have failed to resist this tendency. This may not be surprising. Racial and ethnic categorization is a product of European thought, and in particular of nineteenth century anthropological fantasies; it can scarcely be said to have been expunged from Western social thought.[53] If racial categories play a problematic role in contemporary Western sociology and social policy, the notion of tribalism, concealed beneath the veneer of 'ethnic identification', continues to dominate the analysis of postcolonial Africa. Western social scientists, for this reason, are an uncertain umpire in disputes between conservative and radical in South African social science. Indeed, the influence has been more likely to operate in the other direction: the clearly unsupported assertion of racial categories in South Africa's social analysis may help Western analysts to seek out better concealed assumptions lurking within their own social investigations.

The future of South African political science is likely to be brighter, on this score, than its past. Increasing levels of technical proficiency in quantitative analysis can be expected to bring new scepticism to traditional research practices; and that machinery which political science has developed to challenge, rather than merely to bolster, the presuppositions of its analysts will be brought to bear more consistently. Fascinating research has been conducted already, including at least one important study of political attitudes and the 1994 election which has received little attention.[54] Equally importantly, many analysts are exploring the very different natures of elections and election campaigning in different parts of South Africa without resorting to racialization. Lodge, for example, has sketched out the differences between the kinds of electoral contests that have characterized postcolonial India and parts of the British West Indies from those that taken place in Western Europe and North America.[55] The former, characterized by a liberation movement's fusion of voluntary associations, powerful ideological loyalties and limited tolerance of opposition, in a territorial politics, Lodge takes to lie side by side with a Western media-driven, purportedly issue-centred, and party competitive election in the urban areas. Such an account, based on attention to institutions, political movements and their histories, can capture the diversity of experiences within South Africa without resort to collective psychological attributes.

COMPARATIVE POLITICAL SCIENCE AND THE FUTURE OF SOUTH AFRICA

Explanation, Prediction and Policy

Comparative political science research in South Africa now focuses on the analysis of transition from authoritarian rule and the consolidation of democracy. The formal definitions of democracy needed to make democratizations comparable at all have directed attention away from the consequences that follow from democratization. The transition literature has been retrospective; but the increasing focus on the ways in which the nature of the regime of transition influences the future,[56] and the shift towards the study of consolidation, have helped to make comparative politics more forward-looking. One central interest lies in the sustainability of democracy or in the degree to which it will be 'successful' as a regime type in new circumstances. Almost incidentally this had led to study of the practical consequences of democratic politics in new democracies and the degree to which such politics can be regarded as necessarily (or regularly) benign.[57]

Political scientists have advanced hypotheses about consolidation which may reassure South Africans. Communist regimes bequeath command economies in near-collapse, and military governments leave a need for state reorganization and de-militarization. South Africa, by contrast, has a commercial economy and civilian rule. As elsewhere, however, the organization of executive authority that is required for the first stage of reforms to be successful may well inhibit the creation of the wider coalitions and party system through which democratic rule can be stably perpetuated.[58] The relationships between a powerful working class, populism and capitalist (dis)investment and reaction, moreover, remain opaque. Other factors such as 'political culture', national unity and state infrastructural capacity have been advanced as beneficial for (or even necessary to) consolidation, and in none of these areas does South Africa score highly.[59]

Yet even consolidation analysis is retrospective in the sense that it is shaped by history. Hypotheses are advanced and abandoned in response to the fortunes of the new democracies. The experiences of African states, as with transition, are little registered. Generalizations about the poor, infrastructurally weak and nationally disunited (or never united) states of sub-Saharan Africa are based on a few cases over a short period of time. Observation effects, the role of inter-governmental organizations, other states and international financial and charitable organizations in the prospects of these states, are new phenomena. One major concern of South African political science has been to try to improve on the quality of knowledge within the country of its future 'trends' or 'prospects': this has been a project designed not to predict, but to facilitate, political agency.

Scenarios

Scenario-building has been the most distinctive activity in which South Africa's domestic political analysts have participated to make available to decision-makers projections of the country's possible social and economic futures. Scenario-creation evolved out of attempts by business analysts to predict and influence the major trends affecting their corporate operating environment. Scenarios differ from mere projections in that they incorporate strategy and agency: they provide a set of structured possible futures which represent the outcome not just of trends but also of actions – whether these be the actions of political movements, leaders, bureaucrats, business competitors or the scenario-sponsoring business itself.

Scenarios are therefore ideally the instruments of businesses with very long-range time horizons, heavy fixed investments (requiring protection), a vulnerability to political or economic change and the political muscle to influence the events the scenario is designed to analyse. It was unsurprising, therefore, to find the Anglo-American corporation at the centre of the fashionable scenario-building process that began in the 1980s. Mineral corporations need scenarios more than any: they have massive investments that cannot easily be withdrawn and that pay for themselves only after decades; they are massively dependent on prospecting and property rights; they are vulnerable to creeping taxation levels; and they are extremely demanding in their requirements for labour and infrastructure.

Corporations in South Africa, moreover, face special difficulties. While political risk analysis is often stereotyped as the attempt to predict a political earthquake – a revolution, social collapse, widespread nationalization, military coup – it is actually far more often a modest attempt to avoid domestication. The key threats to business in most 'emerging markets' are not eruptions but encroachments: local content rules, price controls, affirmative action or local representation demands, shipping requirements, tax regime modifications, export controls, sales policy regulations, industrial relations legislation, foreign capital requirements, import controls – and a thousand other potential threats to the profitability of investments. Political risk, moreover, is nearly always specific to a firm or to a sector, since the probability of any event affects each organization in a different way. In South Africa, however, big business was faced with the danger of seemingly genuine unpredictability: nationalization, social disorder and economic collapse all appeared, to some, to be on the cards. In these circumstances, scenario-building became pervasive. It spread from mining to the financial sector and then to South Africa's progressive intellectuals.[60] Today, the fashion has spread still further to the main trade union federation. More important than the proliferation of sources of scenarios has been their transformation into public documents. No business documents these, designed to steal a march on competitors or help shape company–state relations: scenarios, rather, have become an overt means of addressing public opinion and commenting on the prudence of policy choices.

A scenario that is a public document, published and distributed to wide audiences in business, state and civil society, keeps to business scenario protocols for the sake of authority alone. Business scenarios are designed with both positive and negative purposes in mind: the greatest weakness a political risk analysis can display is a failure to treat risk and opportunity as relations. Business projections that paint an unduly gloomy picture create missed opportunities, and so cause commercial harm. Public scenarios, by contrast, have been inherently conservative documents. They have been designed not to create an opportunity for some, on the basis of a commercial logic, but to offer a shared framework for the benefit, purportedly, of all. The audience, moreover, has had to be won over with no logic of profit to which to appeal.

In practice, South African scenarios have been designed for two audiences. The first was White opinion-followers whose fight-or-flight reflexes were equally to be discouraged. Their superstitions – the potential collapse of public order and the coming worthlessness of the Rand – were given starring roles in most scenarios. The second audience was a hypothetical one in the ranks of the ANC: rabid populists with an ideological commitment to nationalization were imagined by many businessmen to dominate the exile movement, and White political leaders saw them as genuine threats to the country's future. The ramifications of populism and nationalization were to be starkly demonstrated in scenarios for the benefit of such hypothetical radicals. Scenarios thus became exercises in reassuring the hysterical about the intentions of the nonexistent.

Political analysts' role in scenario-building projects was important. While the core of every scenario was a politically informed analysis of the (mostly unnegotiable) realities of the worlds of finance and commerce, the main threats and opportunities were perceived to lie in the ideological and social uncertainties that surrounded key groups. The 'socialism' to be found, it was thought, across the ANC leadership; the influences of Soviet, Cuban, Swedish-domiciled exiles; the infiltration of the SACP throughout the ANC leadership; and the populist leaders of the 'township masses' whose unrealistic expectations had to be reined in: all of these were imagined dangers to a business world more isolated than most from the attitudes of potential electors and governors.

The uncertainty about political strategy shown by White business elites was shared not merely by the majority of Whites in professional occupations (including academia, journalism and teaching) but also by many in the ANC themselves. Many of the movement's leaders did in fact believe themselves to be socialists, and many members of the SACP considered themselves communists; and the exiles and Robben Islanders were uncertain about the extent of popular clamour for the redistributive measures that they may already have decided were impossible or counterproductive. Scenarios also promised to bolster ANC leaders' negotiating position. The consequences of stalling by the government could be portrayed in stark terms, as the loss of a possibly bright future and one further turn down a scenario branch line towards chaos. The notion that a range of extremists waited in the wings of the ANC–SACP–COSATU alliance, moreover, provided a counterpoint to the NP's purported worries about extremist Afrikaner nationalism. Just as, for the right, scenarios were designed to discredit populist programmes seeking to meet the 'high expectations' of the 'masses', so, for the left, they could hold up those same quite hypothetical expectations as a threat with which to intimidate conservatives into concession.

All of this suggests that scenarios played a role a long way from that attributed to them by Adam and Moodley, who commented that they were 'useful exercises in opening the apartheid mind among Blacks and Whites alike. Political scenarios can challenge frozen mental maps and stimulate alternative, innovative thoughts and policies for coping with apartheid's fallout.'[61] They seem, rather, to be the vehicles for a setting of limits to mutual intimidation, by showing when and how posturing might spiral into a mutually damaging pitched battle. They are either designed by political elites to promote pre-ordained agreements, or they are directly prescriptive, reinforcing the boundaries of the possible by curtailing responses to the immediate crises of poverty that the new government would face. In both propaganda and prescriptive roles, scenarios proved to be quite effective (and cost-effective) instruments of business.

Policy Science

The coal faces of public administration and public policy analysis are less well populated with political analysts than the high-altitude world of scenario-building. Yet the local and the particular are the most demanding and important areas for research today: the local politics of administrative reorganization (especially in homelands, but elsewhere too as tax bases are reorganized after decades of segregation); community power studies, with a focus on increasing the efficacy and cost-effectiveness of public policy (in the provision of water, electricity, communications, medical care, transport, education, policing); political violence; and the local interfaces between 'traditional' and monetary bases of (collective) resource allocation. Traditional divisions of labour within South African academic life have not fully broken down, and much Black South African politics is regarded as ethnography. Even as analysts increasingly escape these constraints, the obstacles to research remain extreme: there are conventional challenges associated with language, political culture and social fluidity in a fast-changing state; there is the complexity of extended and unique processes of obstructed modernization, proletarianization and urbanization; and there is residual suspicion of the role of academics in a society in which their analysis has been so consistently (and without repentance) an instrument of oppression.

To the degree that South African political science has a common perspective, it is that of White South Africa in retreat. Crime, policing, violence (by Blacks on Whites) and public order are massively over-represented. The lack of familiarity with Black politics, moreover, is manifested repeatedly in the ascription still of diverse (and bizarre) models of cognition to different racial groups. Two kinds of category have dominated discussions of public policy. 'High expectations' have been everywhere in the media, academic analysis and public debate, while it has never been clear to what phenomenon this phrase might refer. In particular, it has been repeatedly suggested that massive, unmet demands for redistribution exist 'in the townships', that metaphysical world as yet empirically little explored by South African political science.

The second prevalent idiom has been the language of human rights. Displaying considerable verbal agility, a whole generation of South African political analysts has become fluent in the international idiom of human rights. This has not prompted constructive reform: the assertion of a right is always easier than the analysis of the institutions through which it might be exercised (or of the history of the institutions by means of which it continues to be denied). Human rights are an important matter in a state such as South Africa. But they lie at some distance from the public policy concerns of most citizens.

This distance weakens policy science all the way through. The reliance of social knowledge on the penetration of society by state institutions is widely recognized. The absence of basic information about South Africa's former homelands therefore provides an unsurprising and powerful obstacle to public policy. The handicap faced by quasi-state institutions is equally sharp. This was demonstrated by the performance of the Independent Electoral Commission during 1994, with its inability to assemble basic information upon which to base its logistical efforts. Universities, however, dependent on the same sources of information, and staffed by similarly isolated academics, have masked their weaknesses behind the myth of academic detachment and the specialist techniques attributed to social science. South Africa's White universities were fertile grounds for opposition to apartheid. Memorable achievements, however, occurred in spite of the specialist techniques of political and social science rather than because of them. The role of such techniques in twentieth-century South Africa was overwhelmingly to aid the definition, organization and prosecution of apartheid rather than to assist in challenging it.

8 Conclusions

This book began with the observation that South Africa's 1994 election attracted unprecedented attention from the publics of the wealthy democracies. The politics of the Republic have also fascinated Western European and North American academic analysts. I have used their professional academic investigations into South Africa's politics to explore the nature of political science as a discipline, and (more tangentially) as a window onto the travails of western liberal democracies themselves.

Chapter 2 introduced the political history of what is today South Africa by means of a fourfold periodization. Organizing the history of a country is never a politically or theoretically innocent activity, and my intention was to challenge a privileging of purportedly pivotal dates in southern Africa that has supported deterministic, racialized or ethnonationalist histories. While the conflicting societies of pre-1870s southern Africa could never be provided with a common history, the minerals revolutions represented a massive common experience for hitherto discrete groups. The ramifications of mineral discoveries – in unification, war, development and quasi-proletarianization – created an otherwise unlikely state and laid institutional foundations for the country's later social trajectory.

Between 1910 and 1960, contingencies and agency, including African collaboration and resistance, shaped the segregationist social order, but could not transform it. The commonplace idea that 1948 represented a 'watershed', on my account, is a hangover from English-speakers' moralizing and Afrikaners' misplaced belief in their own capacity to implement a 'grand plan' apartheid. Recent scholarship has shown the options available to the 1948 government, and its capacity to direct change, were both limited. The 1940s and 1950s displayed remarkable continuity from the earlier segregationist era. By contrast, the age of high apartheid from 1960 represented something quite exceptional internationally, and in the history of this state. The role of ethnic definitions in policy design, the scale of social engineering, the consequent changes in class structure and the extraordinary statism of labour and security controls: this all represented an unprecedented combination.

Chapter 3 explored the academic literature on South Africa and its history, with an eye to how historical writing naturalizes collectivities so creating implicit claims about the rights and obligations of constructed social groups. I examined the weak self-conscious ethnic narratives of Afrikaner, African, Coloured and Indian, before investigating in greater depth the more extensive professional literature of English-speaking liberal South Africa. Afrikaners' historical literature famously played a pivotal role in the creation of Afrikaner nationalism. However, compressed time horizons, the picture-book quality of the tale – colony, trek, war, concentration camp, language movement, election triumph and republic – the limited Afrikaner ethnic vote even in the 1948 election and the adaptability of modern Afrikaner identity, all suggest that the force and constitutive nature of this history have been overrated. Afrikaner history was perpetuated by success: power validated a tale of collective destiny. African, Coloured and Indian South Africans – none constituting a group with obvious unifying historical experiences – had neither the reason nor ability to construct and disseminate ethnic histories.

Four points of departure for political analysis emerged from my survey of English-language historical debates. First, the underdevelopment of comparative political analysis, in contrast to the politics-rich historical literature, resulted from a necessary dependence upon historical analysis in elaborating central categories of social description. Second, functionalism has been widespread in historical-political analysis, and contingency and conflict underemphasized. The South African state has been analysed as the vehicle of an imperial project, and as an instrument of Afrikaner advance. Revisionists initially considered the state the servant of the capitalist class, or of fractions of that class. The common-sense academic template, whatever the content of analysis, remained stubbornly functionalist. Third, and partly in consequence, political and institutional innovation has been poorly understood. Fourth, implicit moral appraisal and self-appraisal within the historical literature has been organised around the self-understandings of liberal Whites.

Chapters 4–7 systematically explored how political analysis might help remedy the weaknesses of historical analysis. Chapter 4 addressed the relationship between the systematic racial oppression of segregation and apartheid, and the ideas and practices associated with liberal democracy. The 'end of apartheid' is generally narrated as an uplifting tale in which the institutions of democracy supplanted the authoritarian institutions of apartheid. An alternative story, common among White liberals in South Africa, sees the unique liberal values represented by English South Africa under apartheid to be threatened by the hegemonic power of the African National Congress. This chapter drew out points of disagreement, and reached unexpected conclusions about the potentially malign role of democracy in the modern state.

First, I exposed the myth that democracy ended apartheid. The global spread of the democratic idea and democratic practice did not cause the demise of the apartheid state. Apartheid's end is best explained by structural economic changes and associated shifts in political organization, in combination with international factors. Indeed, I argued that South Africa was a democracy, albeit a democracy with a limited franchise, from 1910: democracy was thus evidently compatible with segregation and early apartheid. Despite some analysis of the effects of democratic systems, the literature characteristically evades the potential systematic malignity of democratic practice. All such effects are explained away with the evasion that a society is not 'democratic enough' to count as a democracy. By contrast, I here supported the thesis that democracy was in harmony with segregation; I went on to show that it could be considered a cause of high apartheid. Democracy caused high apartheid, first by electoral means, pushing governments to favour White workers and interests over Africans. Second, the ideology of democracy itself had effects through the way it related ideas of territory, membership of community and agency. These notions could only be expressed in South Africa in the 1960s by creating new territorial units and institutional forms with matching 'ethnic' affiliations.

Chapter 5 turned to international comparative political science, which has focused over the past decade on democratization and in particular on the states around the globe that have instituted regular multiparty elections. The idea of democracy has linked the concerns of comparative political scientists with their colleagues in political theory, and it has even provided a bridgehead to the opinions and beliefs of mass publics (who otherwise share few interests with academic analysts). The chapter developed three key themes. First, I provided an overview of the academic literature on democratization. I argued that the literature itself must be understood historically, as a collective endeavour by preoccupied Western analysts to make sense of the emergence of democratic regimes. Second, I showed how academic debate itself played a political role in democratization. Most importantly, for our purposes, scholars rode roughshod over the experiences of the African continent, and treated its politics as anomalous. Finally, assessing the usefulness of this literature for understanding political change in sub-Saharan Africa, I showed how external engineering of democratization rendered most academic models misleading. International scholars, with their comparative explanatory machinery, provided markedly less impressive analysis than South Africa's domestic commentators.

Interventions by political scientists are often policy-influencing by design. Professional academic analysts have advised governments on appropriate courses of action in a range of fields, with science, professionalism and the Western intellectual origin of their discipline as supports. Chapters 6 and 7 investigated how effective the specialized techniques of political science have proved, not only in rendering comprehensible recent political change in South Africa, but also in making the reality of transition more benign.

Chapter 6 explored political scientists' construction of narratives of change out of bewildering events. The boundary line between political science and journalism is often narrow, and academic detachment has been especially hard to maintain in South Africa, especially for overseas visitors. Professionals often created misapprehensions and reinforced the prejudices of White and overseas opinion. Scholars from the United States, in particular, brought domestic preoccupations with them and viewed South Africa through parochial lenses. Circumstances were not conducive to steady intellectual appraisal. Key actors in political parties, the United Democratic Front, civics, women's organizations, youth and churches, all lay across conventional organizational boundaries in political scholarship. The ideological worlds of Black Consciousness, Africanism, charterism and communism, likewise, were elusive in this context. Social science had left largely unexplored the institutional terrain of politics in South Africa. The most rudimentary features of economic, social and political life in homelands and informal settlements were poorly understood.

The filters through which this confusing world were viewed – first- and third worldism, academic Africanism, comparative political studies and scenario-creation – each had selective weaknesses. These styles of analysis rested on diverse sets of assumptions and were generated by distinct scholarly communities in South Africa, Western Europe and North America. They were not, however, merely self-sustaining intellectual worlds. They achieved a degree of interpenetration which served to reinforce the worst misconceptions of each. Their points of greatest agreement were also their greatest errors: each suggested that there existed within South Africa, perhaps within its 'radical' youth in its metaphysical townships, a possibility of state-destabilizing social disorder that might threaten the very integrity of the South African state. Moreover, a threat of civil war purportedly existed in South Africa: Black South Africans, freed from the shackles of the apartheid state, might mobilize against each other in ethnic conflict, and against White South Africans in a populist or redistributive frenzy to satisfy their supposed 'high expectations'. Mutually reinforcing predictions of disaster merged into a shadowy threat which many professional observers saw hanging over the negotiating table. These gloomy messages, fused into predictions of disorder, drew on categories of actor and social location (militant youth, Zulu tribalist, township) of which there had been almost no empirical investigation. Some academic analysts in this way contributed an unduly negative and almost entirely unfounded vision of South African society.

Chapter 7 showed how many (largely foreign) constitutional engineers, specialists in political attitudes and voting behaviour, and (predominantly domestic) scenario and risk analysts, likewise offered ill-grounded speculation about South African society, and sometimes undermined rather than encouraging sound political judgement. Institutional remedies were ill-conceived, and studies shone little light on how South Africa could be made less dangerous for its inhabitants. The country has been the subject of many detailed studies in constitutional design, and these have drawn on the work of international political and legal-constitutional analysts. Political scientists, however, produced mostly unworkable federal and consociational solutions to imagined problems. Western analysts brought with them an ethnocultural essentialism that treated ethnicity in Africa as pre-emptive of all other forms of human identity. The proponents of consociationalism, in particular, drew on naive understandings of social division in South Africa. Their professional training, it seems, offered no protection against this.

Foreign political scientists also influenced the design of more narrowly electoral systems, advised on the necessary conditions for free elections to take place and acted as monitors of the 'free and fair' election process. In order to perform this work, they had to engage with complex problems: how to explain the significance of elections to the citizens of modern states, and how to explore the relationships between social structure, political attitudes and voting behaviour. We observed that the best funded and most extensive efforts to investigate political attitudes in South Africa perpetuated longstanding myths about African society and failed technically as pieces of social science research. The limits to such investigations lie in knowledge-creating institutions, in universities and research funding institutions, in their personnel and in low levels of skill in applied social research.

South African domestic political science contributed to risk assessment and scenario-building exercises which were far more substantial contributions to the stability of transition than anything that their international counterparts accomplished. These scenarios, however, were not open investigations into political possibility. Rather, they set limits to mutual intimidation, by showing when and how posturing might spiral into conflict. They were, moreover, predominantly prescriptive rather than facilitative. In both propagandizing and prescriptive roles, scenarios served primarily the instruments of their business sponsors. In other domestic contributions to policy science, moreover, the implications of public order and White-city crime questions, important to specific audiences, have been disproportionately the focus of professional analysis, confirming how political science can be a prisoner of its conventional audiences as well as of the state and powerful interests.

I now turn to some implications of these chapters and divide my conclusions into three sections. First, I summarize the lessons of South African experience about the nature and limitations of academic political studies. Second, I investigate the light that South Africa's recent past, and the ways in which it has been interpreted, shines on the nature of liberal democracy and its self-congratulatory ideologies of justification. The final section returns to the role of the election in liberal democratic politics.

THE LIMITS OF POLITICAL SCIENCE

International political science was ill-designed to register or remedy the discontents of the majority of South Africans, and poorly placed to perform a facilitatory role in the country's democratic transition. While segregation and apartheid eras had narrowed the subject matter and categories of social description of domestic political studies, South Africa's own academics achieved far more impressive contributions to the practice of transition than did their foreign colleagues.

Nevertheless, domestic academic politics had clear limitations and these reflect on the weaknesses of political science as a discipline.

The politics of White South Africa were organized through institutions derived from the former imperial power, and the ideological justifications of parliamentary democracy surrounded the practice of politics. Political studies, moreover, were conducted through concepts that emerged in quite distinct circumstances and in response to quite different pressures. The study of elections, of party formation and of political attitudes was likewise carried on through lenses from British and American political science. The politics of Black South Africa, by contrast, were viewed as anomalous. While the Republic was comparable with the democracies of Western Europe and it inhabited the world of Western civilization, Black South Africa had third world politics and was the proper object of study of anthropologists and native specialists. There was nothing within the intellectual armoury of political science to prevent its practitioners from accepting Black politics in general, and homeland government in particular, as discrete sets of practices operating according to a quite distinct logic. As we saw in chapters 6 and 7, moreover, borrowings of ideas as diverse as 'underclass', consociational democracy and self-determination from Western political science did not demonstrate the analytic power and practical utility of these concepts, but rather exposed the degree to which the discipline is accommodated to the fields of power of the societies within which it has developed.

Within conventional fields of vision, skills in comparative method and quantitative investigation were weak. Systematic comparative study was hampered by the notion of first and third worldism, and by the myth of Westernization of White South Africa this permitted. The historical weaknesses of comparative politics and quantitative analysis in the United Kingdom, moreover, doubtless helped stunt their development in the Republic. Overwhelmingly the dominant external influence, UK political science partly remade South African political studies in its own unhealthy image. The deepening segregation of South Africa's universities, and the overwhelming concentration of research within historically White universities, accelerated this narrowing of political research.

By contrast, within political studies, bourgeois political theory proved well designed to express the accumulated myths about the nature of the sovereign state and its relations to its citizens that bolstered high apartheid and helped to create it. Political analysts, seeking to attack apartheid, did not find that their discipline readily provided them with intellectual resources to construct a compelling case against separate development. Such a condemnation could only be constructed historically. Liberal political thought rather helped render legitimate both unequal distributions of power between 'sovereign states' and unequal access to resources and power within those states.

Isolation from international political science compounded problems. Peddlers of conservative nostrums were inevitably willing to maintain links across the boycott, and strengthened their influence within South Africa's project-driven political studies community. Moreover, given developments in political science, in particular in the United States, the eventual reconnection of South African political studies to the international community of scholars was bracing. The academic boycott cut off the South African academic community from revolutions in aggregate data analysis that were reshaping social science elsewhere. The emergence of democratization as the central focus of comparative politics, moreover, made South Africa one case among many, and this sat uneasily with the exceptionalism of most South African analysts. Furthermore, the event of democratization itself arrived simultaneously with the literature about it, a conjunction whose intellectual consequences have yet to emerge clearly.

Disciplinary boundaries, in particular the barrier between history and political studies, helped domesticate the discipline. Historians took upon themselves the primary responsibility for critical appraisal of contemporary South African politics and problematized basic categories of social description (concerning identity, nation and social cleavage) taken for granted in political studies. Indeed, one critic has argued that professional historians have been so preoccupied with the politics of the present that they have distorted the past in their efforts to see in it lessons for contemporary actors.[1] Preoccupation with the present is a necessity for a historian in a highly politicized society, and cannot be grounds for criticism. However, historical writing may be inherently incapable of providing the resources for South Africans to think through together the political options open to them. Liberal historians cannot help Black South Africans to place themselves in the same history as Whites, the better to negotiate together a collective future, since Black and White cannot yet meaningfully share a common history. While they integrate the experiences of South Africa's Africans into their historical narratives, and demonstrate the interdependence that has characterized the country's societies over the centuries, historians' moral reflection continues to engage the sensibilities and circumstances of a White audience.

POLITICAL SCIENCE, MORAL APPRAISAL AND POLITICAL ACTION

If social criticism has been concentrated within historical writing, this was not because political studies was a home for conservative or intellectually unadventurous scholars. Political research, rather, while exuding a confident detachment from particular interests and perspectives, has been intensely vulnerable, and this exposure has weakened politics as a critical discipline. Underlying the rhetoric of detachment lie two quite distinct conceptions of political science: a science in the tradition of the natural sciences; and science as technical competency, where authority derives from a possession of specialist skills in social engineering.

The authority of social research everywhere continues to derive from its pseudo-scientific status as a reflection of an independent social reality, even if this scientific aura has been punctured both intellectually and by wholesale failures of prediction and explanation. A quasi-scientific approach to politics at first sight seems an innocent one. Science seems to permit a distancing from moral questions, and an imposition of intellectual order upon the world. However, while neutral political science might have been an intellectual fashion elsewhere, in South Africa it required a suspension of disbelief.

When researching Africans, analysts have been legislators and not just interpreters, prescribing and not merely investigating conditions of social life of their subjects. Moreover, radicals have been acutely aware that even benevolently intended social research can provide the state with data that render populations more vulnerable to state manipulation and social engineering.[2] Research might also, on the radical view, act as a palliative, distracting the masses from the goal of liberation.[3] The plainly oppressive nature of apartheid state institutions, and the evidently racist research commissioned, forced many researchers to take sides. Since the illusion of neutrality was hard to sustain, some social researchers adopted badges of political commitment, including a form of quasi-Marxism, to differentiate themselves from collaborators.[4]

The engineering analogy for political science is based on radically different intellectual foundations. The purpose of political science as technique is to influence human behaviour, rather than to observe it. In particular, political engineers seek to affect the behaviour of the occupants of offices of the state (who commission research and act on its findings) as well as to change the behaviour of wider publics whose understanding of social issues affects political outcomes. Political science as engineering externalizes the world only momentarily, as an aid to practical reflection.

Naturalist and engineering parallels have been important everywhere in shaping the empirical-analytical paradigm that has dominated mainstream social research. Empirical political scientists in South Africa, however, have been unique in almost always treating race and ethnicity as privileged organizing categories, and as factors with independent causal significance. They have not been deflected from this despite the well-documented history of these terms and their reinforcement through apartheid's knowledge-creating institutions. To so use terms that have been deliberately constructed for purposes of social control is, as Taylor and Orkin insist, 'to engage in inscription, not description...to use words that uphold investments of power and privilege.'[5] Political science can avoid this hazard by using sophisticated, skill-intensive and unavoidably expensive quantitative techniques that map changes in the behaviour and self-understandings of subjects over time. But, more importantly, analysts cannot dispense with historical investigation of the construction of contemporary identities and conceptions of social unity and division.

Three problems impede such a development. First, many historians with relevant politico-economic interests have become entrenched in a mainstream of their own. Their quasi-Marxist paradigm revolves around the idea of a class-divided society, and involves its own world of cross-citation, closed academic networks and dogmatic attitudes towards race and ethnicity (but in this case denying them any possible relevance).[6] Secondly, empirical-analytic mainstreamers' authority has depended on their claims to some special insight into social life. To turn political science into a critical discipline would involve repudiating the claims upon which funding and employment depend. To view political research as facilitatory, moreover, is to open up a third problematic area: the recognition that policy sciences, and the academics who participate in them, are intensely vulnerable to the interests they serve.[7]

Academics nonetheless continued not merely to research, but also to teach, and in this role they inevitably helped reproduce South Africa's White managerial, administrative and professional elites. Accepting employment, while rejecting the political system that funds it and that regulates professional activities, is common practice among radical academics everywhere. For South African academics, this role was a great challenge to personal integrity; but, in retrospect, so too should have been that of their radical counterparts in Western European and North American universities, who waged an ineffectual campaign against the capitalist international order through the long decades of the postwar boom.

While generalization is difficult and data scarce, South African political researchers undoubtedly suffer multiple strains. Pressures from student politicization, and the management of student body transformation, combine with frozen or shrinking resources. To conduct research at all in such circumstances is a triumph; self-consciously to modulate the effects of institutional, commercial and political pressures would be something of a miracle.

ESTABLISHED LIBERAL DEMOCRACIES

The extreme experiences of South Africa's professional political analysts illuminate the lesser but parallel travails of their Western counterparts. South African democratization likewise sheds light on the difficulties faced by established liberal capitalist democracies at their time of seeming historical triumph.

While around half of the world's states have become democratic, in the sense that they broadly uphold basic political rights, there remains a widespread perception that reform has been superficial. Politics, according to one commentator, remains 'dominated by clientelistic structures and by political bosses in conjunction with a notably low rate of political participation'. A 'crisis of content' afflicts democratic government in its homelands.[8] In the established democracies, moreover, political leaders have been suffering an extended decline in popularity. Anti-party movements have gained ground, extremism of the right is flourishing and belief in democratic procedures is weakening. Commentators have identified an erosion of 'social capital' that threatens to undermine the foundations of democratic society in participation, trust and civic association. Weakened social connectedness has reduced engagement in collective affairs. After the collapse of communism, moreover, there is no longer any worse alternative against which liberal democracy can be glowingly contrasted.[9]

Contemporary political analysis highlights the putative benefits of democracy while failing to identify its potential hazards. Systematic triumphalism has been reflected in accounts of democratization in South Africa, as elsewhere in the developing world. Democracy is credited with the capacity to act as a self-corrective mechanism within a political system, creating new kinds of information and preventing systematically damaging elite practices from becoming entrenched. It prevents political leaders from squandering or stealing resources, and so rations the rewards of engagement in high politics. Democracy also protects property rights and therefore acts for long-range economic stability, so providing a suitable climate for productive investment. Further purported features of democracy include its ability to generate information that bureaucrats and dictators cannot extract, and to affect the behaviour of subjects by eliciting their consent to be ruled (so making rule potentially more productive).[10]

The protection of property and political rights together seem the backbone of liberal democracy. Democracy defends property, while securing the consent of citizens to the disposal by fellow citizens of vastly unequal endowments of wealth. Its remaining positive qualities, however, depend on a combination of moral appeal and support for the principle of elections. Democracy's significance is thus problematically closely related to the self-understandings of citizens. Notions of popular sovereignty and self-determination, as expressed through electoral politics, give democracy meaning to citizens. Imagined collective assertion is an echo of direct democracy in which the residual magic of representative democracy resides.

The relations between territory, national self-determination, distributive justice and collective assertion together explain the popular significance of democracy. In the remainder of this section, I explore how these relations are understood in contemporary political science. In the final section I address the elusive role of elections in contemporary politics, the arenas in which territory, self-determination and collective assertion are fleetingly brought into contact. Throughout, I use the South African experience, and the ways in which it has been received in the West, to illuminate these issues.

Separate Development in the International State System

Two striking aspects of the relationship between the state and its international setting have been analysed in quite distinct ways in past decades. The first, a perceived threat to the coherence of national politics posed by international economic and political integration, has become a central theme in contemporary political commentary. The second, the guilty stain of international injustice, and the progressive failure of justifications for extreme inequality of power and resources between states, has remained a peripheral issue in Western political argument. Yet these matters are closely related by the tangled but seemingly natural notion of self-determination, an idea that promotes consent as the key to both the sustainability and the legitimacy of states.

Connolly, addressing the first of the questions, has recently emphasized the tensions between 'centrifugal forces' exerting themselves on the modern state – global economic exchange, freer communications, and global environmental threats – and the tight imaginative hold retained by national conceptions of accountability, danger and security. He argues that citizens assume a rough correspondence between territory, action and membership, a relation embodied in the idea of the modern state. 'Correspondence between the scope of common troubles and a territorial place of action [continues] to form the essence of democratic politics'.[11]

For Connolly, the correspondence resides in the 'imagination': in the notion of 'internal' politics grounded in a territory; in the idea of a people or nation living on that territory, related to each other by shared understandings and identities; and in electoral institutions coextensive with the citizen body and territorial limits of the state.[12] On Connolly's reading, today's experiences increasingly fail to live up to expectations, and citizen estrangement, alienation and depoliticization are the sorry consequences. Old states offered seeming security, self-sufficiency and ideological unity; today's states suffer economic interdependence, the threat of global war and the spread of global ideologies. Finance, ecology, communications, travel and migration all challenge the imaginative fusion of agency, territory and national membership that has defined and rendered meaningful processes of domestic democracy.

National self-determination is the imaginative chimera at the heart of Connolly's vision of the state. The idea that the people, a voluntary assembly, united by language, tradition, moral precepts or nature, should be capable of achieving a common will and of governing themselves, has been important in all manner of states, but both democracy and decolonization have received special and parallel justification in the idea that rulers should be accountable to those they rule. Self-determination, however, is both a complex and an opaque notion. Consistent liberals, at first sight, seem obliged to extend their universal principles into a denial of the legitimacy of national affiliations or privileges; and consistent democrats might deny the legitimacy of borders that cut across issues constituencies. Nevertheless liberal democrats are almost all nationalists.[13]

Where disputes have arisen over the grounds for secession or regional autonomy, liberal theory and practice have significantly proved consistently confused and impotent. It remains unclear how the right to self-determination can be derived; it is equally unclear how conflicting claims to the right to self-determination can be refereed; and the degree to which self-determination can be reconciled with sovereignty and territorial integrity is quite little understood.[14] South African experience provides a further powerful corrective to those who view the notion of self-determination as a secure resolution to the problems of conflict in modern politics.

Territoriality in the contemporary state rests upon nationalism, which itself must derive its legitimacy in some way from consent. However, separate development demonstrated the degree to which this complex formula is open to manipulation. It rested on putative historical, biological, social, cultural and linguistic correspondences between people, fused together with a spurious anthropology of African descent, and it created elites who claimed the right to rule on the basis of ethnicity. The apologists of apartheid could draw on certain contemporary liberal themes to justify their actions: on the communitarian notion that constitutive group membership is essential to human flourishing, and is denied in states which lack groups of the necessary inclusive properties; and that the value of such a group provides a justification for self-determination.[15] The international system, according to communitarian thinkers, should make it possible for different ways of life to flourish, and this can only be achieved in communities organized around constitutive states.[16] South Africa's Whites belonged to a community defined by the exclusion of others, and the survival of their constitutive community (as Afrikaners themselves often argued with force) depended on the right to closure. They resisted cosmopolitan duties that confused liberals would try to impose upon them.[17]

On the prevalent optimistic liberal reading, the modern history of democracy represents a widening of the democratic circle as the hitherto excluded have become included within the political community. First came the struggle against class exclusion, and the breaking of the bourgeois stranglehold on political representation, with the extension of the franchise to the working class. Then came the formal inclusion of women into the community of citizens. The struggle to widen the circle then moved to those excluded by virtue of dominant criteria of responsibility and normality (the disabled, the imprisoned, the insane), those belonging to minority nations, migrants, gypsies and indigenous peoples. The young have also been drawn progressively into the fold, with lowered voting ages across the Western democracies. Contemporary debates over the citizenship of refugees and aliens, as Linklater has persuasively argued, bear close resemblance to earlier debates over class, race and gender as criteria of exclusion.[18]

The history of the modern political community has been a progressive struggle for inclusion in order to enjoy a community's moral favouritism. In what terms, then, could separate development be castigated? As South African Whites were aware, their arguments in support of the homelands were highly resistant to the weapons an analytical liberal could deploy. Critics of apartheid relied upon a powerful sense that racial discrimination in itself was wrong and that ethnicity was a mask for race, or that the material deprivation of the homelands itself represented the source of injustice.

Towards a Realist Model of Expanded Citizenship

The right to participate in democratic politics is not just an outcome of struggle but also a generator of consequences. South African Whites' ability to vote created new incentives for politicians to act in their favour at the expense of Blacks. In the history of Western European democracy, as Linklater explains, 'measures to include the hitherto excluded within national communities triggered the closure of community'.[19] In particular, the emergence of the working-class vote, in conjunction with nationalism, created pressures for economic nationalism, protectionism and an end to mass migration. Regardless of the intentions of new citizens, their inclusion in the community modifies political leaders' incentive structures. Politicians, moreover, are never severely punished for exporting evils to non-citizens, even if this creates few real domestic benefits. In a world in which externalities and extraterritorial ramifications are increasingly important, this is a decisive weakness in the argument for the general benevolence of democratic practice.

A rudimentary model of democratic consequences suggests itself. First, citizenship is secured first by the more powerful of the unenfranchised: property owners, organized workers, men, ethnic majorities, those with territorial claims, the normal. Second, democracy affects the structure of incentives facing political leaders. The already powerful, who have secured early citizenship for themselves, displace disbenefits onto those not yet admitted to the fold, and build barriers against entry to full membership of the political community for outsiders. Third, although the franchise continues to expand as a result of struggle, this process has one final limit: the inclusion of the (adult) population of a territory. Yet the ability to impose disbenefits does not cease: the non-empowered merely reside beyond national borders, or hold temporary permits, or live in groups marginalized within the political system. Democracy also provides continued incentives for disbenefits to be transferred to those irredeemably outside the present political community: animals, the natural environment, future generations.

Once we shake off the class-within-nation-state paradigm, democracy certainly need not be empowering. It can help the relatively powerful to displace suffering onto the relatively weak. On the liberal view, democracy will eventually spread to all nations, until everyone is a citizen of a democratic state. This, however, describes not the universal franchise dreamt of in liberal universalism, but a multitude of exclusive franchises, each with incentives to export evil. In such circumstances, the power of a state, and its ability to coerce its neighbours, will be decisive determinants of citizens' possibilities of life.[20]

It is not just that the liberal democratization myth leaves massive inequalities of power and resources between states untouched, and institutionally embeds incentives to export disbenefits to outsiders and to nature. The chimera of democratic accountability also shields the export of suffering in a moral armour of democratic legitimacy. Substantive differences in the nature of citizenship enjoyed by different categories of citizen remain a focus of political struggle within particular states. Men, for example, continue to enjoy privileged exercise of citizenship rights since women's formal citizenship gives them access to rights shaped to be exercisable by men.[21] Between states, however, such inequalities are far starker. Full citizenship relies on possession by a state of the capacity to secure basic rights and protections for its citizens, and to prevent their infringement by overseas powers. It is quite plain that states' capacities to achieve this are wildly uneven.[22]

South Africa shows how the international languages of high politics can make legitimate to western eyes the unequal distribution of resources and power between nations. The creation of the homelands in the 1960s and 1970s was difficult to attack through the conventions of liberal political morality. Afrikaners were using the languages of self-determination quite conventionally in their defences of high apartheid. In South Africa, as elsewhere, 'objective' bases for the division of peoples into distinct nations were easily constructed from the materials of academic anthropology and linguistics, and from narratives of 'national history'. Intellectual and political leaders could always be found to attest to the force of an identity, and to the collective moral life it represented.

Likewise, Afrikaners could not easily be condemned for creating dependent territories, or for giving political independence without the economic self-sufficiency to make this meaningful. Postcolonial states are everywhere bereft of the capacities that might render sovereignty significant. Few states in the world, moreover, can claim economic self-sufficiency, and none in sub-Saharan Africa can credibly claim control over its own destiny.

South Africa's behaviour since 1994 towards its neighbours, in what were the front-line states, indicates that liberal democracy may help make acceptable unequal access to resources, even where (as in South Africa) the political community lacks an easy sense of cultural or national unity. Dependent economically upon South Africa, and vulnerable to its whims on cross-border trade, work permits and foreign workers, these states have increasingly taken second place to the domestic concerns of South Africa's democratic politicians. Much of the machinery designed to implement influx control under the apartheid state is today devoted to rooting out illegal immigrants and returning them to their homelands (in the countries to the North). This is rendered morally defensible by virtue of the democratic status of the Pretoria regime.

From the greater distance of the OECD zone, the democratization of South Africa has radically transformed how Western publics and the 'international community' view the morality of the South African state. Democracy does not just create domestic responsibilities, it discharges external ones. For states which lack the means of creating for their citizens a tolerable standard of living, or for sustaining life at all, the claim to self-determination is nonetheless a declaration of others' non-responsibility. Other states and their citizens are no longer, it seems, morally obliged to intervene. Schmitter has rightly remarked that 'other than pious, unconvincing, and ineffectual protestations of cosmopolitanism, liberal democrats have largely dealt with injustice and inequality in the international system by ignoring both'.[23] The ideology of liberal democracy itself makes it easy for them to do so.

ELECTIONS IN MODERN POLITICS

Elections are the great festivals of modern politics, and the major episodes of mass political participation in contemporary states.

Citizens often view electoral politics as the essence of democracy, and outsiders see them as barometers of the political climate in a foreign state. Yet elections remain poorly understood and great gulfs exist between how political leaders, professional analysts and citizens view them.

For political leaders, elections are potentially dangerous but necessary instruments of rule. Some elections are unavoidable in any state, given their massive size and the quasi-egalitarian doctrines that render hereditary rule illegitimate. Most leaders have won many elections before they compete for the votes of the citizens: leaders have followers, and a ballot records their presence and translates it into legitimate authority. Elections secure popular acquiescence to continued rule, drawing attention to common boundaries and collective problems, and presenting the actions of the state as the outcomes of joint decision.

Politicians may also use elections to change power relations in ways impossible in normal politics. Cunning rulers can undermine interest groups or networks of power; they can change the composition of the ruling elite or recruit new networks in hostile regions; they can also use elections to co-opt elements of the opposition. If carefully designed, elections may also help to marginalize extremists, or ethnic and regional parties, in their challenges to national authority. Elections, crucially, undermine the claims to legitimacy of well-organized opposition movements, so rendering unnecessary the use of violence to crush them.

Western professional politicians treat electors coldly, and sometimes with distaste, in part because of the professionalization of electoral campaigning, and the degree to which campaigns are based around resource distribution and elite negotiation (rather than around collective choice). Leaders, moreover, are ensconced in party systems. Western democracies, with their stable if diversifying class orders, their national political movements, and their traditions of democratic competition, contain long-established parties which socialize, select and present political leaders, spare them from factionalism, and habituate them to the necessity of collective decision-making within the party.[24]

While analysis of elections is the discipline's greatest achievement, political scientists also gaze icily upon electors' behaviour. Their somewhat limited success in predicting and explaining poll results is quite impressive in contrast to the paucity of their understanding of the significance of the modern election for voters. Their forerunners, the founders of modern sociology, forcefully analysed the rationalizing powers of instrumental reason and capital accumulation in the modern state, but said little of the mass democratic public. Fear and disgust have motivated bourgeois commentaries over this century. Contemporary analysis depends heavily on two imaginative constructions: the voter as a child, and passive recipient of political propaganda; and the voter as rational maximizer, calculating interests and their relationship to political leadership.[25]

It is unclear, on such jaded views, why electors participate at all in elections. The democracy of the ancients, it seems, was characterized by near universal engagement of the citizenry in the government of the political community. Yet collective assertion has little place in the practice of modern government (which is incremental, restrained, self-consciously deliberate, inertial, bureaucratically burdened, economically constrained and tied to the vagaries of fate). Moreover, electors are not emancipated from their humanity in the ballot box; they lack autonomy (even if the idea of choosing freely is important to the election process). Modern electors are self-deceived to participate at all.

At the same time, scholars observe that the committed participation of citizens in elections is a precondition for the benevolent product of modern democracy: legitimate, limited, efficient and accountable government. The eliciting of information, the self-correcting properties of democratic systems, the scrutiny of elite behaviour, the displacement of conflict from society to political institutions and the legitimate authority that renders rule productive: all of these depend on alert participation.

The gulf between how electors are believed to be, and how it is desirable that they should be, seems vast. However, it may be that participation is rational and that electors are not entirely unaware of this fact. Elections engage subjects with political realities that they might otherwise evade; in this sense participation is rational in that it discourages self-deceit. Elections also raise awareness of causal relations and of scale, summoning a fleeting vision of a political community, both diverse and massive, that contains both like and different fellow citizens. Campaigning momentarily remakes an active political body capable of a rudimentary collective self-exploration.

Elections thus help to overcome tensions between representative and participatory democracy within liberal democratic ideology. Their magic lies in the sense of collective assertion they bring. Through the personalization of power and the reduction of systemic discontents to the responsibility of individuals, elections re-animate the residual collective assertion that makes democracy personally meaningful.[26]

The South African election was fascinating in part because it seemed to be an exercise of direct collective assertion, an instrument of unambiguous collective choice. Of course, it was not really quite this. Indeed, it may have been our racialized imaginations, rather than those of South African participants, that made this election so special. As observers, our presumption of inevitable antagonism between racial groups, and our assumption of the internal homogeneity within such groups, may have helped to create for us the simple and satisfying triumph that was the election of 1994.

Notes

CHAPTER 1

1. See A.M. Butler, 'Unpopular Leaders: the British Case', *Political Studies* 43 (1995) 48–65; A. Hadenius, 'Victory and Crisis', in Hadenius (ed.), *Democracy's Victory and Crisis: Nobel Symposium No. 93* (Cambridge: Cambridge University Press, 1997) 1–14.

CHAPTER 2

1. P. Maylam, *A History of the African People of South Africa* (London: Longman, 1991, 4th edition); L. Thompson, *A History of South Africa* (London: Yale University Press, 1990), chapter 1. I rely heavily on Thompson's excellent compressed account of pre-1870s South Africa, and also on the collection M. Wilson and L. Thompson, (eds), *A History of South Africa to 1870*, (London: James Currey, 1982, 2nd edition).
2. Thompson, *History of South Africa*, 13; M. Wilson, 'The Nguni People' and M. Wilson, 'The Sotho', in Wilson and Thompson (eds), *History of South Africa*, 75–130, 131–86.
3. Thompson, *History of South Africa*, 24–5.
4. Thompson, *History of South Africa*, 11.
5. J. Guy, 'Ecological Factors in the Rise of Shaka and the Zulu Kingdom', in S. Marks and A. Atmore (eds), *Economy and Society in Pre-industrial South Africa* (London: Longman, 1980) 102–19.
6. J. Cobbing, 'The Mfecane as Alibi', in *Journal of African History* 29 (1988) 487–519.
7. Thompson, *History of South Africa*, 53.
8. Thompson, *History of South Africa*, 53.
9. Thompson, *History of South Africa*, 108.
10. N. Worden, *The Making of Modern South Africa: Conquest, Segregation and Apartheid* (Oxford: Blackwell, 1994) 16.
11. See J. Peires, 'The British and the Cape, 1814–1834', in R. Elphick and H. Giliomee (eds) *The Shaping of South African Society, 1652–1820* (Cape Town: Maskew Miller Longman, 1989).
12. Thompson, *History of South Africa*, 65.
13. Worden, *Making of Modern South Africa*, 17.
14. W. Beinart, *Twentieth Century South Africa* (Oxford: Oxford University Press, 1994) 16.
15. C. Bundy, *The Rise and Fall of the South Africa Peasantry* (London: James Currey, 1988, 2nd edition).
16. See S. Marks and S. Trapido, 'The Politics of Race, Class and Nationalism', in Marks and Trapido (eds), *Politics of Race, Class, and Nationalism in Twentieth Century South Africa* (London: Longman, 1987) 1–70.

17. None of this, of course, makes a purely materialist explanation of segregation possible. Mining capital was never disproportionately politically powerful; and existing forms of segregation that preceded mineral discoveries were important forces in social change.
18. S. Terreblanche and N. Nattrass, 'A Periodization of the Political Economy from 1910', in N. Nattrass and E. Ardington (eds), *The Political Economy of South Africa* (Cape Town: Oxford University Press, 1990) 6–23.
19. Beinart, *Twentieth Century South Africa*, chapter 5.
20. H. Bradford, *A Taste of Freedom: The ICU in rural South Africa, 1924–30* (New Haven: Yale University Press, 1987).
21. This narrative has drawn extensively on Beinart, *Twentieth Century South Africa*, chapter 5.
22. Under the second reading, apartheid was segregation by another name; but with vastly worse conditions in the over-populated reserves and more intrusive exploitation of Black labour in the urban and mining economies.
23. 'The Cornerstone of the Later High Apartheid System was the Division of all South Africans by Race', Worden, *Making of Modern South Africa*, 95.
24. The biggest effect of this Act was on Indians and Coloureds, of whom 600,000 were removed from their homes in Cape Town and Durban. Enforcement was especially slow in Cape Town. Here, however, contrary to White liberal mythology, the key obstruction seems to have been the interests of the Cape's slum-lords, rather than an unwillingness to cause inconvenience to Cape Town's Coloured population.
25. F. Wilson, *Labour in the South African Gold Mines 1911–1969* (Cambridge: Cambridge University Press, 1972).
26. P. Bonner, P. Delius and D. Posel, 'The Shaping of Apartheid: Contradiction, Continuity and Popular Struggle', in Bonner et al. (eds), *Apartheid's Genesis* 1–41, esp. 15–21.
27. D. Posel, *The Making of Apartheid* (Oxford: Clarendon, 1991) 60.
28. Posel, *Making of Apartheid*, 6.
29. Bonner et al., 'Shaping of Apartheid', 31; see also S.B. Greenberg, *Legitimating the Illegitimate: State, Markets, and Resistance in South Africa* (Berkeley: University of California, 1987), chapters 2 and 3.
30. N. Nattrass, 'Economic Aspects of the Construction of Apartheid', in P. Bonner, P. Delius and D. Posel (eds) *Apartheid's Genesis 1935–1962* (Johannesburg: Witwatersrand University Press, 1993) 42–64, 53.
31. Bonner et al., 'Shaping of Apartheid', 31.
32. See M. Szfeitzel, 'Ethnicity and Democratization in South Africa', *Review of African Political Economy* 60 (1994) 185–99.
33. This system of rule was known to the British as 'indirect rule'; to the French it was known as *association*. Mamdani, *Citizen and Subject*, 7–8.
34. L. Vail (ed.), *Creation of Tribalism in Southern Africa* (London: James Currey, 1989); S. Bekker, *Ethnicity in Focus: the South African Case* (Durban: Indicator South Africa, 1993).
35. Worden, *Making of Modern South Africa*, 112.

36. Elsewhere, where Afrikaner intellectuals struggled to create histories of African nations from thin material, and to locate homelands in barren areas, manufactured identity achieved little purchase.
37. As Bonner et al. comment, 'The more effective the apartheid regime was in stalling African urbanization and forcing migrancy on people who would otherwise have settled permanently in the towns the greater the threat to the migrant labour system'. Bonner et al., 'The Shaping of Apartheid', 34.

CHAPTER 3

1. S. Marks and S. Trapido, 'The Politics of Race, Class and Nationalism', in S. Marks and S. Trapido (eds), *The Politics of Race, Class and Nationalism in 20th Century South Africa* (London: Longman, 1987) 1–70.
2. N. Worden, *The Making of Modern South Africa* (Oxford: Blackwell, 1994) 87.
3. For examples available in English, see W. de Klerk, *The Puritans in Africa* (Harmondsworth, Penguin, 1976); C. Muller, *Five Hundred Years: A History of South Africa* (Pretoria: Academica, 1975, 2nd edition).
4. A. Du Toit, 'No Chosen People: the Myth of the Calvinist Origins of Afrikaner Nationalism and Racial Ideology', in *American Historical Review* 88 (1983) 920–52.
5. L. Thompson, *History of South Africa* (New Haven: Yale University Press, 1990) 135.
6. F. A. van Jaarsveld, *The Awakening of Afrikaner Nationalism, 1868–1881*, trans. F. R. Metrowich (Cape Town: Human and Rousseau, 1961); and *The Afrikaner Interpretation of South African History* (Cape Town: Simondium, 1964); T. Dunbar Moodie, *The Rise of Afrikanerdom* (Berkeley: University of California Press, 1975).
7. Worden, *Making of Modern South Africa*, 87–94; Marks and Trapido (eds), *Race, Class and Nationalism*, Introduction.
8. Worden, *Making of Modern South Africa*, 90.
9. Worden, *Making of Modern South Africa*, 91.
10. M. Eldridge and J. Seekings, 'Mandela's Lost Province', *Journal of Southern African Studies* 22:4 (1996) 517–40; R. Mattes, *The Election Book* (Cape Town: IDASA, 1995).
11. Thompson, *History of South Africa*, 66, 171. This optimistic tale seems most feasible in Cape Town and its immediate surroundings. A strong element within right-wing Afrikanerdom continues to champion the cultural and ethnic unity of Afrikaner and Coloured.
12. Marks and Trapido, 'Politics of Race, Class and Nationalism', 29.
13. B. Nasson, 'Political Ideologies in the Western Cape', in T. Lodge, B. Nasson, S. Mufson, K. Shubane and N. Sithole, *All, Here, and Now* (London: Hurst, 1992) 206–32.
14. S. Biko, *I Write What I Like* (London: Heinemann, 1978).
15. Worden, *Making of Modern South Africa*, 85.

16. T. Karis and G. Carter, *From Protest to Challenge: a Documentary History of African Politics in South Africa, 1822–1964* (Stanford: Hoover Press, 1973) vol. 1, 18; cited Worden, *Making of Modern South Africa*, 81.
17. But for the importance of Afrikaner ethnicity as a defence against perceived vulnerability, see H. Giliomee, 'The Growth of Afrikaner Identity', in H. Hadden and H. Giliomee, *Ethnic Power Mobilised: Can South Africa Change?* (New Haven: Yale University Press, 1979).
18. For detailed analysis and extended references see S. Saunders, *The Making of the South African Past: Major Historians on Race and Class* (Cape Town: David Philip, 1985).
19. C. W. de Kiewiet, *A History of South Africa: Social and Economic* (London: 1941) Chapter 3; Saunders, *Making of South African Past*.
20. H. Wolpe, 'Capitalism and Cheap Labour Power in South Africa: From Segregation to Apartheid', in *Economy and Society* 4:4 (1972) 425–56.
21. For a fuller statement of Wolpe's position with responses to the early challenges, see H. Wolpe, *Race, Class and the Apartheid State* (London: James Currey, 1988). For other powerful quasi-materialist analyses, see F. Johnstone, *Class, Race and Gold* (London: Routledge and Keegan Paul, 1976) and R. Davies, *Capital, State and White Labour in South Africa in 1900–1960: an Historical Materialist Analysis of Class Formation and Class Relations* (Brighton: Harvester, 1979); for a critique see P. Harries, 'Capital, State and Labour on the 19th Century Witwatersrand: a Reassessment', in *South African Historical Journal* (1986) 25–45. On the economics of the mines and their labour supplies, see F. Wilson, *Labour in the South African Gold Mines, 1911–1969* (Cambridge: Cambridge University Press, 1972); J. Crush, A. Jeeves and D. Yudelman, *South Africa's Labour Empire: a History of Black Migrancy to the Gold Mines* (Cape Town: David Philip, 1991); A. Jeeves, *Migrant Labour in South Africa's Mining Economy: the Struggle for the Gold Mines Labour Supply 1890–1920* (Johannesburg: Witwatersrand University Press, 1985).
22. M. Lipton, *Capitalism and Apartheid: South Africa, 1910–84* (Aldershot: Gower, 1985).
23. See P. Bonner, P. Delius and D. Posel, 'The Shaping of Apartheid: Contradiction, Continuity and Popular Struggle', in P. Bonner, P. Delius and D. Posel (eds), *Apartheid's Genesis 1935–62* (Johannesburg: Witwatersrand University Press, 1993) 1–41.
24. D. Posel, 'The Meaning of Apartheid before 1948: Conflicting Interests and Forces within the Afrikaner Nationalist Alliance', *Journal of Southern African Studies* 14 (1987) 123–39; *The Making of Apartheid 1948–61: Conflict and Compromise* (Oxford: Clarendon, 1991); J. Lazar, 'Verwoerd versus the "Visionaries": the South African Bureau of Racial Affairs (SABRA) and Apartheid, 1948–61', in Bonner et al., *Apartheid's Genesis*, 362–92.
25. Posel, *The Making of Apartheid*, 16.
26. S. B. Greenberg, *Legitimating the Illegitimate: State, Markets, and Resistance in South Africa* (Berkeley: University of California Press, 1987).
27. I. Smith, 'The Revolution in South African Historiography', in *History Today* 38 (1988) 8–10.

28. D. Welsh, *The Roots of Segregation: Native Policy in Colonial Natal, 1845–1910* (Cape Town: Oxford University Press, 1971). For magnificent comparative analysis of colonial labour recruitment strategies in British and French Africa in the mid-years of the century, see F. Cooper, *Decolonisation and African Society: the Labour Question in French and British Africa* (Cambridge: Cambridge University Press, 1996).
29. S. Marks, *Reluctant Rebellion: The 1968 Disturbances in Natal* (Oxford: Clarendon, 1970); 'Natal, the Zulu Royal Family and the Ideology of Segregation', in *Journal of South African Studies* 4 (1978) 172–94; *The Ambiguities of Dependence in South Africa: Class, Nationalism and the State in 20th-century Natal* (Johannesburg: Ravan, 1986).
30. See M. Legassick, 'British Hegemony and the Origins of Segregation in South Africa, 1901–14', in W. Beinart and S. Dubow (eds), *Segregation and Apartheid in 20th Century South Africa* (London: Routledge, 1995) 43–59; see also S. Marks and S. Trapido, 'Lord Milner and the South African State', in *History Workshop Journal* 2 (1979) 50–80.
31. Beinart, *Twentieth Century South Africa*, 3.
32. M. Legassick, 'The Frontier Tradition in South African Historiography', in S. Marks and A. Atmore (eds), *Economy and Society in Pre-Industrial South Africa* (London: Longman, 1980) 44–79; see also C. van Onselen, 'Race and Class in the South African Countryside: Cultural Osmosis and Social Relations in the Share Cropping Economy of the South Western Transvaal, 1900–50', in *American Historical Review* 95:1 (1980) 99–123.
33. See M.W. Swanson, 'The Sanitation Syndrome: Bubonic Plague and Urban Native Policy in the Cape Colony, 1900–19', *Journal of African History* 18 (1977) 387–410.
34. S. Dubow, *Segregation and the Origins of Apartheid in South Africa* (London: Macmillan, 1989).
35. W. Beinart and S. Dubow, 'Historiography of Segregation and Apartheid', in Beinart and Dubow (eds), *Segregation and Apartheid*, 8–9; see also P. Delius, 'Migrant Labour and the Pedi 1840–80', in Marks and Atmore (eds), *Economy and Society*, 293–312.
36. W. Beinart and C. Bundy, *Hidden Struggles in Rural South Africa: the Politics and Popular Movements in the Transkei and Eastern Cape, 1890–1930* (Johannesburg: Ravan, 1987).
37. See, for example, the otherwise excellent R. Price, *The Apartheid State in Crisis: Political Transformation in South Africa, 1975–1990* (Oxford: Oxford University Press, 1991).
38. See, for example, T. Sisk, *Democratization in South Africa* (Princeton: Princeton University Press, 1995); and A.W. Marx, *Lessons of Struggle: South African Internal Opposition, 1960–1990* (Oxford: Oxford University Press, 1991).
39. C. Bundy, *Remaking the Past* (Cape Town: University of Cape Town Press, 1987).
40. See B. Bozzoli, 'Marxism, Feminism and South African Studies', *Journal of Southern African Studies* 9 (1983); see also Bozzoli, *Women of Phokeng* (Portsmouth NH: Heinemann, 1991); J. Wells, 'Why Women Rebel', *Journal of Southern African Studies*, 10 (1983); and articles by Beinart

and Bradford, in B. Bozzoli (ed.), *Class, Community and Conflict* (Johannesburg: Raven, 1987); C. Walker, *Women and Gender in Southern Africa to 1945* (London: James Curry, 1990).

41. For the latter, see in particular, Legassick, 'British Hegemony and the Origins of Segregation', and Swanson, 'Sanitation Syndrome', both in Beinart and Dubow (eds), *Segregation and Apartheid*.
42. See, in particular, the devastating indictment by C. McCarthy, 'Apartheid Ideology and Economic Development Policy', in N. Nattrass and E. Ardington (eds), *Political Economy of South Africa* (Cape Town: Oxford University Press, 1990) 43–54.
43. See T. Moll, 'From Booster to Brake: Apartheid and Economic Growth in Comparative Perspective', in Nattrass and Ardington (eds), *Political Economy*, 73–87.
44. S.B. Greenberg, *Legitimating the Illegitimate: State, Markets and Resistance in South Africa* (Berkeley: University of California Press, 1987) 5–14.
45. See D. Innes, *Anglo American and the Rise of Modern South Africa*; on the development of labour control mechanisms and the minefields, Yudelman, *South Africa's Labour Empire*; R. Turrell, *Capital and Labour on the Kimberley Diamond Fields 1871–1890* (Cambridge: Cambridge University Press, 1987); Jeeves, *Migrant Labour in South Africa's Mining Economy*; Wilson, *Labour in the South African Goldmines*.
46. See, for example, M. Mann, 'The Giant Stirs: South African Business in the Age of Reform', in P. Frankel, N. Pines and M. Swilling (eds), *State, Resistance and Change in South Africa* (Johannesburg: Southern Books, 1988) 52–86.
47. See however the attempts by Truth and Reconciliation Commission in November 1997 to investigate the activities of business from 1960 to 1990.
48. For a tracing of these networks, see the path-breaking article, R. Taylor and M. Orkin, 'The Racialisation of Social Scientific Research on South Africa', *South African Sociological Review* 7:2 (1995) 43–69.
49. Posel, *Making of Apartheid*, chapter 10.
50. See the third dimension of power in S. Lukes, *Power: a Radical View* (Oxford: Oxford University Press, 1974).
51. T.R.H. Davenport, *South Africa: a Modern History* (London: Macmillan, 1991, 4th edition); L. Thompson, *A History of South Africa* (New Haven: Yale University Press, 1990).
52. Just as, in the crudest technological example, the QWERTY keyboard secured permanent ascendancy over more logical and later potential competitors, so public policies, once embarked upon, can shape followers in their stead. See D.C. North, *Institutions, Institutional Change and Economic Performance* (Cambridge: Cambridge University Press, 1990), chapter 11; J. Knight, *Institutions and Social Conflict* (Cambridge: Cambridge University Press, 1992).
53. P. Pierson, 'When Effect Becomes Cause: Policy Feedback and Political Change', in *World Politics* 45 (1993) 595–628.
54. For reflection on these questions, see G. Hawthorn, *Plausible Worlds* (Cambridge: Cambridge University Press, 1990).

55. See S. Gelb (ed.), *South Africa's Economic Crisis* (Cape Town: David Philip, 1991).
56. E. H. Carr, *What Is History?* (New York, 1962).
57. C. Van Onselen, *The Seed is Mine: The Life of Kas Maine, a South African Sharecropper 1894–1988* (Cape Town: David Philip, 1996).
58. See, for example, D. Welsh, *Roots of Segregation*. Similarly, economists often approach contemporary analysis of the economy by way of long-range historical analysis. See, for example, Wilson, *Labour in the South African Gold Mines*, and N. Nattrass, 'A Periodization of the South African Political Economy since 1910', in Nattrass and Ardington (eds), *Political Economy of South Africa* (Cape Town: Oxford University Press, 1990).

CHAPTER 4

1. M. Kaase and K. Newton, *Beliefs in Government* (Oxford: Oxford University Press, 1995) vol. 5, chapter 2.
2. Kaase and Newton, *Beliefs in Government*, vol. 5, chapter 4.
3. A.M. Butler, 'Unpopular Leaders: the British Case', *Political Studies* 43:1 (1995) 48–65. Protest, however, is usually couched in terms of institutional or, more commonly, personal failure: established political structures are viewed as self-serving, or political leaders are viewed as corrupt. Democracy is being failed, rather than itself failing.
4. See S.P. Huntington, *The Third Wave: Democratization in the Late Twentieth Century* (Norman: University of Oklahoma Press, 1991).
5. F. Fukuyama, *The End of History and the Last Man* (New York: Free Press, 1992).
6. Following S.M. Lipset, *Political Man: the Social Bases of Politics* (Baltimore: Johns Hopkins University Press, 1961).
7. See W.R. Keech, *Economic Politics: The Costs of Democracy* (Cambridge: Cambridge University Press, 1995), especially 211–22.
8. J. Buchanan and R. Wagner, *Democracy in Deficit: the Political Legacy of Lord Keynes* (New York: Academic Press, 1977); but see the cautions in M.S. Lewis-Beck, *Economics and Elections* (Ann Arbor: University of Michigan Press, 1988).
9. R.D. Arnold, *The Logic of Congressional Action* (New Haven: Yale University Press, 1990).
10. T. Garton Ash, 'Eastern Europe: the Year of Truth', *New York Review of Books* 15 June (1990) 17.
11. Democracy is a limited variable, assuming only positive values. See A. Przeworski and F. Limongi, 'Modernization: Theories and Facts', *World Politics* 49 (1997) 155–83, fn. 4.
12. See, especially, M. Lipton, *Capitalism and Apartheid* (Aldershot: Gower, 1985).
13. S. Gelb (ed.), *South Africa's Economic Crisis* (Cape Town: Philip, 1991).
14. All the while, the region in general and South Africa in particular were undergoing a steady economic marginalization. The end of the postwar

boom had ended a golden age in South Africa as elsewhere in the developing world. See T. Moll, 'From Booster to Brake?', in N. Nattrass and E. Ardington (eds), *Political Economy of South Africa* (Cape Town: Oxford University Press, 1990).

15. In this section I rely heavily on T. Lodge, *Black Politics in South Africa since 1945* (London: Longman, 1985).
16. As Parekh comments of their Victorian forebears, these liberal new democrats in fact favour representative *government* – the government of the people by their representatives – and not representative *democracy*'. B. Parekh, 'The Cultural Particularity of Liberal Democracy', in D. Held (ed.), *Prospects for Democracy* (Cambridge: Polity Press, 1993) 156–75.
17. The massive discipline of ANC procedures such as expulsion from parliament allows this volatile entity to avoid disintegration while retaining formal democracy.
18. Even here, analysts have misread the role of black consciousness in the 'democratic' struggle against the apartheid state. They have often failed to locate the strengths of black consciousness in its continuity from pre-existing forms of cultural organization for the Youth, and have instead treated the movement as an aspect of 'democratization'. See, for example, T. Sisk, *Democratization in South Africa* (Princeton: Princeton University Press, 1995); A.W. Marx, *Lessons of Struggle* (Oxford: Oxford University Press, 1991). This could never have been so: in a country in which Africans are so overwhelmingly in the majority, the key system of ideas around which black consciousness revolved had to be exclusionary and designed to serve the self-government of Africans.
19. See H. Bradford, *A Taste of Freedom* (New Haven: Yale University Press, 1987).
20. Lodge, *Black Politics*, chapter 1.
21. Lodge's studies of women's protest campaigns in the 1950s, the Evanton and Alexandra bus boycotts of 1955/7, and the Sharpeville crisis, demonstrate that Black political protest should not be conceived as the steady application of liberal democratic principles to an authoritarian regime. Lodge, *Black Politics*, chapters 6, 7 and 9. Women, angrily aware of the ways in which migrant labour robbed men of their ability to perform their traditional roles as protector, had not been humiliated by and accustomed to unskilled industrial work and constant pass checks. The threat of the women's pass system being enforced by the National Party after 1948 worried both low-paid, foreign and domestic labourers and brought the threat of sexual harassment at the hands of pass control officialdom.
22. Lodge, *Black Politics*, 181.
23. See chapter 3 for detailed discussion of these tendencies.
24. Madison's separation of powers and representative system of government were designed explicitly to exclude the democracy of the deliberation of the common will. The 'true distinction' of America's governments, according to Madison, 'lies in the total exclusion of the people, in their collective capacity, from any share'. *The Federalist*, no.

63, cited in G.S. Wood, 'Democracy and the American Revolution', in J. Dunn (ed.), *Democracy* (Oxford: Oxford University Press 1992), 91–105, 97. See also T. Ball, *Transforming Political Discourse* (Oxford: Oxford University Press, 1988) 59–78.
25. Dunn (ed.), *Democracy*, 247.
26. Dunn (ed.), *Democracy*, 248.
27. J. Schumpeter, *Capitalism, Socialism and Democracy* (New York: Harper, 1947).
28. J.F. Revel, *Democracy against Itself: the Future of the Democratic Impulse*, trans. R. Kaplan (New York: Free Press, 1993) viii–ix.
29. P. Ricoeur, 'The Political Paradox', in W. Connolly (ed.), *Legitimacy and the State* (New York: New York University Press, 1984).
30. See, in particular, H. Lever, *The South African Voter: Some Aspects of Voting Behaviour* (Cape Town: Juta Books, 1972).
31. It is mostly economists who have tried to understand economic and social change as framed by the decisions of elected politicians. See, for example, Lipton, *Capitalism and Apartheid*.
32. Dunn, *Democracy*, 264.
33. Wood, 'Democracy', 91.
34. R. Maidment, 'Democracy in the USA since 1945', in D. Potter, D. Goldblatt, M. Kiloh and P. Lewis (eds.), *Democratization* (Cambridge: Polity Press, 1997) 118.
35. Freedom House, *Freedom in the World: Political Rights and Civil Liberties* (University of America, 1997).
36. Przeworski and Limongi, 'Modernization', 178–9.
37. Przeworski and Limongi, 'Modernization', 178.
38. Worden, *Making of Modern South Africa*, 39.
39. Worden, *Making of Modern South Africa*, 41.
40. S. Greenberg, *Race and State in Capitalist Development* (Johannesburg: Ravan, 1980) 391.
41. B. Hirson, *Yours for the Union: Class and community struggles in South Africa 1930–47* (London: Zed Books, 1989) especially chapter 3.
42. Greenberg, *Race and State*, 391–2.
43. Greenberg, *Race and State*, 392.
44. Greenberg, *Race and State*, 392–3.
45. Posel, *Making of Apartheid*, chapter 9, for definition of phases.
46. Posel, *Making of Apartheid*. See also chapter 2 above.
47. These states were not granted international recognition but received the blessing of a number of UK parliamentarians.
48. Worden, *Making*, chapter 6.
49. High apartheid also created new administrative structures and thereby progressively created a new class structure. The African politicians, bureaucrats and entrepreneurs who took advantage of the systems of patronage, power and incentive in the new Bantustans developed into 'a new class of collaborators'. Worden, *Making*, 113.
50. P. Bonner, P. Delius and D. Posel, 'The Shaping of Apartheid: Contradiction, Continuity and Popular Struggle', in Bonner, Delius and Posel (eds), *Apartheid's Genesis 1935–62* (Johannesburg: Witwatersrand University Press, 1993) 34.

51. H.L.A. Hart and M. Honore, *Causation and the Law* (Oxford: Oxford University Press, 1956).
52. See S. Lukes, *Marxism and Morality* (Oxford: Clarendon, 1985) on the coexistence of historical inevitability and moral appraisal within Marxist political thought. Lukes isolates the problem by identifying within Marxism a consequentialist perfectionism. On the problem of historical inevitability and human agency in Marxism, see G.A. Cohen, 'Historical Inevitability and Human Agency', in Cohen, *History, Labour, and Freedom: Themes from Marx* (Oxford: Clarendon, 1987) 51–82.
53. See, for example, Greenberg, *Race and State*; see also, J. Cell, *the Highest State of White Supremacy: The Origins of Segregation in South Africa and the American South* (Cambridge: Cambridge University Press, 1982).
54. See chapter 3 for extended discussion of the literature.
55. N. Worden and C. Crais (eds), *Breaking the Chains: Slavery and Emancipation in the Nineteenth-century Cape Colony* (Johannesburg: Witwatersrand University Press, 1993); D. Posel, *Making of Apartheid*, chapter 9; M. Legassick, 'British Hegemony and the Origins of Segregation in South Africa, 1900–09', in W. Beinart and S. Dubow (eds), *Segregation and Apartheid in Twentieth Century South Africa* (London: Routledge, 1995) 43–59.
56. Posel, *Making of Apartheid*, chapter 9.
57. J. Lazar, 'Verwoerd versus the Visionaries: The South African Bureau of Racial Affairs (SABRA) and Apartheid, 1948–1961', in Bonner et al., *Apartheid's Genesis*, 373.
58. Beinart, *Twentieth Century*, 134.
59. J.S. Mill, cited in M. Legassick, 'British Hegemony and the Origins of Segregation', in Beinart and Dubow (eds), *Segregation and Apartheid* 59, 51; source of Mill citation not identified.
60. J. Bryce, *Impressions of South Africa*, cited in Legassick, 'British Hegemony', 50.
61. J.H. Plumb, *England in the Eighteenth Century* (Baltimore: Penguin, 1950) 50.
62. See W.E. Connolly, 'Democracy and Territoriality', in M. Ringrose and A. Lerner (eds), *Re-imagining the Nation* (Oxford: Oxford University Press, 1993) 49–75.
63. See A.M. Butler, *Transformative Politics: the Future of Socialism in Western Europe* (London: Macmillan, 1995) chapter 2.
64. Connolly, 'Democracy and Territoriality', 59.
65. Union of South Africa, *Native Laws Commission* (Fagan Commission) (1946) 19, cited in Posel, *Making of Apartheid*, 48.
66. Much of the best land, inevitably, was on the borders of the reserves; in particular, control over water supplies would be lost in many areas by small expansions of the reserve boundaries.
67. Posel, *Making of Apartheid*, 50.
68. SABRA, *Integration or Separate Development* (Stellenbosch: SABRA, 1952) 11, cited Posel, *Making of Apartheid*, 50–1.
69. Cited in Dubow, 'Elaboration of Segregationist Ideology', in Beinart and Dubow, *Segregation and Apartheid*, 160.
70. See Beinart, *Twentieth Century South Africa*, chapter 5.

71. Quoted J. Lazar, 'Verwoerd versus the Visionaries', in Bonner et al., *Apartheid's Genesis*, 372.
72. Dunn, 'How Democracies Succeed', 5–18.
73. F. Cooper, *Decolonization and African Society: The Labour Question in French and British Africa* (Cambridge: Cambridge University Press, 1996) 469.
74. See S.N'Z. Grovogui, *Sovereigns, Quasi-Sovereigns, and Africans: Race and Self-determination in International Law* (Minneapolis: University of Minnesota Press, 1996).

CHAPTER 5

1. These figures are from D. Potter, 'Explaining Democratization', in D. Potter, D. Goldblatt, M. Killoh and P. Lewis (eds), *Democratization* (Cambridge: Polity Press, 1997) 1, 5 and 9. I have drawn very heavily on this excellent collection in this chapter.
2. S. P. Huntingdon, *The Third Wave: Democratization in the Late Twentieth Century* (Norman: University of Oklahoma Press, 1991).
3. Potter, 'Explaining Democratization', 9–10.
4. L. Diamond, 'Economic Development and Democracy Reconsidered', in *American Behavioural Scientist* 35:4/5 (1992) 450–99.
5. See A. Przeworski and F. Limongi, 'Modernization: Theories and Facts' in *World Politics* 49 (1997) 155–83. For versions of Lipset's initial thesis, see S.M. Lipset, *Political Man* (London: Heinemann, 1983); and S. M. Lipset, 'Some Social Requisites of Democracy', *American Political Science Review* 53 (1959).
6. On whether the relationship should be viewed as linear, see Przeworski and Limongi, 'Modernization', 156, n. 4.
7. Przeworski and Limongi, 'Modernization', 156–7. On this thesis, of course, it might have been possible that the establishment of democracy varies inversely with the level of development, but that survival nevertheless establishes the positive relationship with development. As Przeworski and Limongi show, however, this is not the case.
8. Przeworski and Limongi, 'Modernization', 159.
9. Przeworski and Limongi, 'Modernization', 159.
10. Data from 1950–90, with US dollar 1985 values; regimes classified as democracy or authoritarian only.
11. S.P. Huntingdon, *Political Order in Changing Societies* (New Haven, Yale University Press, 1968) 43.
12. Przeworski and Limongi, 'Modernization', 160.
13. Przeworski and Limongi, 'Modernization', 165.
14. Przeworski and Limongi, 'Modernization', 165–6.
15. B. Moore, *Social Origins of Dictatorship and Democracy: Lord and Peasant in the Making of the Modern World* (Boston: Beacon Press, 1965).
16. Moore, *Social Origins*, 4 and 3.
17. Moore, *Social Origins*, 4 and 4.
18. Moore, *Social Origins*, 430–1.

19. D.R. Rueschemeyer, E.H. Stephens and J.D. Stephens, *Capitalist Development and Democracy* (Cambridge: Polity Press, 1992).
20. Potter 'Explaining Democratization', 22.
21. A. Przeworski and F. Limongi, 'Modernization', 176; A. Przeworski, *Democracy and the Market: Political and Economic Reform in Eastern Europe and Latin America* (Cambridge: Cambridge University Press, 1991).
22. D. Rustow, 'Transitions to Democracy', *Comparative Politics* 2 (1970) 337–63, 340; cited Potter et al., *Democratization*, 14.
23. See, in particular, G. O'Donnell, P. Schmitter and L. Whitehead (eds), *Transitions from Authoritarian Rule* (Baltimore: Johns Hopkins University Press, 1986) 4 vols; and, for the implications of transition upon future political reforms, Y. Shain and J. Linz (eds), *Between States: Interim Governments and Democratic Transitions* (Cambridge: Cambridge University Press, 1995).
24. See L. Whitehead, 'Democratic Transitions', in J. Krieger (ed.) *Oxford Companion to Politics of the World* (Oxford: Oxford University Press, 1993). I have drawn heavily on Whitehead's incisive analysis here.
25. Whitehead, 'Democratic Transitions', 225.
26. Whitehead, 'Democratic Transitions'.
27. Whitehead, 'Democratic Transitions', 225.
28. Whitehead, 'Democratic Transitions', 225.
29. A. Przeworski, 'Democracy as a Contingent Outcome of Conflict', in J. Elster and R. Slagstad (eds), *Constitutionalism and Democracy* (Cambridge: Cambridge University Press, 1988) 63.
30. Przeworski, 'Democracy as Contingent Outcome', 61.
31. S.M. Lipset, 'The Social Requisites of Democracy Revisited', in *American Sociological Review* 59 (1994) 1–22, 16.
32. Lipset, 'Social Requisites', 18.
33. A. Leftwich, 'From Democratization to Democratic Consolidation', in Potter et al. (eds), *Democratization*, 517–37, 522.
34. Marxist theory has likewise accommodated itself to the vagaries of contingency and human agency within a deterministic framework.
35. Whitehead, 'Democratic Transitions', 226.
36. P. Lewis, 'Democratization in Eastern Europe', in Potter et al. (eds), *Democratization*, 414.
37. Lewis, 'Democratization in Eastern Europe', 410.
38. Lewis, 'Democratization in Eastern Europe', 413.
39. A. Leftwich, 'From Democratization to Democratic Consolidation', in Potter et al. (eds) *Democratization*, 521.
40. Rueschemeyer et al., *Capitalist Development and Democracy*, 159. See Leftwich, in 'From Democratization', 522.
41. Potter, 'Explaining', 23.
42. See A. Kohli, P. Evans, P. Katzenstein, A. Przeworski, S. Rudolf, J. Scott and T. Skocpol, 'The Role of Theory in Comparative Politics: a Symposium', *World Politics* 48 (1995) 1–49.
43. Przeworski and Limongi, 'Modernization', 177.
44. Leftwich, 'From Democratization', 523.
45. Leftwich, 'From Democratization', 523.

46. See also Przeworski and Limongi, 'Modernization', 167–8.
47. See the discussion in M. Mamdani, *Citizen and Subject: Contemporary Africa and the Legacy of Late Colonialism* (Princeton: Princeton University Press, 1996) 9–11.
48. See S. Kaviraj, 'On State, Society and Discourse in India', in J. Manor (ed.), *Rethinking Third World Politics* (London: Longman, 1991).
49. J. Wiseman, 'Democracy in Africa' in Potter et al., *Democratization*, 272–93, 285.
50. T. Young, 'Elections and Electoral Politics in Africa' in *Africa* 63: 3 (1993) 299–312, 299.
51. Young, 'Elections and Electoral Politics', 310, n. 6.
52. Young, 'Elections and Electoral Politics'.
53. Young, 'Elections and Electoral Politics', 300.
54. J. A. Wiseman (ed.), *Democracy and Political Change in Sub-Saharan Africa* (London: Routledge, 1995); Wiseman, *The New Struggle for Democracy in Africa* (Aldershot: Avebury, 1996).
55. L. Diamond, 'Rethinking Civil Society', in *Journal of Democracy*, 5:3 (1994) 4–17; D.E. Apter and C.G. Rosberg (eds), *Political Development and a New Realism in Sub-Saharan African* (Charlottesville: University of Virginia Press, 1994); P. Gifford (ed.), *The Christian Churches and the Democratisation of Africa* (Leiden: E. J. Brill, 1995).
56. Wiseman, *Democracy in Africa*, 288.
57. J. Dunn, 'How Democracies Succeed' in *Economy and Society*, 25: 4 (1996) 511–628, 515; see also T. Skocpol, *States and Social Revolutions* (Cambridge: Cambridge University Press, 1979).
58. See M. Mann, 'The Autonomous Power of the State', in J. A. Hall (ed.), *States in History* (Oxford: Blackwell, 1986).
59. Whitehead, 'Political Transitions', 226–7.
60. W. Galenson, 'Introduction' to Galenson (ed.), *Labour and Economic Development* (New York: Wiley, 1959) 3; K. De Schweinitz Jr, 'Industrialization, Labour Controls and Democracy', in *Economic Development and Cultural Change*, 7 (July 1959); both quoted in Przeworski and Limongi, 'Modernization', 177.
61. See T. Young, 'Governance, the World Bank and Liberal Theory', in *Political Studies* 42 (1994) 84–100.
62. Samuel Huntingdon's career is fascinating in this regard. His work has provided the justification for (and seeming celebration of) the engineering of both authoritarian regimes and democratic ones over the past three decades. See the conclusion to Przeworski and Limongi 'Modernization'; compare Huntingdon, *Third Wave*, Conclusion.
63. See J. Herbst, 'The Structural Adjustment of Politics in Africa', in *World Development*, 18: 7 (1990) 949–58; L. Diamond and M. Plattner (eds), *Economic Reform and Democracy* (Baltimore: Johns Hopkins University Press, 1995); S. Haggard and R.R. Kaufman, *Political Economy of Democratic Transitions* (Princeton: Princeton University Press, 1995).
64. The US was willing to prolong the war in Angola until the MPLA was willing to accept a multi-party system.

65. C.R. Crocker, *High Noon in Southern Africa: Making Peace in a Rough Neighbourhood* (New York: W.H. Norton, 1992).
66. Wiseman, *New Struggle*, 36.
67. See G. Hawthorn, 'The Crises of Southern States', in J. Dunn (ed.), *Contemporary Crisis of the Nation State?* (Oxford: Blackwell, 1994).

CHAPTER 6

1. R.M. Unger, *Social Theory: Its Situation and its Task* (Cambridge: Cambridge University Press, 1987).
2. See, for example, Y. Shain and J. Linz (eds), *Between States: Interim Governments and Democratic Transitions* (Cambridge: Cambridge University Press, 1995); and L. Diamond and M. Plattner (eds), *Economic Reform and Democracy* (Baltimore: Johns Hopkins University Press, 1995).
3. I have found particularly useful the following papers: N. Etherington, 'Is it too Early to Start Devising Historical Explanations for the End of Apartheid?', in P.B. Rich (ed.), *The Dynamics of Change in Southern Africa* (London: Macmillan, 1994), and K. Asmal, 'The Making of a Constitution', *Southern African Review of Books* 36 (1995).
4. See J.B. Goodman and L.W. Pauly, 'The Obsolescence of Capital Controls? Economic Management in an Age of Global Markets', *World Politics* 46 (1993) 50–82.
5. J. Herbst, 'South Africa: Economic Crises and Distributional Imperative', in S.J. Stedman (ed.), *South Africa: The Political Economy of Transformation* (London: Lynne Rienner, 1994) 29–45.
6. Asmal, 'Making of a Constitution'.
7. Asmal, 'Making of a Constitution', section III.
8. Asmal, 'Making', section III. In particular, Asmal points to the ANC's concession of 'sunset clauses' to the advantage of retired and near-retired military, security and police officers and civil servants, as instruments of advance.
9. A. Johnston, 'South Africa: the Election and the Emerging Party System', *International Affairs* 70:4 (1994) 721–36, 722.
10. Asmal, 'Making', section IV.
11. For coherent analysis of the South African state, see R. Schrire (ed.), *Malan to de Klerk: Leadership in the Apartheid State* (London: Hurst, 1994); on the influx control state, see Posel, *Making of Apartheid*; on the security state, see K.W. Grundy, *The Militarization of South African Politics* (Bloomington: University of Indiana Press, 1986).
12. The NP itself was riven by historical and ideological divides and the process predicted for the ANC – disintegration once a common enemy had vanished – has instead been inflicted on the NP. The historical gulf between Cape and Transvaal has widened; and the 'enlightened' wing of the party may break away into new parties.
13. T. Lodge, 'Rebellion: the Turning of the Tide', in T. Lodge et al., *All, Here, and Now: Black Politics in South Africa in the 1980s* (London:

Hurst, 1992) 29; I have relied heavily on Lodge's account of the UDF here.

14. Notably the Industrial Relations Act of 1979 which legalized unions in order to control them, but resulted in their growth and militancy; and the new constitution of 1983, designed to incorporate Coloured and Indian into the political system, but in effect stimulating debate and opposition.
15. Lodge, 'Rebellion', 34.
16. Lodge, 'Rebellion', 38.
17. See J. Seekings, *Heroes or Villains? Youth Politics in the 1980s* (Johannesburg: Ravan, 1993); see also C. Bundy, 'Street Society and Pavement Politics: Some Aspects of Student/Youth Consciousness during the 1985 Schools Crisis in Greater Cape Town', *Journal of Southern African Studies* 13:3 (1997) 303–30; D. Everatt and E. Sisulu (eds), *Black Youth in Crisis: Facing the Future* (Johannesburg: Ravan, 1992).
18. See, for example, T. Lodge, *Black Politics in South Africa Since 1945* (London: Longman, 1983) chapter 6; J.C. Wells, 'Why Women Rebel: a Comparative Study of South African Women's Resistance in Bloemfontein (1913) and Johannesburg (1958)', *Journal of Southern African Studies* 10:1 (1983) 55–70.
19. C. Walker (ed.), *Women and Gender in Southern Africa to 1945* (London: James Currey, 1990); B. Bozzoli (ed.), *Class, Community and Conflict* (Johannesburg: 1987); E. Unterhalter, 'Class, Race and Gender', in J. Lonsdale (ed.), *South Africa in Question* (Cambridge: Cambridge University Press, 1988) 154–71.
20. But see R. Southall, *South Africa's Transkei: the Political Economy of an 'Independent' Bantustan* (London: Heinemann, 1982); and C. Murray, 'Displaced Urbanization: South Africa's Rural Slums', in J. Lonsdale (ed.), *South Africa in Question*. For historical perspectives on agriculture, see W. Beinart, 'Agrarian Historiography and Agrarian Reconstruction', in J. Lonsdale (ed.) *South Africa in Question*; and M. de Klerk, *A Harvest of Discontent* (Cape Town: IDASA, 1991).
21. See, in particular, J. Comaroff, *Body of Power, Spirit of Resistance* (Chicago: Chicago University Press, 1985); M. West, *Bishops and Prophets in a Black City* (Cape Town: David Philip, 1975).
22. For overviews, see S. Friedman, *Building Tomorrow Today: African Workers in Trade Unions, 1970–1985* (Johannesburg: Raven, 1987); J. Baskin, *Striking Back: a History of COSATU* (London: Verso, 1991); G. Kraak, *Breaking the Chains: Labour in South Africa in the 1970s and 1980s* (London: Pluto, 1993); and issues of *South African Labour Bulletin*.
23. For analysis of the ideological influences on the ANC, especially on its left, see Lodge, 'Rebellion', Part III.
24. Lodge, 'Rebellion', Part III.
25. C. McCarthy, 'Apartheid Ideology and Economic Development Policy', in N. Nattrass and E. Ardington (eds), *The Political Economy of South Africa* (Cape Town: Oxford University Press, 1990) 43–54, 46.
26. See A.M. Butler, 'Political Attitudes in South Africa', *Government and Opposition* 32:1 (1997) 145–52.

27. See R. Taylor and M. Orkin, 'The Racialisation of Social Scientific Research on South Africa', *South African Sociological Review* 7:2 (1995) 43–69.
28. See C. Carter, *The Politics of Inequality: South Africa since 1948* (London: Thames and Hudson, 1958); K. Heard, *General Elections in South Africa, 1943–1970* (Oxford: Oxford University Press, 1974).
29. For proof that well-constructed research was possible for a determined analyst in even the most difficult circumstances, see M. Kentridge, *An Unofficial War: Inside the Conflict in Pietermaritzburg* (Capetown: David Philip, 1990).
30. M. Mamdani, *Citizen and Subject* (Princeton: Princeton University Press, 1996) chapter 1.
31. Mamdani, *Citizen and Subject*, 24.
32. Mamdani, *Citizen and Subject*, 24, 13, 7, 8.
33. Mamdani, *Citizen and Subject*, 289, 286.
34. Frederick Cooper's analysis of colonial labour recruitment and control, by contrast, recognizes the capacity of individuals to adopt complex strategies in response to the circumstances they face. See F. Cooper, *Decolonization and African Society: the Labour Question in French and British Africa* (Cambridge: Cambridge University Press, 1996).
35. For an excellent concise history of the subject, see P. Schmitter, 'Comparative Politics', J. Krieger (ed.), *Oxford Companion to the Politics of the World* (Oxford: Oxford University Press, 1993) 171–7.
36. See S. Greenberg, *Race, State, and Capitalist Development* (Johannesburg: Ravan, 1980).
37. T. Sisk, *Democratization in South Africa* (Princeton: Princeton University Press, 1995) 4.
38. Schmitter, 'Comparative Politics', 173.
39. A. Lijphart, *Power Sharing in South Africa* (Berkeley: University of California Institute of International Studies, 1985) 19–20.
40. See, for example, S. Gelb (ed.), *South Africa's Economic Crisis* (Capetown: David Philip, 1991).

CHAPTER 7

1. Economists, likewise, resorted to high-level generalities (of the 'urban, informal sector') when exploring township economics. They address phenomena that are neither urban (given the networks connecting city and country around which they are often based), nor informal (given that they involve highly structured relationships), nor even sectoral (in that they involve activities spanning across conventionally distinct institutional arenas). See F. Cooper, *Decolonization and African Society* (Cambridge: Cambridge University Press, 1996), Conclusion.
2. MacDonald reports that Lijphart's name was often raised in interviews by South African parliamentarians in 1991, one day in consecutive interviews by three members from three different parties, and with no prompting from MacDonald. See M. MacDonald, 'The Siren's Song:

the Political Logic of Power-sharing in South Africa', *Journal of Southern African Studies* 18:4 (1992) 709–25, n.13.
3. Cited M. Mamdani, *Citizen and Subject* (Princeton: Princeton University Press, 1996) 5.
4. M. Murray, *South Africa: Time of Agony, Time of Destiny* (London: Verso, 1987) 112.
5. T. Sisk, *Democratization in South Africa* (Princeton: Princeton University Press, 1995) 70.
6. But for powerful criticism, see S.C. Nolutshungu, *Changing South Africa: Political Considerations* (Manchester: Manchester University Press, 1982).
7. A. Lijphart, 'Consociational Democracy', in J. Krieger (ed.), *Oxford Companion to Politics of the World* (Oxford: Oxford University Press, 1993).
8. Lijphart, 'Consociational Democracy', 189.
9. A. Lijphart, *Power Sharing in South Africa* (Berkeley: University of California, 1985) 22, 27, 28.
10. I. Shapiro and C. Jung, 'South African Democracy Revisited', *Politics and Society* 24:3 (1996) 237–47.
11. These preconditions are drawn from A. Lijphart, *Democracy in Plural Societies: a Comparative Explanation* (New Haven: Yale University Press, 1977); 'Electoral Systems, Party Systems and Conflict Management in Segmented Societies', in R. Schrire (ed.), *Critical Choices in South Africa: An Agenda for the 1990s* (Cape Town: Oxford University Press, 1990); P. Ferdinand, 'Nationalism, Community and Democratic Transition in Czechoslovakia and Yugoslavia', D. Potter et al. (eds), *Democratization* (Cambridge: Polity, 1997), 466–89.
12. The key quasi-state studies were: Quail Commission, *Ciskei Commission Report* (Pretoria: Conference Associates, 1980); Lombard Report, *Alternatives to the Constitution of KwaZulu* (Pretoria: BEPA, 1980); Buthelezi Commission, *Requirements for Stability and Development in KwaZulu and Natal* (Durban: H&H Publishers, 1982). On the corporate and parastatal funding sources for these projects, see R. Taylor and M. Orkin, 'The Racialisation of Social Scientific Research on South Africa', *South African Sociological Review* 7:2 (1995) 43–69.
13. Lijphart, *Power Sharing*, 19–20, emphasis added.
14. R. Price, 'South Africa: the Political Economy of Growth and Democracy', in S.J. Stedman (ed.), *South Africa: the Political Economy of Transformation* (London: Lynne Rienner, 1994) 181–98, 184.
15. MacDonald shows how Horowitz's affirmed historical-contextual understanding of ethnicity is at odds with his affirmations of the timeless priority of ethnicity in African society. See 'Siren's Song', 722–4. Shapiro and Jung, 'South African Democracy', 243.
16. MacDonald, 'Siren's Song', 722.
17. D. Welsh, 'Ethnicity in sub-Saharan Africa', *International Affairs* 72:3 (1996) 485.
18. MacDonald, 'Siren's Song', 725.
19. G van N. Viljoen, 'Constitutional Safeguards and the Negotiating Process', speech of 27 September 1990, quoted MacDonald, 'Siren's Song', 715.

20. R.W. Johnson and L. Schlemmer, *Launching Democracy in South Africa* (New Haven: Yale University Press, 1996) 209.
21. E.N. Tjonneland (ed.), *South Africa's 1994 Elections* (Oslo: Norwegian Institute of Human Rights, 1994) 1 .
22. Sisk, *Democratization*, 297.
23. T. Young, 'Elections and Electoral Politics in Africa', *Africa* 93:3 (1993) 300.
24. J. Lonsdale, 'Political Accountability in African History', in P. Chabal (ed.), *Political Domination in Africa* (Cambridge: Cambridge University Press, 1986) 126–57, 129.
25. Lonsdale, 'Political Accountability', 137.
26. Debates over whether political attitudes among Africans should rightly be understood as 'group' or collective attributes, as crude tribalists insist, overlook the obvious fact that arguments about political accountability and demands that authority be brought to account can only be conducted within social institutions. Where ethnic associations are the most vibrant of social institutions, they may be the only arenas within which such argument can be pursued.
27. Lonsdale, 'Political Accountability', 126–7.
28. This robust finding of political science is especially firmly grounded in states with deregulated public transport systems.
29. See M.S. Lewis-Beck, *Economics and Elections* (Ann Arbor: Michigan University Press, 1988).
30. Cited Young, 'Elections', 306.
31. See, in particular, A. Campbell, P. Converse, W. Miller and D. Stokes, *The American Voter* (New York: Wiley, 1960); and N. Nie, S. Verba and J. Petrocik, *The Changing American Voter* (Cambridge: Harvard University Press, 1976).
32. Taylor and Orkin, 'Racialisation of Social Scientific Research', 48.
33. Johnson and Schlemmer, *Launching Democracy*, 368.
34. Johnson and Schlemmer, *Launching Democracy*, 362.
35. Johnson and Schlemmer, *Launching Democracy*, 61
36. The presence of questions designed for different racial groups is revealed by 'You African like Big Leader?' questions, e.g. Johnson and Schlemmer, *Launching Democracy*, 196, 255.
37. Johnson and Schlemmer, *Launching Democracy*, 208.
38. Johnson and Schlemmer, *Launching Democracy*, 196
39. Johnson and Schlemmer, *Launching Democracy*, 254.
40. Johnson and Schlemmer, *Launching Democracy*, 152, 146, 147.
41. Johnson and Schlemmer, *Launching Democracy*, 64.
42. Johnson and Schlemmer, *Launching Democracy*, 86.
43. Johnson and Schlemmer, *Launching Democracy*, 205, 194, 209.
44. Johnson and Schlemmer, *Launching Democracy*, 215, 214.
45. Johnson and Schlemmer, *Launching Democracy*, 208.
46. Johnson and Schlemmer, *Launching Democracy*, 262–3.
47. Johnson and Schlemmer, *Launching Democracy*, 358, 359, 364.
48. Johnson and Schlemmer, *Launching Democracy*, 3.
49. *Weekly Mail and Guardian*, 29 November (1996).
50. Johnson and Schlemmer, *Launching Democracy*, 88, 364–5, 372, 360

51. See Taylor and Orkin, 'Racialisation of Social Scientific Research', 51.
52. Taylor and Orkin, 'Racialisation of Social Science Research', 46.
53. See E. Barkan, *The Retreat of Scientific Racism* (Cambridge: Cambridge University Press, 1982).
54. R. Mattes, *The Election Book: Judgement and Choice in South Africa's 1994 Election* (Cape Town: IDASA, 1995); on the Western Cape, see M. Eldridge and J. Seekings, 'Mandela's Lost Province: the ANC and the Western Cape Electorate in the 1994 elections', *Journal of Southern African Studies* 22:4 (1996) 517–40.
55. T. Lodge, 'South Africa 1994: Election of a Special Kind', *Southern African Review of Books* 6:2 (1994) 3–5. Lodge's analysis of Western elections seems a little flattering to them; and his reading has not necessarily been supported by events, and in particular by local election results.
56. Shain and Linz (eds), *Between States*.
57. Consolidation is normally defined by means of a two-election test, or a transfer of power criterion. For a useful review, see D. Beetham, 'Conditions for Democratic Consolidation', *Review of African Political Economy* 60 (1993) 157–72.
58. S. Haggard and R.R. Kaufman, *The Political Economy of Democratic Transition* (Princeton: Princeton University Press, 1995).
59. On culture and religion, see Huntington, *Third Wave*; on national unity and the idea of the people, see G. Nodia, 'Nationalism and Democracy', *Journal of Democracy* 3:4 (1992) 3–22; on state capacity, see G. Hawthorn, 'Sub-Saharan Africa', in D. Held (ed.), *Prospects for Democracy* (Cambridge: Polity, 1993) 330–54.
60. R. Tucker and B. Scott, *South Africa: Prospects for a Successful Transition* (Kenwyn: Juta, 1992); Frankel Max Pollak Vinderine, Sanlam, Ernst and Young, and The Human Sciences Research Council, *Platform for Investment* (Human Sciences Research Council, 1993); Institute for Social Development, *Mont Fleur Scenarios* (Bellville: University of the Western Cape, 1993); Professional Economists Panel, *Growing Together* (Johannesburg: Nedcor and Old Mutual, 1993).
61. H. Adam and K. Moodley, *The Negotiated Revolution* (Johannesburg: Ravan, 1993).

CHAPTER 8

1. H. Wright, *Burden of the Present* (Cape Town: David Philip, 1977).
2. S. Bekker, 'Social Research and the Politics of Pre-negotiations', in P. Hugo (ed.), *Truth Be in the Field: Social Science Research in South Africa* (Pretoria: UNISA, 1990) 1–14.
3. See J. Cock, 'Guilt, Fear, and Other Difficulties in Researching Domestic Relations', in Hugo (ed.) *Truth*, 15–23.
4. C. Cross, 'Africa and the People without Numbers', in Hugo (ed.), *Truth*, 24–44.
5. R. Taylor and M. Orkin, 'Racialisation of Social Scientific Research in South Africa', in *South African Sociological Review* 7:2 (1995) 49.

6. This parallel is sharply drawn by J. Seekings, 'Some Comments of "The Racialisation of Social Research in South Africa"', *South African Sociological Review*, 7:2 (1995) 60–9.
7. Heated debates about academic freedom show how difficult it can be for even professional social analysts to register the multiple purposes served by the institutions in which they are embedded, and the influence of state funding, commercial sponsorship, markets, bureaucratically powerful academic peers and the social experiences of the researcher.
8. A. Hadenius, 'Introduction', to A. Hadenius (ed.), *Democracy's Victory and Crisis* (Cambridge: Cambridge University Press, 1997) 2.
9. A.M. Butler, 'Unpopular Leaders: the British Case', *Political Studies*, 43 (1995) 48–65; D. Putnam, *Making Democracy Work* (Princeton: Princeton University Press, 1993); P. Schmitter, 'Explaining the Problematic Triumph of Liberal Democracy', in Hadenius, *Democracy's Victory*, 297–307.
10. For reflections on these claimed properties, see A. Przeworski and F. Limongi, 'Democracy and development', in Hadenius, *Democracy's Victory*, 163–94; J. Lonsdale, 'Political Accountability in African History', in P. Chabal (ed.), *Political Domination in Africa* (Cambridge: Cambridge University Press, 1986) 226–57.
11. W.E. Connolly, 'Democracy and Territoriality', in M. Ringrose and A. Lerner (eds), *Reimagining the Nation* (Buckingham: Open University Press, 1993) 49–75.
12. Contemporary visions of the relations between state, nation and territory have a protracted history, with legacies of territoriality, universalism, sovereignty, nationality and territorial ideology. These have been cemented within newly stabilized international frontiers, suffused by the mystifications of international law and reinforced by great political settlements through which international elites have agreed frontiers. See M. Anderson, *Frontiers: Territory and State Formation in the Modern World* (Cambridge: Polity, 1996).
13. Schmitter, 'Explaining the Problematic Triumph', in Hadenius, *Democracy's Victory*, 300–1.
14. See M. Freeman, 'Democracy and Dynamite: the People's Right to Self-determination', *Political Studies* 44 (1996) 746–61; M. Moore, 'On National Self-determination', *Political Studies* 45 (1997) 900–13.
15. A. Margalit and J. Raz, 'National Self-determination', *Journal of Philosophy* 87 (1990) 439–62.
16. T. Nardin, *Law, Morality and the Relations of States* (Princeton: Princeton University Press, 1983).
17. M. Walzer, *Spheres of Justice* (Oxford: Oxford University Press, 1983) chapter 2.
18. A. Linklater, 'The Transformation of Political Community', *Review of International Studies* 23 (1997) 321–8, 336.
19. Linklater, 'Transformation', 327.
20. Collectively rational international agreements, moreover, as solutions to collective action problems thrown up by the relations between states, may be harder for embattled democratic politicians to negotiate than for authoritarian leaders.

21. See A. Phillips, *Engendering Democracy* (Cambridge: Polity Press, 1991).
22. Jackson has explored the nature of sovereignty in the quasi-states of the post colonial world, with their formal rights but their lack of capacity to make them meaningful. See R.H. Jackson, *Quasi-states: Sovereignty, International Relations and the Third World* (Cambridge: Cambridge University Press, 1990). Such states do not possess the capacity to make meaningful the formal claims to citizenship.
23. Schmitter, 'Explaining', 301.
24. Where leaders emerge outside party structures, by contrast, as is the case in many developing countries, they are often inclined to discourage the development of just such structures. This can perpetuate cycles of instability, short-term populism, and personal rule which make elections still more personally exposing. See A. Kohli, 'On Sources of Social and Political Conflict in Follower Democracies', in Hadenius, *Democracy's Victory*, 71–80.
25. This dichotomy is not necessarily sharp. Identification may be a rational strategy helping voters to overcome collective action problems and avoid costly information processing. An instrumentally rational elector, moreover, may rationally support a candidate speaking in familiar idioms, recognising social realities, articulating wants in comprehensible terms, and identifying potential political allies.
26. These are also the features that make it most potentially destructive.

Nothing by Bond, Desai, H. Marais

Bibliography

Adam, H. and K. Moodley, *The Negotiated Revolution* (Johannesburg: Ravan, 1993).
Anderson, M., *Frontiers: Territory and State Formation in the Modern World* (Cambridge: Polity, 1996).
Apter, D.E. and C. G. Rosberg (eds), *Political Development and a New Realism in Sub-Saharan African* (Charlottesville: University of Virginia Press, 1994).
Arnold, R.D., *The Logic of Congressional Action* (New Haven: Yale University Press, 1990).
Asmal, K., 'The Making of a Constitution', *Southern African Review of Books* 36 (1995).
Ball, T., *Transforming Political Discourse* (Oxford: Oxford University Press, 1988).
Barkan, E., *The Retreat of Scientific Racism* (Cambridge: Cambridge University Press, 1982).
Baskin, J., *Striking Back: A History of COSATU* (London: Verso, 1991).
Beetham, D., 'Conditions for Democratic Consolidation', *Review of African Political Economy* 60 (1993) 157–72.
Beinart, W. and S. Dubow (eds), *Segregation and Apartheid in 20th Century South Africa* (London: Routledge, 1995).
Beinart, W., *Twentieth Century South Africa* (Oxford: Oxford University Press, 1994).
Beinart W. and C. Bundy, *Hidden Struggles in Rural South Africa: the Politics and Popular Movements in the Transkei and Eastern Cape, 1890–1930* (Johannesburg: Ravan, 1987).
Bekker, S., *Ethnicity in Focus: the South African Case* (Durban: Indicator South Africa, 1993).
Biko, S., *I Write What I Like* (London: Heinemann, 1978).
Bonner, P., P. Delius and D. Posel (eds), *Apartheid's Genesis 1935–1962* (Johannesburg: Witwatersrand University Press, 1993).
Bozzoli, B., *Women of Phokeng* (Portsmouth, NH: Heinemann, 1991).
Bradford, H., *A Taste of Freedom: The ICU in Rural South Africa, 1924–30* (New Haven: Yale University Press, 1987).
Buchanan, J. and R. Wagner, *Democracy in Deficit: the Political Legacy of Lord Keynes* (New York: Academic Press, 1977).
Bundy, C., *The Rise and Fall of the South Africa Peasantry*, 2nd edn (London: James Currey, 1988).
Butler, A.M., 'Unpopular Leaders: the British Case', *Political Studies* 43 (1995) 48–65.
Butler, A.M., *Transformative Politics: the Future of Socialism in Western Europe* (London: Macmillan, 1995).
Butler, A.M., 'Political Attitudes in South Africa', *Government and Opposition* 32 (1997) 145–52.
Campbell, A., P. Converse, W. Miller and D. Stokes, *The American Voter* (New York: Wiley, 1960).

Carter, C., *The Politics of Inequality: South Africa since 1948* (London: Thames and Hudson, 1958).
Cell, J., *The Highest State of White Supremacy: the Origins of Segregation in South Africa and the American South* (Cambridge: Cambridge University Press, 1982).
Chabal, P. (ed.), *Political Domination in Africa* (Cambridge: Cambridge University Press, 1986).
Cobbing, J., 'The Mfecane as Alibi', *Journal of African History* 29 (1988) 487–519.
Cohen, G.A., *History, Labour, and Freedom: Themes from Marx* (Oxford: Clarendon, 1987).
Comaroff, J., *Body of Power, Spirit of Resistance* (Chicago: Chicago University Press, 1985).
Connolly, W. (ed.), *Legitimacy and the State* (New York: New York University Press, 1984).
Cooper, F., *Decolonisation and African Society: the Labour Question in French and British Africa* (Cambridge: Cambridge University Press, 1996).
Crocker, C.R., *High Noon in Southern Africa: Making Peace in a Rough Neighbourhood* (New York: W.H. Norton, 1992).
Crush, J., A. Jeeves and D. Yudelman, *South Africa's Labour Empire: a History of Black Migrancy to the Gold Mines* (Cape Town: David Philip, 1991).
Davenport, T.R.H., *South Africa: A Modern History* (London: Macmillan, 1991) 4th edition.
Davies, R., *Capital, State and White Labour in South Africa in 1900–1960: an Historical Materialist Analysis of Class Formation and Class Relations* (Brighton: Harvester, 1979).
Delius, P., 'Migrant Labour and the Pedi 1840–80', in S. Marks and A. Atmore (eds), *Economy and Society*, (London: Longman, 1980).
Diamond, L., 'Economic Development and Democracy Reconsidered' in *American Behavioural Scientist* 35 (1992) 450–99.
Diamond, L. and M. Plattner (eds), *Economic Reform and Democracy* (Baltimore: Johns Hopkins University Press, 1995).
Dubow, S., *Segregation and the Origins of Apartheid in South Africa* (London: Macmillan, 1989).
Dunn, J. (ed.) *Democracy: The Unfinished Journey* (Oxford: Oxford University Press, 1992).
Dunn, J. (ed.), *Contemporary Crisis of the Nation State?* (Oxford: Blackwell, 1994).
Dunn, J., 'How Democracies Succeed', *Economy and Society* 25: 4 (1996) 511–628.
Eldridge, M. and J. Seekings, 'Mandela's Lost Province', *Journal of Southern African Studies* 22:4 (1996) 517–40.
Elphick, R. and H. Giliomee (eds), *The Shaping of South African Society, 1652–1820* (Cape Town: Maskew Miller Longman, 1989).
Elster, J. and R. Slagstad (eds), *Constitutionalism and Democracy* (Cambridge: Cambridge University Press, 1988).
Etherington, N., 'Is it Too Early to Start Devising Historical Explanations for the End of Apartheid?', in P.B. Rich (ed.), *Dynamics of Change in Southern Africa* (London: Macmillan, 1994).

Frankel, P., N. Pines and M. Swilling (eds), *State, Resistance and Change in South Africa* (Johannesburg: Southern Books, 1988).
Freeman, M., 'Democracy and Dynamite: the People's Right to Self-determination', *Political Studies* 44 (1996) 746–61.
Fukuyama, F., *The End of History and the Last Man* (New York: Free Press, 1992).
Gelb, S. (ed.), *South Africa's Economic Crisis* (Cape Town: David Philip, 1991).
Gifford, P. (ed.), *The Christian Churches and the Democratisation of Africa* (Leiden: E. J. Brill, 1995).
Giliomee, H., 'The Growth of Afrikaner Identity', in H. Hadden and H. Giliomee, *Ethnic Power Mobilized* (New Haven: Yale University Press, 1979).
Goodman, J.B. and L.W. Pauly, 'The Obsolescence of Capital Controls? Economic Management in an Age of Global Markets', *World Politics* 46 (1993) 50–82.
Greenberg, S.B., *Race and State in Capitalist Development* (Johannesburg: Ravan, 1980).
Greenberg, S.B., *Legitimating the Illegitimate: State, Markets, and Resistance in South Africa* (Berkeley: University of California, 1987).
Grundy, K.W., *The Militarization of South African Politics* (Bloomington: University of Indiana Press, 1986).
Guy, J., 'Ecological Factors in the Rise of Shaka and the Zulu Kingdom', in S. Marks and A. Atmore (eds), *Economy and Society* (London: Longman, 1980).
Hadden, H. and H. Giliomee, *Ethnic Power Mobilised: Can South Africa Change?* (New Haven: Yale University Press, 1979).
Hadenius, A. (ed.), *Democracy's Victory and Crisis: Nobel Symposium No. 93* (Cambridge: Cambridge University Press, 1997).
Haggard, S. and R. R. Kaufman, *Political Economy of Democratic Transitions* (Princeton: Princeton University Press, 1995).
Hall, J.A. (ed.), *States in History* (Oxford: Blackwell, 1986).
Harries, P., 'Capital, State and Labour on the 19th Century Witwatersrand: a Reassessment', *South African Historical Journal* (1986) 25–45.
Hart, H.L.A. and M. Honore, *Causation and the Law* (Oxford: Oxford University Press, 1956).
Hawthorn, G., *Plausible Worlds* (Cambridge: Cambridge University Press 1990).
Hawthorn, G., 'The Crises of Southern States', in J. Dunn (ed), *Contemporary Crisis of the Nation State?* (Oxford: Blackwell, 1994).
Heard, K., *General Elections in South Africa, 1943–1970* (Oxford: Oxford University Press, 1974).
Held, D. (ed.), *Prospects for Democracy* (Cambridge: Polity Press, 1993).
Herbst, J., 'South Africa: Economic Crises and Distributional Imperative', in S.J. Stedman (ed.), *South Africa: The Political Economy of Transformation* (London: Lynne Rienner, 1994).
Hirson, B., *Yours for the Union: Class and Community Struggles in South Africa 1930–47* (London: Zed Books, 1989).
Hugo, P. (ed.), *Truth Be in the Field: Social Science Research in South Africa* (Pretoria: UNISA, 1990).

Huntingdon, S.P., *Political Order in Changing Societies* (New Haven: Yale University Press, 1968).
Huntington, S.P., *The Third Wave: Democratization in the Late Twentieth Century* (Norman: University of Oklahoma Press, 1991).
Jaarsveld, F.A. van, *The Awakening of Afrikaner Nationalism, 1868–1881*, translated F. R. Metrowich (Cape Town: Human and Rousseau, 1961).
Jackson, R.H., *Quasi-States: Sovereignty, International Relations and the Third World* (Cambridge: Cambridge University Press, 1990).
Jeeves, A., *Migrant Labour in South Africa's Mining Economy: the Struggle for the Gold Mines' Labour Supply 1890–1920* (Johannesburg: Witwatersrand University Press, 1985).
Johnson, R.W. and L. Schlemmer, *Launching Democracy in South Africa* (New Haven: Yale University Press, 1996).
Johnston, A., 'South Africa: the Election and the Emerging Party System', *International Affairs* 70:4 (1994) 721–36.
Johnstone, F., *Class, Race and Gold* (London: Routledge and Kegan Paul, 1976).
Kaase, M. and K. Newton, *Beliefs in Government* (Oxford: Oxford University Press, 1995) Vol. 5.
Karis, T. and G. Carter (eds), *From Protest to Challenge: a Documentary History of African Politics in South Africa, 1822–1964* (Stanford: Hoover Press, 1973) vol 1.
Keech, W.R., *Economic Politics: the Costs of Democracy* (Cambridge: Cambridge University Press, 1995).
Kentridge, M., *An Unofficial War: Inside the Conflict in Pietermaritzburg* (Cape Town: David Philip, 1990).
Klerk, M. de, *A Harvest of Discontent* (Cape Town: IDASA, 1991).
Knight, J., *Institutions and Social Conflict* (Cambridge: Cambridge University Press, 1992).
Kohli, A., P. Evans, P. Katzenstein, A. Przeworski, S. Rudolf, J. Scott and T. Skocpol, 'The Role of Theory in Comparative Politics: A Symposium', *World Politics* 48 (1995) 1–49.
Kraak, G., *Breaking the Chains: Labour in South Africa in the 1970s and 1980s* (London: Pluto, 1993).
Lazar, J., 'Verwoerd versus the "Visionaries": the South African Bureau of Racial Affairs (SABRA) and Apartheid, 1948–61', in P. Bonner et al., *Apartheid's Genesis, 1935–1962* (Johannesburg: Witwatersrand University Press, 1993).
Legassick, M., 'The Frontier Tradition in South African Historiography', in S. Marks and A. Atmore (eds), *Economy and Society* (London: Longman, 1980).
Legassick, M., 'British Hegemony and the Origins of Segregation in South Africa, 1901–14' in W. Beinart and S. Dubow (eds), *Segregation and Apartheid in 20th Century South Africa* (London: Routledge, 1995).
Lever, H., *The South African Voter: Some Aspects of Voting Behaviour* (Cape Town: Juta Books, 1972).
Lewis-Beck, M.S., *Economics and Elections* (Ann Arbor: University of Michigan Press, 1988).

Lijphart, A., *Power Sharing in South Africa* (Berkeley: University of California Institute of International Studies, 1985).
Lijphart, A., *Democracy in Plural Societies: a Comparative Explanation* (New Haven: Yale University Press, 1977).
Lijphart, A., 'Electoral Systems, Party Systems and Conflict Management in Segmented Societies', in R. Schrire (ed.), *Critical Choices in South Africa* (Cape Town: Oxford University Press, 1990).
Linklater, A., 'The Transformation of Political Community', *Review of International Studies* 23 (1997) 321–8.
Lipset, S.M., *Political Man: the Social Bases of Politics* (Baltimore: Johns Hopkins University Press, 1961).
Lipset, S.M., 'The Social Requisites of Democracy Revisited', *American Sociological Review* 59 (1994) 1–22.
Lipton, M., *Capitalism and Apartheid: South Africa, 1910–84* (Aldershot: Gower, 1985).
Lodge, T., *Black Politics in South Africa since 1945* (London: Longman, 1985).
Lodge, T., B. Nasson, S. Mufson, K. Shubane and N. Sithole, *All, Here, and Now* (London: Hurst, 1992).
Lonsdale, J. (ed.), *South Africa in Question* (Cambridge: Cambridge University Press, 1988).
Lonsdale, J., 'Political accountability in African History', in Chabal (ed.), *Political Domination in Africa* (Cambridge, Cambridge University Press, 1986).
Lukes, S., *Power: a Radical View* (Oxford: Oxford University Press, 1974).
Lukes, S., *Marxism and Morality* (Oxford: Clarendon, 1985).
MacDonald, M., 'The Siren's Song: the Political Logic of Power-sharing in South Africa', *Journal of Southern African Studies* 18:4 (1992) 709–25.
McCarthy, C. 'Apartheid Ideology and Economic Development Policy', in N. Nattrass and E. Ardington (eds), *Political Economy of South Africa* (Cape Town: Oxford University Press, 1990).
Mamdani, M., *Citizen and Subject: Contemporary Africa and the Legacy of Late Colonialism* (Princeton: Princeton University Press, 1996).
Mann, M. 'The Giant Stirs: South African Business in the Age of Reform' in Frankel, P., N. Pines and M. Swilling (eds), *State, Resistance and Change in South Africa* (Johannesburg: Southern Books, 1988).
Marks, S., *Reluctant Rebellion: the 1968 Disturbances in Natal* (Oxford: Clarendon Press, 1970).
Marks, S., 'Natal, the Zulu Royal Family and the Ideology of Segregation' in *Journal of South African Studies* 4 (1978) 172–94.
Marks, S., *The Ambiguities of Dependence in South Africa: Class, Nationalism and the State in 20th Century Natal* (Johannesburg: Ravan, 1986).
Marks, S. and S. Trapido, 'Lord Milner and the South African State', in *History Workshop Journal* 2 (1979) 50–80.
Marks, S. and A. Atmore (eds), *Economy and Society in Pre- Industrial South Africa* (London: Longman, 1980).
Marks, S. and S. Trapido (eds), *Politics of Race, Class, and Nationalism in Twentieth Century South Africa* (London: Longman, 1987).

Marx, A.W., *Lessons of Struggle: South African Internal Opposition, 1960–1990* (Oxford: Oxford University Press, 1991).
Mattes, R., *The Election Book* (Cape Town: IDASA, 1995).
Maylam, P., *A History of the African People of South Africa* (London: Longman, 1991) 4th edition.
Moll, T., 'From Booster to Brake: Apartheid and Economic Growth in Comparative Perspective', in N. Nattrass and E. Ardington (eds), *Political Economy of South Africa* (Cape Town: Oxford University Press, 1990).
Moodie, T. Dunbar, *The Rise of Afrikanerdom* (Berkeley: University of California Press, 1975).
Moore, B., *Social Origins of Dictatorship and Democracy: Lord and Peasant in the Making of the Modern World* (Boston: Beacon Press, 1965).
Moore, M., 'On National Self-determination', *Political Studies* 45 (1997) 900–13.
Muller, C., *Five Hundred Years: a History of South Africa* (Pretoria: Academica, 1975), 2nd edition.
Murray, M., *South Africa: Time of Agony, Time of Destiny* (London: Verso, 1987).
Nardin, T., *Law, Morality and the Relations of States* (Princeton: Princeton University Press, 1983).
Nattrass, N. and E. Ardington (eds), *Political Economy of South Africa* (Cape Town: Oxford University Press, 1990).
Nie, N., S. Verba, J, Petrocik, *The Changing American Voter* (Cambridge: Harvard University Press, 1976).
Nolutshungu, S.C., *Changing South Africa: Political Considerations* (Manchester: Manchester University Press, 1982).
North, D.C., *Institutions, Institutional Change and Economic Performance* (Cambridge: Cambridge University Press, 1990).
O'Donnell, G., P. Schmitter and L. Whitehead (eds), *Transitions from Authoritarian Rule* (Baltimore: Johns Hopkins Press, 1986) 4 vols.
Onselen, C. van, 'Race and Class in the South African Countryside: Cultural Osmosis and Social Relations in the Share Cropping Economy of the South Western Transvaal, 1900–50', *American Historical Review* 95 (1980) 44–79.
Onselen, C. van, *The Seed is Mine: the Life of Kas Maine, a South African Sharecropper 1894–1988* (Cape Town: David Philip, 1996).
Parekh, B., 'The Cultural Particularity of Liberal Democracy', in D. Held (ed.), *Prospects for Democracy* (Cambridge: Polity Press, 1993).
Phillips, A., *Engendering Democracy* (Cambridge: Polity Press, 1991).
Pierson, P., 'When Effect Becomes Cause: Policy Feedback and Political Change', in *World Politics* 45 (1993) 595–628.
Plumb, J.H., *England in the Eighteenth Century* (Baltimore: Penguin, 1950).
Posel, D., 'The Meaning of Apartheid before 1948: Conflicting Interests and Forces within the Afrikaner Nationalist Alliance', *Journal of Southern African Studies* 14 (1987) 123–39.
Posel, D., *The Making of Apartheid* (Oxford: Clarendon, 1991).
Potter, D., D. Goldblatt, M. Kiloh and P. Lewis (eds.), *Democratization* (Cambridge: Polity Press, 1997).
Price, R., *The Apartheid State in Crisis: Political Transformation in South Africa, 1975–1990* (Oxford: Oxford University Press, 1991).

Przeworski, A., *Democracy and the Market: Political and Economic Reform in Eastern Europe and Latin America* (Cambridge: Cambridge University Press, 1991).
Przeworski, A., 'Democracy as a Contingent Outcome of Conflict', in J. Elster and A. Slagstad (eds), *Constitutionalism and Democracy* (Cambridge: Cambridge University Press, 1988).
Przeworski, A. and F. Limongi, 'Modernization: Theories and Facts', *World Politics* 49 (1997) 155–83.
Putnam, D., *Making Democracy Work* (Princeton: Princeton University Press, 1993).
Revel, J.F., *Democracy Against Itself: the Future of the Democratic Impulse*, trans. R. Kaplan (New York: Free Press, 1993).
Rich, P.B. (ed.), *The Dynamics of Change in Southern Africa* (London: Macmillan, 1994).
Ringrose, M. and A. Lerner (eds), *Re-imagining the Nation* (Oxford: Oxford University Press, 1993).
Rueschemeyer, D.R., E.H. Stephens and J.D. Stephens, *Capitalist Development and Democracy* (Cambridge: Polity Press, 1992).
Saunders, S., *The Making of the South African Past: Major Historians on Race and Class* (Cape Town: David Philip, 1985).
Schrire, R. (ed.), *Critical Choices in South Africa. an Agenda for the 1990s* (Cape Town: Oxford University Press, 1990).
Schrire, R. (ed.), *Malan to de Klerk: Leadership in the Apartheid State* (London: Hurst, 1994).
Schumpeter, J., *Capitalism, Socialism and Democracy* (New York: Harper, 1947).
Seekings, J., *Heroes or Villains? Youth Politics in the 1980s* (Johannesburg: Ravan, 1993).
Seekings, J., 'Some Comments on "The Racialisation of Social Research in South Africa"', *South African Sociological Review*, 7:2 (1995) 60–9.
Shain, Y. and J. Linz (eds), *Between States: Interim Governments and Democratic Transitions* (Cambridge: Cambridge University Press, 1995).
Sisk, T., *Democratization in South Africa* (Princeton: Princeton University Press, 1995).
Skocpol, T., *States and Social Revolutions* (Cambridge: Cambridge University Press, 1979).
Smith, I., 'The Revolution in South African Historiography' in *History Today* 38 (1988) 8–10.
Southall, R., *South Africa's Transkei: the Political Economy of an 'Independent' Bantustan* (London: Heinemann, 1982).
Stedman, S.J. (ed.), *South Africa: the Political Economy of Transformation* (London: Lynne Rienner, 1994).
Swanson, M.W., 'The Sanitation Syndrome: Bubonic Plague and Urban Native Policy in the Cape Colony, 1900–19', *Journal of African History* 18 (1977) 387–410.
Szfeitzel, M., 'Ethnicity and Democratization in South Africa', *Review of African Political Economy* 60 (1994) 185–99.
Taylor, R. and M. Orkin, 'The Racialisation of Social Scientific Research on South Africa', *South African Sociological Review* 7:2 (1995) 43–69.

Terreblanche, S. and N. Nattrass, 'A Periodization of the Political Economy from 1910', in N. Nattrass and E. Ardington (eds), *Political Economy of South Africa* (Cape Town: Oxford University Press, 1990).
Thompson, L., *A History of South Africa* (London: Yale University Press, 1990).
Tjonneland, E.N. (ed.), *South Africa's 1994 Elections* (Oslo: Norwegian Institute of Human Rights, 1994).
Toit, A. Du, 'No Chosen People: the Myth of the Calvinist Origins of Afrikaner Nationalism and Racial Ideology', in *American Historical Review* 88 (1983) 920–52.
Toit, A. Du, *The Afrikaner Interpretation of South African History* (Cape Town: Simondium, 1964).
Turrell, R., *Capital and Labour on the Kimberley Diamond Fields 1871–1890* (Cambridge: Cambridge University Press, 1987).
Unger, R.M., *Social Theory: Its Situation and its Task* (Cambridge: Cambridge University Press, 1987).
Vail, L. (ed.), *Creation of Tribalism in Southern Africa* (London: James Currey, 1989).
Walker, C., *Women and Gender in Southern African to 1945* (London: James Curry, 1990).
Walzer, M., *Spheres of Justice* (Oxford: Oxford University Press, 1983).
Welsh, D., *The Roots of Segregation: Native Policy in Colonial Natal, 1845–1910* (Cape Town: Oxford University Press, 1971).
Welsh, D., 'Ethnicity in Sub-Saharan Africa', *International Affairs* 72:3 (1996).
West, M., *Bishops and Prophets in a Black City* (Cape Town: David Philip, 1975).
Wilson, F., *Labour in the South African Gold Mines 1911–1969* (Cambridge: Cambridge University Press, 1972).
Wilson, M. and L. Thompson, (eds), *A History of South Africa to 1870*, 2nd edn (London: James Currey, 1982).
Wiseman, J.A. (ed), *Democracy and Political Change in Sub- Saharan Africa* (London: Routledge, 1995).
Wiseman, J.A., *The New Struggle for Democracy in Africa* (Aldershot: Avebury, 1996).
Wolpe, H., 'Capitalism and Cheap Labour Power in South Africa: From Segregation to Apartheid', *Economy and Society* 4 (1972) 425–56.
Wolpe, H., *Race, Class and the Apartheid State* (London: James Currey, 1988).
Wood, G.S., 'Democracy and the American Revolution', in J. Dunn (ed.), *Democracy*.
Worden, N., *The Making of Modern South Africa: Conquest, Segregation and Apartheid* (Oxford: Blackwell, 1994).
Worden, N. and C. Crais (eds.), *Breaking the Chains: Slavery and Emancipation in the Nineteenth-century Cape Colony* (Johannesburg: Witwatersrand University Press, 1993).
Wright, H., *Burden of the Present* (Cape Town: David Philip, 1977).
Young, T., 'Elections and Electoral Politics in Africa', *Africa* 63 (1993) 299–312.
Young, T., 'Governance, the World Bank and liberal theory', *Political Studies* 42 (1994) 84–100.

Index

Act of Union (1910), 14, 45, 63, 68, 128
Adam, H., 153, 194 n
African National Congress (ANC)
 history and politics, 52, 58, 59, 60, 69, 108, 109, 110, 111, 113, 115, 116, 141, 146, 158, 183 n
 political analysis, 152–3
 undemocratic, 59, 60, 157–8
 Women's League, 59, 114–15
 Youth League, 17, 59, 114–15
African People's Organization, 34
African South Africans
 African polities, 8, 12
 conquest, 7, 8, 12
 historical writing, 8, 35–6, 42
 politics pre-1870, 7, 10
 resistance, 7, 8, 12, 13, 28, 110–16
 terminology, ix
Africanism
 politics, 34, 35, 116
 scholarship, 117, 118, 121–3
Afrikaner
 Broederbond, 21, 27, 70, 72, 76, 79, 81
 Cape, 9, 10
 historical writing, 9, 30–4, 37–8
 liberal/Marxist debate, 38–9
 nationalism, 7, 16, 18, 32, 33, 70, 82
 responsible for apartheid, 41, 66–72
agriculture, 14, 15, 28, 69, 76
Anderson, M., 195 n
Anglo American Corporation, 45, 46
Angola, 108
anthropology, 25, 84, 115, 162, 171
apartheid
 demise, 57–8, 108–9
 early apartheid, 7, 15–22
 explanations, 75–82
 grand plan, 19, 20
 high apartheid, 7, 22–8, 71, 74–82
 indirect rule, 122–3

responsibility, 44
slogan, 18, 19
see also, Separate Development, liberal/Marxist debate
Apter, D.E., 188 n
Ardington, E., 177 n, 181 n, 182 n, 183 n, 190 n
Argentina, 65
Arnold, R.D., 182 n
Ash, T. Garton, 156, 182 n
Asmal, Kader, 109, 110, 111, 189 n
Atmore, A., 176 n, 180 n
Australia, 64
Azanian People's Organization (AZAPO), 116–17

Ball, T., 184 n
Bantu Affairs Department (BAD), 27, 75, 76, 133
Bantu Authorities Act (1951), 20
Bantustans, *see* Separate Development
Barkan, E., 194 n
Baskin, J., 194 n
Beetham, D., 190 n
Bekker, S., 177 n, 194 n
Beinart, W., 41, 42, 76, 176 n, 177 n, 180 n, 181 n, 185 n, 190 n
Belgium, 124
Biko, Steve, 178 n
Black
 political agency, 42–3
 terminology, ix
Black Consciousness, 34, 35, 43, 116–17, 121
Bodin, Jean, 61
Boer War, *see* South African War
Bonner P., 21, 22, 40, 177 n, 178 n, 179 n, 184 n, 185 n
Boputhatswana, 72
Botha, Pieter Willem, 109
Botswana, 23, 80
Bozzoli, B., 180 n, 181 n, 190 n
Bradford, H., 177 n, 181 n, 183 n

Britain
  apartheid, 41–2
  Commonwealth, 58
  democracy, 94
  imperial power, 9–11
  interests pre-1870, 10
  racism, 11
  settlers, 8, 10–11
Broederbond, see Afrikaner Broederbond
Bryce, James, 77, 185 n
Buchanan, J., 182 n
Bundy, C., 176 n, 180 n, 190 n
bus boycotts, 17
Buthelezi, Mangosuthu, 117, 131
Buthelezi Commission, 133, 192 n
Butler, A.M., 176 n, 182 n, 185 n, 190 n, 195 n

Campbell, A., 193 n
Canada, 64
Cape
  Colony, 6–9, 9–10, 14, 42
  franchise, 16, 21, 36, 64–5, 68
  liberalism, 23, 39
  Province, 20
  Town, 6, 13, 33, 177 n
  Western, 116, 143
capitalism
  creation of capital, 13–15
  research funding, 4, 46
  South African, 45–6
  Third World, 1
  see also, liberal/Marxist debate
Caribbean, 11
Carr, E.H., 50, 182 n
Carter, C., 191 n
Carter, G., 179 n
Carter, President James, 94
cattle complex, 16
causation, 73–4
Cell, J., 185 n
Chabal, P., 195 n
Charterism, 34, 60, 116
Ciskei, 72
civic associations, 4, 114–15
civil society
  African Studies, 122
  concept, 101
  consociational, 129–35
  South Africa, 132–3
civilized labour policy, 19–20
Cohen, G.A., 185 n
Cobbing, J., 176 n
Cock, J., 194 n
colour bar, 5
Coloured South Africans
  Africanism, 35
  Black Consciousness, 34–5
  history and identity, 33–5, 70, 120–1
  political attitudes, 143–4
  politics, 34–5, 115–6
  terminology, ix, 34–5
Comaroff, J., 190 n
Commonwealth, 58
communism, see South African Communist Party
communitarianism, 169
community mobilization, 145–6
comparative politics
  Africa, 92–4
  democratization, 92–3, 106
  North American, 3, 4, 158–9
  prediction, 149–50
  retrospective, 93, 162
  scenarios, 150–3
  weaknesses, 106–26
  Western European, 4, 158–9
  see also democracy, political science
Confederation of South African Trade Unions (COSATU), 4, 59, 115, 116, 147
Connolly, W., 78, 168, 184 n, 185 n, 195 n
Conservative Party (CP), 113
constitutions
  consociational, 129–35
  Constitutional Principles, 110, 111
  engineering, 4, 10, 105, 124, 128–35, 160
  federal, 130–5
  interim, 110, 111
  tricameral, 129–32
  union, 128
Convention for a Democratic South Africa (CODESA), 109

Index

Converse, W., 193 n
Cooper, F., 84, 180 n, 186 n, 191 n
Crais, C., 185 n
Crocker, Chester R., 189 n
Cross, C., 194 n
Crush, J., 179 n

Davenport, T.R.H., 181 n
Davies, R., 179 n
De Beers Consolidated Mines Company, 68
De Klerk, F.W., 109
De Klerk, M., 190 n
De Klerk, W., 178 n
De Kock, C., 142, 144
De Schweinitz, K., 102, 188 n
decolonization, 3, 38
Delagoa Bay, 9
Delius, P., 177 n, 179 n, 180 n, 184 n
democracy
　African, 86, 93, 8–103
　cause of apartheid, 56–82
　consequences, 170–1
　consociational 129–35
　consolidation, 97–8, 149–50
　contemporary critics, 55–6
　definitions, 66
　democratization analysis, 86–104
　fragility, 1, 54, 166
　liberal, 166–72, 169–70
　participatory and representative, 60–1
　purported triumph, 1, 54–5, 86–7, 166–7
　strengths, 166–7
Democratic Party (DP), 111
Diamond, L., 87, 186 n, 188 n, 189 n
diamonds, *see* minerals
difaqane, *see* mfecane
Du Toit, A., 178 n
Du Toit, S.J., 32
Dubow, S., 42, 180 n, 181 n, 185 n
Dunn, J., 61, 83, 101, 184 n, 186 n, 188 n
Dutch East India Company, 6, 7, 8, 33
Dutch Reformed Church, 32, 35

Eastern Cape, 10, 35–6
Economic Commission (1930–2), 16

Eldridge, M., 178 n, 194 n
elections
　apartheid, 17–18, 27, 68–71
　effects, 139–40
　integrity, 139
　observers, 136
　magic, 167, 172–3, 174
　participation, 139
　political science, 5, 94, 137–8, 140–9
　proliferation, 1
　role and significance, 136–9, 172–5
Elster, J., 187 n
Etherington, N., 189 n
ethnicity
　attributed, 125, 128, 129, 140
　conflict, 4, 107
　constitutional design, 129–35
　constructivism, 25–6
　contested notion, 37–8, 165
　creation, 23–8, 72, 80
　essentialism, 24–5
　instrumentalism, 25
　political attitudes, 140–8
　retribalization, 20, 23–8
　territory and agency, 82
　transition, 128–35
　tribalism, 24–6
　western notion, 8, 72
European Union, 95
Evans, P., 187 n
Everatt, D., 190 n

Fagan Commission (1946), 21, 78
federalism, 130–5, *see also* constitutions
Ferdinand, P., 192 n
First and Third Worldism, 119–21, 162
France, 10, 94
Frankel, P., 181 n
Freedom House, 66, 184 n
Freeman, M., 195 n
Friedman, S., 190 n
Fukuyama, F., 54, 182 n
functionalism, 51, 64

Galeson, W., 188 n
Gauteng, 145

Index

Gelb, S., 182 n, 191 n
gender, 43, *see also* women's politics
Ghana, 122
Gifford, P., 188 n
Giliomee, H., 176 n, 179 n
gold, *see* minerals
Gold Standard, 16
Goldblatt, D., 184 n, 186 n
Goodman, J.B., 189 n
Gotz, G., 145
Government of National Unity, 144
Great Trek, 6, 10, 33
Greece, 93
Greenberg, S.B., 40, 45, 69, 177 n, 179 n, 181 n, 184 n, 185 n, 191 n
Group Areas Act (1950), 19, 71, 72
Grovogui, S.N'Z., 186 n
Grundy, K.W., 189 n
Guy, J., 176 n

Hadden, H., 179 n
Hadenius, A., 176 n, 195 n
Haggard, S., 188 n, 194 n
Harries, P., 179 n
Hart, H.L.A., 73, 185 n
Hawthorn, G., 181 n, 189 n, 194 n
Heard, K., 191 n
Held, D., 183 n
Herbst, J., 188 n, 189 n
Hertzog, J.B.M., 16
high expectations, 14
historical writing
    African, 42–3
    African South African, 35–6
    Afrikaner, 31–3
    Coloured, 33–5
    contemporary identities, 6,7
    democracy, 92–8
    incoherence, 7–9, 11, 12, 49–50
    institutionalism, 47–8
    periodization, 6
    political analysis, 92–8, 163
    romanticism, 9
    social, 43
    watersheds, 6, 17
Hirson, B., 184 n
Hobbes, Thomas, 61, 144
homelands, *see* Separate Development

Honore, M., 73, 185 n
Horowitz, D., 192 n
Hugo, P., 194 n
Human Rights Commission, 112
Human Sciences Research Council, 46, 121, 133, 148
Hungary, 95
Huntingdon, S.P., 86, 87, 89, 182 n, 186 n, 188 n, 194 n

Independent Electoral Commission, 154
India, 87
Indian South Africans
    history, 17, 35, 120
    terminology, ix, 35
Industrial and Commercial Workers Union of South Africa (ICU), 16, 59
influx control, 14, 15, 28, 40
Inkatha Freedom Party, 4, 110, 116, 117, 130, 142, 147
Innes, D., 181 n
Institute for Multi-Party Democracy, 141
institutional engineering, 55, *see also* constitutions
Israel, 87
Italy, 87

Jaarsveld, F.A. van, 178 n
Jackson, R.H., 196 n
Japan, 80, 87
Jeeves, A., 179 n, 181 n
job reservation, 68–9
Johannesburg, 13, 14
Johnson, R.W., 140–8, 193 n
Johnston, A., 110, 189 n
Johnstone, F., 179 n
Jung, C., 192 n

Kaase, M., 182 n
Karis, T., 179 n
Katzenstein, P., 187 n
Kaufman, R.R., 188 n, 194 n
Kaviraj, S., 188 n
Keech, W.R., 182 n
Kentridge, M., 191 n
Khoisan, 7, 8, 10, 11, 33

Index

Kiewiet, C.W. de, 179 n
Kiloh, M., 184 n, 186 n
Knight, J., 181 n
Kohli, A., 187 n, 196 n
Kraak, G., 190 n
Krieger, J., 191 n
Kruger, J., 147
KwaZulu, 26, 117, 143

labour, 13, 47–8
Labour Party, 16
Lazar, J., 76, 179 n, 185 n, 186 n
League of Nations, 129
Leftwich, A., 95, 96, 98, 187 n
Legassick, M., 42, 77, 180 n, 181 n, 185 n
legitimacy and legitimation, 137–8
Lesotho, 23, 80
Lever, H., 184 n
Lewis, P., 96, 184 n, 186 n, 187 n
Lewis-Beck, M.S., 182 n, 193 n
liberal/Marxist debate
   debate, 38–9
   developments, 38–42, 57–8
   Regulation School, 49, 58
   weaknesses, 41–5, 49
Lijphart, A., 124–5, 128, 130–1, 132, 133, 191 n, 192 n; *see also* constitutions
Limongi, F., 56, 57, 66, 88, 89, 97, 182 n, 184 n, 187 n, 188 n, 195 n
Linklater, A., 170, 195 n
Linz, J., 187 n, 189 n, 194 n
Lipset, S.M., 87, 88, 90, 91, 95, 97, 182 n, 186 n, 187 n
Lipton, M., 40, 179 n, 182 n, 184 n
Lodge, T., 114, 149, 183 n, 189 n, 190 n, 194 n
Lombard Report, 192
Lonsdale, J., 138, 190 n, 195 n
Lukes, S., 181 n, 185 n

MacDonald, M., 134–5, 191 n, 192 n
McCarthy, C., 120, 181 n, 190 n
Macmillan, Harold, 71
Madison, T., 183 n
Maidment, R., 184 n
Malan, D.F., 16
Mamdani, M., 122–3, 177 n, 188 n, 191 n, 192 n

Mandela, Nelson, 17, 109
Manor, J., 188 n
Mann, M., 181 n, 188 n
Marks, S., 41, 141, 176 n, 177 n, 178 n, 180 n
Marx, A.W., 180 n, 183 n
Marxism, *see* liberal/Marxist debate
Mattes, R., 144, 178 n, 194 n
Maylam, P., 176 n
Metrowich, F.R., 178 n
mfecane, 6, 9
migrant labour, 7, 14, 26, 39, 42
military
   British dominance, 8
   coup, 4
   settler superiority, 9
   transition, 10
Mill, J.S., 77, 185 n
Miller, W., 193 n
Milner, High Commissioner Alfred, 14, 49
minerals
   Chamber of Mines, 15
   diamonds, 13
   gold, 13
   mineral corporations, 14, 15, 46
   mining, 45–6
   revolutions, 7–8, 12–15, 32
   segregation, 20
   state formation, 12–15, 46
   tribalism, 26
missionaries, 24, 25, 46
Moll, T., 181 n, 183 n
Moodie, T. Dunbar, 178 n
Moodley, K., 153, 194 n
Moore, Barrington, 89–90, 94, 186 n
Moore, M., 195 n
Mufson, S., 178 n
Muller, C., 178 n
Murray, M., 190 n, 192 n

Namibia, 21, 108, 129
Nardin, T., 195 n
Nasson, B., 178 n
Natal, 10, 41, 75, 116
National Party (NP), 4, 6, 16, 17, 18, 19, 20, 21, 23, 27, 33, 58, 64, 70, 71, 75, 76, 81, 84, 108, 109, 110, 111, 113, 129, 133, 135, 144

Native Affairs Department (NAD), 21, 27
Native Economic Commission (1930–2), 80
Natives Land Act (1913), 15
Natives Resettlement Act (1954), 70–1
Nattrass, N., 21, 177 n, 181 n, 182 n, 183 n, 190 n
negotiated transition, 108–12, 113
Negotiating Council, 110
Netherlands, 124
New Zealand, 64
Newton, K., 182 n
Nie, N., 193 n
Nodia, G., 194 n
Nolutshungu, S.C., 192 n
Non-European Unity Movement, 34
North, D.C., 181 n

O'Donnell, G., 94, 187 n
Orange Free State, 17, 20, 71
Organization for Economic Cooperation and Development (OECD) zone, 1, 5, 81, 172
Orkin, M., 148, 165, 181 n, 191 n, 192 n, 193 n, 194 n

Pan-Africanist Congress (PAC), 60, 111
Parekh, B., 183 n
Pauly, L.W., 189 n
Peires, J., 176 n
Petrocik, J., 193 n
Phillips, A., 196 n
Pierson, P., 48, 181 n
Pines, N., 181 n
Plattner, M., 188 n, 189 n
Plumb, J.H., 77, 185 n
Poland, 95
policy science, 153–5
political risk, 151
political science
  limits, 106–26, 161–4
  modern state, 103
  policy influence, 153–5
  political attitude surveys, 121, 140–9
  research funding, 120–1

South African, 123–5, 161–6
systematic error, 119–26
see also, comparative politics, democracy, elections
political theory
  communitarianism, 135
  constitutions, 128–35
  democratic theory, 55–6, 60–1, 66, 166–72
  legitimacy, 137–8
  liberal democracy, 112, 168–72, 174
  Separate Development, 167–75
Population Registration Act (1950), 71, 129
Portugal, 9, 58, 93
Posel, D., 20, 21, 46, 71, 75, 177 n, 179 n, 181 n, 184 n, 185 n
Potter, D., 97, 184 n, 186 n, 187 n, 192 n
Price, R., 180 n, 192 n
proletarianization, 7, 12, 36
Promotion of Bantu Self Government Act (1959), 22, 80
Przeworski, A., 56, 57, 66, 88, 89, 94, 97, 182 n, 184 n, 186 n, 187 n, 188 n, 195 n
Public Protector, 112
Putnam, D., 195 n

Quail Commission, 192 n

race
  Afrikaners, 38
  historical writing, 38–9
  political attitudes, 140–8
  responsibility, 74
  see also, apartheid, ethnicity, segregation
Rand Revolt, 16
Raz, J., 195 n
Reagan, Ronald, 58
religion, 4, 17, 36, 114
Reservation of Separate Amenities Act (1953), 19
reserves, 14, 26, *see also* Separate Development
resistance, 12, 16, 17, 21, 42–3, 113
Revel, J.F., 62, 184 n
Ricoeur, P., 61, 184 n

Rich P.B., 189 n
Robben Island, 59
Rosberg, C.G., 188 n
Rueschemeyer, D.R., 90, 97, 187 n
Rustow, D., 91, 187 n

Sauer Report (1947), 20
Saunders, S., 179 n
Scandinavia, 1
scenarios, 4, 103, 105, 118–19, 125, 150–3
Schlemmer, L., 140–8, 131, 193 n
Schmitter, P., 94, 172, 187 n, 191 n, 195 n, 196 n
Schrire, R., 189 n, 192 n
Schumpeter, J., 61, 62, 184 n
Scott, B., 194 n
Seekings, J., 114, 178 n, 190 n, 194 n, 195 n
segregation
  amenities, 19
  early apartheid, 7, 14, 15–22
  see also apartheid
self-determination, 81, 168–71
Separate Development
  democracy, 82–5
  forced removals, 24
  homelands, 22–3
  international legitimacy, 167–72
  policy and practice, 22, 23–8, 63, 72–3, 169–70
Shain, Y., 187 n, 189 n, 194 n
Shapiro, I., 192 n
Sharpeville, 6, 60
Shaw, M., 145
Sheptsone system, 49
Shubane, K., 178 n
Sisk, T., 124, 180 n, 183 n, 191 n, 192 n, 193 n
Sisulu, E., 190 n
Sisulu, Walter, 109
Sithole, N., 178 n
Skocpol, T., 187 n, 188 n
Slagstad, R., 187 n
slavery, 47
Smith, I., 179 n
Smuts, General Jan Christian, 17, 80, 129
social capital, 1

Social Darwinism, 14, 15, 34, 42
Sotho, 10
South African Agricultural Union (SAAU), 28, 76
South African Bureau of Racal Affairs (SABRA), 27, 79, 185 n
South African Communist Party (SACP), 4, 17, 59, 116, 152
South African Institute of Race Relations (SAIRR), 148
South African National Civics Organization (SANCO), 115
South African Native Congress, 36
South African War, 6, 12, 34, 68
South Korea, 122
Southall, R., 190 n
Soweto, 6, 60, 147
Spain, 93
state
  Afrikaner, 112
  capital, 45
  formation, 2, 12–15, 40
  functionalism, 40, 51
  idea, 61
  instrumentalism, 40–1
  legitimacy, 45
  structural crisis, 108
  territory, 168
  unitary actor, 51
State of Emergency, 109
Stedman, S.J., 192 n
Stephens, E.H., 90, 187 n
Stephens, J.D., 90, 187 n
Stokes, D., 193 n
Strydom, J.G., 81
Suppression of Communism Act (1950), 129
survey research, 140–8
Suzman, Helen, 131
Swanson, M., 180 n, 181 n
Swaziland, 23, 80
Swilling, M., 181 n
Szfeitzel, M., 177 n

Tambo, Oliver, 17
Taylor, R., 140, 148, 165, 181 n, 191 n, 192 n, 193 n, 194 n
technology transfer, 108
Terreblanche, S., 177 n

Thatcher, Margaret, 58
Thompson, L., 176 n, 178 n, 181 n
Tjonneland, E.N. 193 n
Tomlinson Commission (1955), 80
townships, 20, 114, 117–18, 126–7, 154, 159, 160
Transitional Executive Council, 110
Transkei, 26, 72
Transvaal, 10, 20, 32
Trapido, S., 176 n, 178 n, 180 n
tribalism, see ethnicity
tricameral system, 129–32
Trotskyism, 34, 35
Truth and Reconciliation Commission (TRC), 191
Tucker, R., 194 n
Turrell, R., 181 n

Unger, R.M., 106, 189 n
unification, 6, 12, see also state formation
Union of Soviet Socialist Republics (USSR), 58, 96, 102, 108
unions, 17, 58, see also COSATU
United Democratic Front (UDF), 34, 109, 113, 114, 159
United Kingdom, 1, 162, see also Britain
United Party (UP), 17, 18, 20, 21, 22, 7, 78
United States, 10, 14, 27, 58, 64, 71, 80, 94, 108, 163
universities, 127, 155, 162
Unterhalter, E., 190 n
Urban Areas Act (1923), 15
urbanization, 17, 18, 21, 69, 78

Vail, L., 177 n
Van Onselen, C., 50, 180 n, 182 n
Venda, 72
Verba, S., 193 n
Verwoerd, Hendrik Frensch, 80
Viljoen, G. Van N., 192 n

Wage Act (1925), 20
Wagner, R., 182 n

Walker, C., 181 n, 190 n
Walzer, M., 78, 195 n
Weber, Max, 137
Wells, J., 180 n, 190 n
Welsh, D., 41, 180 n, 182 n, 192 n
West, M., 190 n
West Germany, 87
Western Cape, 116, 143
Westminster Foundation, 141, 148
White South Africans
  divisions, 11
  liberalism, 43, 136, 157–8
  misapprehensions, 114, 119–20, 154
  terminology, ix, 125
  see also, Afrikaner, Britain
White Supremacy, 18, 22, 27, 42
Whitehead, L., 94, 95, 102, 187 n
Wilson, F., 19, 20, 177 n, 179 n, 181 n, 182 n
Wilson, M., 176 n
Wiseman, J.A., 100, 101, 188 n, 189 n
Witwatersrand, 13
Wolpe, H., 179 n
women
  political attitudes, 142
  political behaviour, 4, 65, 114–5, 183 n
Wood, G.S., 65, 184 n
Worden, N., 31, 176 n, 177 n, 178 n, 184 n
Wright, H., 194 n

Xhosa polity, 36

Young, T., 100, 101, 136, 139, 188 n, 193 n
youth, 4, 17, 114, 126, 127–8, 159, see also ANC Youth League
Yudelman, D., 179 n, 181 n

Zulu
  polity, 8, 12, 36
  resistance, 9, 10, 160
Zulu, P., 143